D1438098

Founded in 1972, the Institute for Research on Public Policy is an independent, national, nonprofit organization. Its mission is to improve public policy in Canada by promoting and contributing to a policy process that is more broadly based, informed and effective.

In pursuit of this mission, the IRPP

- identifies significant public policy questions that will confront Canada in the longer term future and undertakes independent research into these questions;

- promotes wide dissemination of key results from its own and other research activities;

- encourages non-partisan discussion and criticism of public policy issues in a manner which elicits broad participation from all sectors and regions of Canadian society and links research with processes of social learning and policy formation.

The IRPP's independence is assured by an endowment fund, to which federal and provincial governments and the private sector have contributed.

Créé en 1972, l'Institut de recherche en politiques publiques est un organisme national et indépendant à but non lucratif.

L'IRPP a pour mission de favoriser le développement de la pensée politique au Canada par son appui et son apport à un processus élargi, plus éclairé et plus efficace d'élaboration et d'expression des politiques publiques.

Dans le cadre de cette mission, l'IRPP a pour mandat :

- d'identifier les questions politiques auxquelles le Canada sera confronté dans l'avenir et d'entreprendre des recherches indépendantes à leur sujet;

- de favoriser une large diffusion des résultats les plus importants de ses propres recherches et de celles des autres sur ces questions ;

- de promouvoir une analyse et une discussion objectives des questions politiques de manière à faire participer activement au débat public tous les secteurs de la société canadienne et toutes les régions du pays, et à rattacher la recherche à l'évolution sociale et à l'élaboration de politiques.

L'indépendance de l'IRPP est assurée par les revenus d'un fonds de dotation auquel ont souscrit les gouvernements fédéral et provinciaux, ainsi que le secteur privé.

INSTITUTE FOR RESEARCH ON PUBLIC POLICY

INSTITUT DE RECHERCHE EN POLITIQUES PUBLIQUES

PETER AUCOIN

the new public management

CANADA

IN COMPARATIVE PERSPECTIVE

IRPP
GOVERNANCE

Bibliothèque nationale du Québec
Dépôt légal 1995

Canadian Cataloguing in Publication Data

Aucoin, Peter, 1943-
The new public management: Canada in comparative perspective

Includes bibliographical references

ISBN 0-88645-180-9

1. Public administration—Canada. 2. Public administration.
3. Civil service reform—Canada. 4. Civil service reform.
5. Bureaucracy—Canada. 6. Bureaucracy.
I. Institute for Research on Public Policy. II. Title.

JF1411.A82 1996   354.71001   C95-920812-7

Marye Ménard-Bos
Executive Director, IRPP

F. Leslie Seidle
Research Director, Governance Program, IRPP

Copy Editing
Penny Williams, PMF Editorial Services Inc.

Editorial Assistance
Félice Schaefli

Design and Production
Studio Duotone Inc.

Cover Design
Studio Duotone Inc.

Published by
Institute for Research on Public Policy (IRPP)
Institut de recherche en politiques publiques
1470 Peel Street, Suite 200
Montreal, Quebec H3A 1T1

Distributed by
Renouf Publishing Co. Ltd.
1294 Algoma Road
Ottawa, Ontario K1B 3W8
Tel.: 613-741-4333
Fax: 613-741-5439

Contents

Foreword

In Canada, as elsewhere, the common wisdom is that the public sector should be reduced, both in size and cost. Governments are facing the need to make choices between the programs they consider essential to administer themselves and those that may be transferred to other organizations or discontinued. A new vision of how government should function has recently emerged, notably with greater emphasis on performance and results.

Three years ago, IRPP launched a major initiative titled Rethinking Government. As part of this project, we have commissioned research that addresses how government is structured, manages change and serves the public.

The first initiative was a roundtable in June 1993 which featured presentations by Ted Gaebler, co-author of *Reinventing Government*, and Bill Jenkins, a leading British scholar. Three senior Canadian academics also presented papers. The proceedings, *Rethinking Government: Reform or Reinvention?*, followed later that year.

The research program continued as part of IRPP's Governance activities. It led to the 1994 publication *The Road to Better Public Services: Progress and Constraints in Five Canadian Federal Agencies*, by Professor Bruce Doern of Carleton University. Recently, the Institute published *Rethinking the Delivery*

i

of Public Services to Citizens, a comparative monograph by Leslie Seidle, IRPP Governance Research Director. Other research in progress will lead to further publications.

In the present study, Peter Aucoin, Professor of Public Administration and Political Science at Dalhousie University and a Fellow of IRPP, analyzes the impact of an increasingly influential paradigm, the "new public management," on the public services of four countries: Canada, Australia, New Zealand and the United Kingdom. The common elements he observes across these four parliamentary systems derive from what he labels a "confluence of perceptions" about major challenges facing governments. These include bureaucracies with undue power over the management of the state; organizational designs that restrict ministers' capacity to lead and manage their individual portfolios; and rigid rules and procedures that stand in the way of implementing change.

Based on extensive research, including interviews with some 90 officials and former officials in the four countries, this study reviews the various reform initiatives that have been launched in response to these challenges. The author's canvas is a broad one, and he devotes considerable attention to the relation between the principles of the new public management and those of parliamentary responsible government. In this context, he provides a highly thoughtful assessment of the implications of such reforms for accountability – to senior levels of the public service, Parliament and the public.

Professor Aucoin's study confirms that the Canadian government has been rather timid compared to the other countries in implementing change in the public sector. With an eye toward Ottawa, he presents an agenda for public management centred on organizational separation of responsibilities for policy and operations; contractual relations between ministers and the heads of operational agencies; devolution of authority for the management of operations; rigorous performance measurement; a robust accountability regime; and steps to protect the independence of the public service.

IRPP is pleased to publish this important study by one of Canada's senior scholars of public management. We are confident it will be read and discussed with great interest both in Canada and abroad.

Monique Jérôme-Forget
President, IRPP

Acknowledgements

This study of Canadian public management in comparative perspective was made possible by the intellectual assistance of a great number of scholars and experts in Canada and elsewhere. I am particularly grateful to Professors Colin Campbell of Georgetown University and Guy Peters of the University of Pittsburgh for encouraging me to participate in the Structure and Organization Research Committee of the International Political Science Association. I have learned much from my colleagues in this international college of scholars. My debt to them is only partly expressed in the numerous citations of their works in this book.

My knowledge of Canadian public management has benefited enormously from my contacts with the faculty of the Canadian Centre for Management Development, an institution I am proud to be associated with as a Senior Fellow. I am especially grateful to Dr. Ralph Heintzman, Vice Principal – Research, who has made it possible for me to discuss my work with a considerable number of senior public servants at the Centre. These opportunities have proved to be of immense value in complementing my interviews with practitioners in Canada and abroad.

The field work for this study, as well as research assistance, was made possible by the financial support of the Social Sciences and Humanities Research Council of Canada. In particular, this support enabled me to conduct interviews in person with officials and former officials from each of the four governments. This field work also made possible the collection of unpublished materials, in some cases confidential documents, that otherwise would not have come to my attention.

My interviews with officials and former officials were conducted on a confidential, not-for-attribution basis. These conversations were not recorded, nor were those interviewed quoted directly. In most cases, I approached them on the recommendations of others (scholars, other officials, former officials and those previously interviewed). In this way I was able to talk to people who were most knowledgeable and who had thoughtful perspectives on the initiatives of interest to me. My primary objective in interviewing officials and former officials was not to obtain a documented account of experiences but to learn about the ideas underpinning the principal reforms initiated in each system. I sought to be sensitive to the fact that ideas about public management, while they may have universal application, must always be adapted to the particular circumstances of a specific political and governmental system.

Most of these interviews and discussions took place in Ottawa, Canberra, London and Wellington. A number of conversations with visiting foreign officials and former officials took place in Ottawa and at various conferences and workshops in other locations. In several cases, a discussion was not confined to a single occasion, but became an ongoing dialogue, either in person or by telephone. In all, approximately 60 officials and former officials in the three foreign jurisdictions were formally interviewed, with a fairly even split between the number for each country. In Canada, approximately 30 officials and former officials were interviewed specifically for this project, although during the same period a much greater number of less formal discussions, in various forums, also contributed to my research. Given the conditions of my interviews, and the confidences assumed in less formal discussions, I must express my gratitude to these officials and former officials without identifying them.

My knowledge of the experiences of the three other countries examined here has benefited immensely from my association with John Holmes and Tom Wileman of the Office of the Auditor General of Canada, who were examining public management developments not only in Canada but also in Australia, New Zealand and Great Britain, at the same time I was. I am grateful to them both for sharing their extensive knowledge and for their incisive and thorough commentaries on my initial draft of this book.

Professor Evert Lindquist, University of Toronto, also read the entire manuscript in first draft and provided invaluable suggestions for improvements. I thank him for both his expert assistance and personal encouragement.

I am grateful to Professor John Halligan, University of Canberra, and Professor Jonathan Boston, Victoria University of Wellington, who graciously hosted me in Canberra and Wellington respectively and provided generously of their time in securing interviews with government officials. Mr. Ravi Kapil, Deputy Head of the Public Management Committee, Organisation for Economic Co-operation and Development, made it possible for me to interview the experts resident at the OECD, an organization which has become a mine of information for students of comparative public management.

I thank Candace Redden for her research assistance, in particular her constant efforts to introduce a degree of efficiency to my data collection and documentation.

My Dalhousie colleague, Professor Herman Bakvis, worked with me in studying various aspects of the Australian experience, and our joint undertaking resulted in the publication of "Consolidating cabinet portfolios: Australian lessons for Canada" (*Canadian Public Administration*, Vol. 36, no. 3 (Fall 1993), pp. 392-420). I have learned much from our continuing collaboration and appreciate his willingness to devote time to my scholarly interests.

Professor Donald Savoie, Université de Moncton, my Acadian *confrère* in public administration, has generously given of his time to discuss our mutual interests in public management reform, and I express my appreciation for his contribution to my work.

Finally, I am especially indebted to Dr. Leslie Seidle, Director of Research (Governance) for the Institute for Research on Public Policy. He not only secured the Institute's approval to publish this work but also shepherded my manuscript through to publication with great forbearance and careful attention to logic and detail. Equally important, he brought his own considerable expertise in the area of comparative public management to bear upon my study. I thank him for his support throughout.

I wish to express my appreciation to Penny Williams of PMF Editorial Services Inc. for her excellent copy editing of the manuscript and to Félice Schaefli for her meticulous editorial assistance.

This book is dedicated to Margot. Without her constant emotional support and encouragement, this work would not have been brought to fruition. Her great patience with my numerous absences from Halifax and long evenings at the university allowed me the time to research and write this book.

Dalhousie University
December 1995

ONE

Introduction:
the New Public Management

When Margaret Thatcher became Prime Minister of Great Britain in May 1979, virtually all governments in the major Western democracies were "under stress."[1] The politics and management of "restraint in government" had become the order of the day.[2] Thatcher differed from other leaders of these democracies at the time, however, in at least one important respect: she actually welcomed the challenge, even relished the prospects, of rolling back the liberal welfare state with its extensive interventions in the socio-economic order.

Thatcher's desire to reduce the dominance of the state did not entail a comprehensive plan to overhaul British government and public administration. However, she was adamant that three dimensions of British governance be reformed. First, the power of the civil service was to be diminished to make the state apparatus more responsive to political direction. Second, private sector management practices were to be introduced to promote economy and efficiency in government. And, third, the freedom of individual citizens was to be enhanced to counter the dominance of state control over the design and delivery of public services. Over the following decade, her government gradually but consistently introduced major changes in organizational designs and managerial practices. The result was the introduction of what Christopher Hood has called the "new public management."[3]

The revolution in public management launched by Thatcher in 1979 was viewed at the time as little more than the logical consequence of her particular neo-conservative policy agenda. The role of the state was to be reduced and what remained was to be subject to enhanced political direction, increased managerial discipline and greater responsiveness to citizens. Over the following decade, however, the new public management became an international phenomenon. Its logic and approach were adopted by governments formed by political parties from across the political spectrum, including parties on the traditional left, most notably Labour governments in Australia and New Zealand.

Governments in all Western democracies have been driven to seek significant changes in public policy and management by three major determinants. First, and most obvious, national economic realities have required restraint in public sector spending. Although levels of debt and deficit have varied across the Western democracies, efforts to reduce public spending have been a universal political priority.[4] Second, widespread decline of public confidence in the effectiveness of public policies and the quality of public services has resulted in calls for, as the United States National Performance Review put it, "government that works better and costs less."[5] Third, in the new international economic order, the impacts of what governments do, and do not do, across a wide range of public policy areas are no longer regarded as merely internal or domestic matters having little or no effect on the global competitiveness of national economies. Notwithstanding the diminished role of national governments in this new world order, the management of the state, as the public household, is acknowledged as crucial to national economic prosperity.[6]

Across the Western democracies, government efforts to cope with this trinity of developments have varied in their particulars. Strategies have varied because political systems have different starting points from which they can seek to roll back the state, improve public services and promote national competitiveness. Priorities have varied because the parties in power in these Western democracies have changed over the last two decades. Finally, successes have varied because political leaders have demonstrated different degrees of conviction, willingness or ability to effect change.

In almost all Western political systems, nevertheless, changes in public policy have encompassed the privatization, or at least the commercialization, of public enterprises; increased contracting out of public services; an expansion of user charges for public services; and, more generally, a wide variety of expenditure restraint initiatives, including those that seek to reduce the size of the public service as well as the public service payroll. These responses have been accompanied by equally significant efforts to change the structures, systems and practices of public management, broadly defined.

Although astute observers of public management, and especially those who are also practitioners, may find themselves retching with each new attempt to coin catchy slogans to advance the fads and fashions of the day, rhetoric has long been recognized as a central feature of change. Rhetoric has been an important element in public management reforms precisely because of its role in affecting what Christopher Hood and Michael Jackson label the "acceptance factor."[7] Public management reform has "come of age"[8] not because it is based on novel ideas, but because new paradigms of public management have gained ascendency. How political reformers have packaged reforms has thus had a significant influence on their acceptance.[9] The contours of change to public management are shaped not only by ideas about best practices but also, and more important, by normative visions and guiding philosophies for administering public affairs. It is this latter dimension that counts most. By definition, it constitutes the political dynamic of change in public management. The reason is clear. Changes in public management are not merely changes to administrative processes and practices; they are also changes to governance itself.

The New Public Management in Westminster Systems

The new public management that emerged during the 1980s in the four Westminster systems of Australia, Canada, New Zealand and the United Kingdom clearly has entailed the acceptance of new paradigms for the administration of public affairs. Although there have been significant differences in the particular public management reforms that have been pursued and adopted in each of these systems, several common elements are found across all of them. It is the commonality of these elements that enables commentators to speak of a new public management that extends beyond the boundaries of any one of the systems.

These common elements derive from a confluence of perceptions about the challenges confronting governments as they seek to respond to the exigencies of the times. First was the widespread perception by political leaders in each system that the career public service, or state bureaucracy, had assumed too great an influence over the management of the state. In each case, public management reform has tried to check, counter and constrain this influence. Second was the perception that the organizational designs of the central executive systems had come to restrict not only the capacity of those at the strategic apex, including prime ministers, to provide leadership in the management of government, but also the capacity of ministers to manage their individual portfolios. In each case, efforts have been made to enhance these capacities. Third was the perception that management in government had become excessively preoccupied with adherence to rigid rules and procedures and thus too prone to bureaucratic pathologies. In each system, efforts have been made to introduce a greater emphasis on performance, an increased focus on responsiveness to citizens and accountability for results.

Reforms on these three fronts over the last decade have resulted in each of the four systems adopting measures that have sought to give new life to three traditional tenets of the Westminster system. There is, of course, a certain irony in the fact that political reformers in these four systems have returned to their "roots" to find new paradigms for public management. In one sense, this is an indication of the extent to which these systems had veered, or were perceived to have veered, from the Westminster model. In another sense, it is a testimony to the genius of the Westminster model itself. To accommodate their structures, systems and practices to the realities of contemporary governance, governments in these four systems have sought to reassert political control over the state apparatus in order to direct change in accordance with political priorities; to reconfigure the balance of power within cabinet government in order to promote greater strategic direction and discipline in public policy management; and to devolve responsibilities for the management of policy implementation in order to pursue enhanced performance and responsiveness in government operations. In so doing, the pendulum of power has swung in two directions simultaneously. Such a paradox, however, is not a new phenomenon.

On the contrary, the Westminster model has always sought to accommodate what appear at first glance to be contradictory purposes: to secure policy and administrative coordination across government, while assigning individual ministers responsibility for the direction of the executive departments of government, on the one hand; and to distinguish between partisan and nonpartisan responsibilities in the executive administration of law and public policy, on the other. The former represents a recognition of the fact that cabinet government within the Westminster system of responsible parliamentary government is both a constitutional principle – the government must have the confidence of the elected legislative assembly – as well as a practical method to control the state bureaucracy – authority is vested in ministers and not in appointed state officials. The latter represents a recognition that while cabinet government is "party government," with political parties in Parliament constituting the mechanism whereby governments are formed, maintained and held accountable, "good government" also requires a state bureaucracy that is constituted and managed on a nonpartisan basis, lest partisanship override fairness, probity and efficiency in the design and delivery of public services as well as the enforcement of regulations.

At least two features of the Westminster system have afforded the four countries the opportunity to be among the international leaders in promoting and adopting the new public management. In comparison to the United States, with its system of divided government, for example, prime ministers and Cabinets in these Westminster systems have considerable discretion to change the machinery of government and administrative practices without recourse to legislative change. And, even when legislative changes have been pursued, executive dominance in these systems of parliamentary government has meant that parliamentary opposition is unlikely to forestall change.

Second, in comparison to parliamentary systems where coalition governments are the norm, and thus diverse partisan forces must be accommodated, the governments of these four systems have been formed by a single political party. Their political leaders have considerable leverage to effect change without seeking support from outside their own partisan circles. Moreover, insofar as the new public management has sought to reinforce traditional tenets of the Westminster model, reforms have been legitimized by reference to longstanding principles. To the degree that reforms have failed to take effect or have stalled, they have done so largely as a consequence of either a lack of ministerial commitment or the indifference of ministers to reform measures.

The New Politics

The new public management, as implemented by governments on both the right and the left of the political spectrum, is partly an effort to return to the roots of parliamentary government. But it is also an effort to cope with a new politics emerging in almost all Western systems. This new politics has entailed a greater politicization of governance. From the outset, there has been an insistence that the state apparatus, as constituted by the permanent bureaucracy, be responsive to political leadership. That the right and the left approach governance with different ideological goals has not diminished the common perception that public management must first and foremost be re-established as a responsibility of those elected to govern as the delegates or agents of citizens.

It perhaps comes as no surprise then that citizens have come to be increasingly regarded as "customers" or "clients." While these terms are often used interchangeably in political discourse, they portray a greater willingness on the part of governments, and elected representatives generally, to be responsive to their constituents. For those on the right, citizens as taxpayers deserve the same attention afforded paying customers or consumers by private business. The mistrust of government, viewed from this perspective, is similar to the mistrust of private monopolies wherein the interests of the monopoly take precedence over those of their customers/consumers. For those on the left, citizens deserve the same attention clients receive from professionals who give primacy to the interests of their clients. The mistrust of government, viewed from this perspective, is similar to the mistrust of professionals when client interests take a back seat to professional interests.[10]

This changing vocabulary of politics reflects more than an effort on the part of governments and their administrators to establish a new discourse to counter discontent with bureaucracy and demands for "quality service." It also reflects an emergent crisis in representative democracy. Everywhere there has been a deepening public cynicism regarding the institutions of representative government that goes beyond bureaucracy bashing, however much certain political leaders have sought to capitalize on this sentiment. Government is mistrusted because those elected to public office are increasingly viewed as motivated not by public interests but by self-serving interests: the perks and privileges of a political class.

The hugely popular British Broadcasting Corporation's sitcom on ministerial-public service relations, "Yes, Minister," portrays the career public service as engaged in a conspiracy against those elected representatives who constitute the government and thus are its political masters. This popular mythology has been fostered by many politicians. However, the flip side, also part of the mythology, is the depiction of politicians in ways that undermine public confidence in representative democracy. They are viewed as driven not by the public interest in governance, but primarily by their own personal survival in office. This cynicism is partly the reason for a decreasing attachment to what have been the primary political organizations of representative democracy, namely political parties. The political class that leads political parties, accordingly, has increasingly fewer partisan followers to confront the current political crisis of representative democracy.

This crisis in contemporary democratic governance is perhaps most clearly illustrated by the extent to which populist coalitions on the right of the political spectrum and social movements on the left share common ground, if not common cause, in challenging the legitimacy of political elites. The new democracy represented by these forces is evidence of the declining cohesion of Western democratic societies; their civic cultures no longer provide the necessary deference to authority that our practice of representative democracy traditionally assumed. While the use of "direct democracy" measures such as referendums may constitute inadequate answers to the conundrums of contemporary governance, they signify the extent to which the consent of the governed can no longer be considered exclusively in terms of an electoral democracy in which partisan political preferences are expressed every three to five years by the voting public.

As governments struggle to cope with these new realities, they are also confronted by an increasingly aggressive mass media in a new information environment where less and less can be kept from public view. In part, of course, governments have contributed to a more open style of government, especially where they have adopted access to government information legislation. They have furthered this development by enhancing the review powers and capacities of parliamentary committees and legislative agencies, especially various kinds of auditing bodies. And, in some governments, they have encouraged greater public access by adopting formal mechanisms and processes for public consultation. The net result of all these developments has been more exposed government.

As political leaders confront these new realities, public servants must also adjust to them. First, they no longer can expect to monopolize the policy advisory function in government; there are now competitors. Some are brought into government by their political masters; some are outside government but have the ears of their masters. Some are partisan strategists *cum* policy advisers; some are independent policy experts in their own right. Second, the expertise of public servants in administering the affairs of government is increasingly challenged by those constituencies to whom they provide public services or whom they regulate in the name of the state. This is especially true where these constituencies are well organized to advance their political interests in public policy making and/or implementation. Finally, public servants are increasingly subject to demands for a public accounting of their behaviour by legislative committees, various public auditors of administration and the mass media. Their anonymity, once a powerful force in securing their influence, has been breached.

The New Managerialism

The rise of a new public management has not been restricted to an increased politicization of governance. It has also entailed the emergence of a new "managerialism."[11] In some important respects, reforms to public management have been consciously modelled on management practices from the private sector. There is little that is new in the demand that government emulate business in its management of public services. In the development of a career public service in Great Britain in the last century, for instance, the aim was to have ministers assisted by "men of business" in the administration of the affairs of state.[12] The longstanding assumption that politics and administration must be distinct in order to promote economy and efficiency in the administrative dimensions of governance has fostered a dichotomy between the appropriate roles of ministers and public servants. While this division sits uneasily with the constitutional and political accountability of ministers for administration as well as the responsibility of public servants in advising ministers on public policy, it has served to legitimize calls for businesslike practices in public administration.

All too often, however, proposals to adopt the methods of the private sector in public administration have floundered precisely because they have prescribed a degree of autonomy for public servants that has not been acceptable to ministers. The new public management has resulted in a revolution in public administration, primarily because much of its reform program has been designed *within* government. Advisers from outside government have played a major role in some cases, but they have had to cast their ideas in ways that meet the essential character of public administration.

This has required adherence to at least three conditions. First, the superior position of ministers, and therefore the subordinate position of public servants, has had to be respected. Hierarchy remains a fundamental principle of government, even where efforts are made to separate policy and operational responsibilities between ministers and public servants respectively. Second, the continuing need for the corporate management of government, which inevitably restrains discretion, has had to be acknowledged. Even where there is a significant measure of delegated authority, departments and agencies as parts of government must be subject to at least a minimum set of values and standards. Third, the business of government must still be governed by law, however much the operations of government are re-engineered in response to the dictates of economy and efficiency, opportunities provided by new information technologies or demands for quality service. In respecting the primacy of these three conditions, public administration remains subject to democratic control.

The new managerialism in public management has been driven by the same forces experienced in private-sector management, namely a greater need to pay attention to the bottom line in terms of the relationship between revenues and expenditures, on the one hand, and increased demands for quality products and services, on the other. Although the dynamics of the economic marketplace are obviously not similar in every respect to those in the political arena, governments are not immune from either economic realities or citizen demands. Confronted simultaneously by declining fiscal capacities and increasing pressures for quality public services, governments have sought to enhance their own productivity, in part by resorting to new management practices. Concerns for economy and efficiency have thus been given a new priority in public management. Enhancing cost-consciousness, doing more with less and achieving value for money became the objectives of this finance-centred perspective on public management reform.[13]

Efforts to pursue this first objective have entailed a significant measure of centralized control as political leaders have sought to rein in public spending. At the same time, new financial management systems have devolved authority to ministers and officials in ways that have afforded them greater scope to effect economies and efficiencies. As might be expected, these twin features of the new public management in relation to budgeting and financial management have led to differing interpretations throughout government as to where effective power over the public purse actually resides. The designers of the new systems have tried to balance centralization to achieve strategic directions and corporate discipline with decentralization of managerial authority over the use of allocated resources joined to a greater accountability for results. For many in the trenches of government operations, however, the reality has been viewed as a massive centralization of power using both direct and indirect measures; managers have fewer resources with which to operate and yet are expected to generate even more in the way of savings but without diminishing the quantity or quality of services.

The second major focus of the new managerialism is on performance or results. Citizens, especially as voters, now judge governments not only on their management of public finances but also on the quality of public services they obtain from the state. Indeed, the latter can be more significant for citizens generally, given that the state of public finances is often not joined to the quality of service. Traditions and expectations respecting entitlements, even rights, to public services have done much to create a political dynamic wherein the relationships between cost and quality are ignored.

In this context, governments have little choice but to attempt to do more with less. This requires an increased emphasis on results. The operative assumption of much of the reform focused on this dimension of public management is that governments can do better if three conditions are met. First, greater attention must be given to the views of citizens in the design and delivery of public services. Second, sufficient authority must be devolved to those who are responsible for the operational aspects of public services, especially those on the front lines of service provision. Third, citizens must be well informed about the services to which they are entitled and the costs of these services; service targets and standards must be set for those providing them; and public service managers and their organizations must be accountable for respecting citizen entitlements and meeting their targets and standards within the limits of the resources provided.

The Canadian Experience

By the end of the 1970s, the Canadian state was obviously not immune to the developments that gave impetus to the new public management. The federal government was clearly one of those major Western democratic governments under stress. In May 1979, the same month that Margaret Thatcher became Prime Minister in Great Britain, the Progressive Conservative party, led by Joe Clark, defeated the long-serving Liberal government of Pierre Trudeau. Although Clark had always been viewed as being on the left of the federal Conservative party in Canada (a "red

Tory," or a "wet" as Thatcher would have labelled him), Colin Campbell has noted that:

> Before his victory on 22 May 1979, Clark sounded like a Canadian counterpart to the "iron lady"...Rumblings from the Tory camp seemed to signal radical reform of executive leadership in Canada: the Cabinet would be reorganized into a two-tier system...[A] mercifully swift purge of senior officials strongly identified with Trudeau would assure that the bureaucracy would place itself at the disposal of the Conservatives; the aggrandizement of the bureaucracy would cease; and the public service would be cut by 20 percent.[14]

Unlike Thatcher, however, Prime Minister Clark stumbled badly; within a year his government had lost a non-confidence vote in the House of Commons on its first budget and, subsequently, the 1980 general election. Trudeau returned from retirement to lead the Liberal party in this election, won a majority in the Commons and formed a new Liberal government.

In some respects, Trudeau's paradigm of "rational management"[15] incorporated elements of the new public management. From the outset of his first government in 1968, for instance, he had been concerned that ministers not be captured by their departmental bureaucrats. Government decisions were to be made by ministers, especially in Cabinet and Cabinet committees. At the same time, however, he considered himself neither an ideological nor a party partisan. Consequently, he was more than content to surround himself with a coterie of senior officials, especially in the Privy Council Office (the prime minister's department and cabinet secretariat), who, as "super-bureaucrats,"[16] could advise both him and his ministers, coordinate the policy process and, more generally, provide for the management of government.[17] This style of governance and management persisted throughout Trudeau's 1980-84 government, although the lustre of this paradigm and its elaborate architecture for decision making and management began to fade well before Trudeau resigned a second time in 1984.

By the end of the Trudeau era it appeared that what had begun in Great Britain with Thatcher, and had now spread elsewhere, had apparently only been postponed in Canada when the Clark government had forfeited the opportunity to emulate the Thatcher revolution. With Clark replaced as Conservative leader by Brian Mulroney, the stage was set to begin again.

Mulroney's attacks on government generally, and the public service in particular, obviously struck a responsive chord; four years of international attention to Thatcherism, coupled with the rise of neo-conservatism and extensive government and bureaucracy bashing south of the border in two successive American presidential elections, had more than conditioned the Canadian polity to these new forces. When campaigning in the 1984 election, "Mulroney never missed the opportunity to make political mileage with stories of government mismanagement and blunders. His apparent need to make his listeners feel good...encouraged him to regale his audiences with stories of bureaucratic wastage with special emphasis on those instances of bureaucratic arrogance and incompetence" – hence his oft-quoted remark that he would dismiss public servants "with a pink slip and a pair of running shoes."[18] Under a Conservative government, he declared, "the minister will run his department. And any Deputy Minister who doesn't understand that will have a career notable for its brevity."[19]

Much less publicized, nevertheless, were Mulroney's views on public management reform. He had stated, for example, that:

It is clear that the government has lost sight of a basic truth – good managers don't manage systems, they manage people. And people are motivated not by rules and guidelines imposed from head office, but by leadership, the value of the job, the chance to contribute and to achieve, and the sense of being needed and rewarded for their work...[T]he problem [of productivity] in the federal government is not caused by indolent public servants...What we have is a management problem. A problem which stems from a lack of political direction and leadership. What to do to end the malaise? First, instill a positive approach to productivity management that will permeate the entire government.[20]

It came as no surprise that the party's campaign promises included a commitment to make "productive management...a top political priority." Its principal statement on the public service claimed that a Conservative government would establish "a management philosophy of government... based on accountability, appropriate delegation of authority and the encouragement of creative and efficient management within the civil service." Its goal, it stated, was "to shift from reliance on regulations, controls and detailed procedures towards greater reliance on managers' competence and the achievement of results...to simplify government – and to let managers manage."[21]

What Mulroney and the Conservatives had promised was put to the test in the aftermath of the September 1984 election when they achieved the largest majority ever in the House of Commons, winning 211 of 282 seats. Almost a decade later, and following a second electoral victory in 1988, the Conservatives were out of power, having been subjected to the worst defeat ever suffered by a governing party, winning merely two of 295 seats in the House of Commons. Over the course of this period of Conservative rule, the Mulroney government, and its Conservative successor under Prime Minister Kim Campbell, pursued a range of organizational and managerial changes. These followed, in many respects, the major patterns of public management reform in the other Westminster systems.[22] As elsewhere, for instance, increased efforts at centralization, coordination and control were paralleled by increased efforts to decentralize, deregulate and delegate. Yet in comparison to the other three systems, Canada appeared to fall short of the mark. The legacy of the Conservative era in respect to public management reform was ambiguous at best.

A 1993 study by the Office of the Auditor General of Canada,[23] for instance, expressed the opinion that reforms in the three Westminster systems most comparable to Canada, namely Australia, New Zealand and the United Kingdom, have had "a more strategic focus and greater coherence and consistency" than the reforms in Canada.[24] Although it did not suggest that the basic principles of Canadian reform were deficient, it noted that the relative success of reforms in each of these other three countries was considered by those involved in them to be due to "visible political leadership and commitment" and "sustained leadership from the 'centre'."[25] In stating that "the Canadian federal public service could benefit from the adoption of a more strategic approach to public management and public service reform,"[26] the study implied that Canadian reforms under the Conservatives had met with less than the desired success precisely because the required political and public service leadership had been lacking.

For its part, the Liberal party under John Turner and then Jean Chrétien had not evinced a great deal of interest in public management reform throughout its time in opposition. However, it continually criticized the Tories for what it claimed was a corrosive politicization of public administration generally and was highly critical of the massive restructuring of government departments initiated by Campbell shortly before the 1993 election. During the election campaign, it had much to say about the need for new policy directions, yet its position on public management reform was limited to promises to restore integrity in governance and to improve relations between ministers and the public service. On the latter, Marcel Massé, the Liberal's leading spokesperson on the subject, declared: "Good government requires a close and congenial relationship between public servants of every level and politicians. In particular, ministers and deputy ministers have to work together intimately and must share a mutual trust."[27] Massé, a former deputy minister and Clerk of the Privy Council/Secretary to Cabinet under Clark, whom Chrétien personally recruited and nominated as a Liberal candidate, obviously had a receptive audience for his campaign speech to a conference of federal public servants in which he argued: "Reinforcing simplistic biases, government and the people who work in it are always portrayed by the Tories as inefficient, bureaucratic and unreliable."[28]

Since assuming office, the Chrétien government has taken a number of steps to undo some of the changes put in place by the Mulroney government. At the same time, it continued the restructuring of departments begun by Campbell, with only one major change, and adopted a streamlined cabinet structure similar in most respects to that put in place by Campbell. By 1995, it had also unveiled a new Expenditure Management System, the principles of which maintained the directions in which the federal government had been heading for some time. Associated management reforms have continued to be implemented, or at least announced as government plans. By far the most significant initiatives, however, have centred on a series of major policy and program reviews to tackle the fiscal crisis and, in the words of Massé, later appointed Minister responsible for Public Service Renewal, to "get government right."

If it were still necessary, in 1993, to "get government right" in these regards, what had gone wrong? Was it merely that the Conservatives had failed to establish "a close and congenial relationship" with the public service? Did Mulroney and his ministers fail to adhere to his stated philosophy of "productive management"? Was there a failure on the part of the leadership of the public service to implement reforms effectively? Was the Canadian public service immune to reform as a consequence of almost three decades of constant turmoil over changes in public management, and was it thus suffering from a "saturation psychosis," as one participant-observer put it, after merely one decade of change?[29] Or, notwithstanding the changes in the United Kingdom, Australia and New Zealand, is there a fundamental contradiction between the philosophy underlying the new public management and the essential dynamics of responsible government within the parliamentary system?[30] Finally, as Donald Savoie has recently argued, did political leaders intent on managerial reform, such as Thatcher, Mulroney and Reagan in the United States, set out to fix the very things that were not broken in government, namely the bureaucratic delivery of public services?[31]

Whatever one's view of the merits of the new public management, it is difficult to disagree with the implied conclusion of the Office of the Auditor General's study that the relative lack of success in the Canadian experience to 1993 was due, in some large measure, to shortcomings in political leadership. There is too much evidence that the Conservatives were not sufficiently interested in public management reform, and many of the key ministers simply did not understand the issue. They did not see it as centrally connected to the dilemmas they faced. Nor did they see any votes in advancing good management. For them, management reform was essentially an internal bureaucratic preoccupation that could be tolerated so long as it did not detract from their political agenda.

While it is undoubtedly the case that the Conservatives' lacklustre and inconsistent approach to public management diminished their capacity to effect significant reform, it is also true that the leadership of the federal public service throughout this period did not possess a radically different vision or plan to reform public management. While there was perhaps a measure of agreement on the need to consolidate the cabinet system and to provide deputy ministers with greater authority to manage their departments, there was little support for the major initiatives that were beginning to emerge from the other three Westminster systems. A gradualist, experimental approach was deemed more appropriate.

To some considerable extent, this attitude of the senior mandarins was due to what were perceived to be past failures during the Trudeau era of attempts to apply rational choice and managerialist techniques to public management. Senior bureaucrats who were in the public service throughout this period were highly sceptical about anything done elsewhere that appeared to resemble what had already been attempted in Canada and, it was agreed, found wanting. It was paradoxical, therefore, that when the senior public service sought to initiate major change in the second term of the Mulroney government, beginning in 1989 with its Public Service 2000 program, it embraced wholeheartedly, at least at the level of official rhetoric, the new paradigm of managerialism extant in the private sector.

It was able to do so, without apparent contradiction with its scepticism to what was being done elsewhere, because it adopted the view that attitudes, rather than structures or systems, were what had to be transformed.

Unfortunately, this new approach was deemed to be no more successful than prior efforts to reform public management using different means. Even before the Liberals came to power in 1993, positive references to Public Service 2000 had diminished considerably; following the election that year, they disappeared altogether. Indeed, not long after the transition in government, the former Clerk of the Privy Council under Mulroney, Paul Tellier, by then ensconced as president of a major Crown corporation, offered a public apology of sorts for his failure to take more than "half measures...in re-engineering" the organization and management of the public service.[32] In defence of what had been done to date, the then outgoing Secretary to the Treasury Board, Ian Clark, not only took issue with his former superior's call for radical measures,[33] but also asserted that there was "little evidence to suggest that the more radical structural reforms enacted by other countries [that is, Australia, the United Kingdom and New Zealand]...have achieved greater results in terms of controlling operating expenditures and increasing accountability."[34]

Whether Canada could or should have adopted a more radical approach to public management reform during the Mulroney era, major surgery to the machinery of government was initiated by Campbell and completed by the Liberals. Moreover, the current leadership of the federal public service, headed by the Clerk of the Privy Council, Jocelyne Bourgon, has had to respond to the challenge of major policy and especially program reviews initiated by the Liberals. In combination, these two developments have had profound implications for public managers and their staff. At the same time, there appears to be no interest in mounting a comprehensive program of public management reform. It is acknowledged that improvements on a number of fronts are required, but these are to be pursued in the normal course of ongoing change and innovation. This pause in the pursuit of major and systemic reform initiatives offers an appropriate time to assess the Canadian experience in comparative perspective, especially since the basic designs of the new public management in each of the three other Westminster systems appear to have been accepted as established. In both the United Kingdom and Australia, for instance, recent government assessments of the current state of affairs endorse staying the basic courses set during the last decade.[35]

Studying Canada in Comparative Perspective

This study analyses the experience of the Canadian government and that of three other Westminster systems in response to the major forces that have given rise to the new public management. As indicated, these forces have encompassed the full spectrum of governance. At one level, the focus has been on the critical relations between ministers and public servants as governments seek to manage the affairs of state. At a second level, the focus has been on securing strategic direction and control as well as economy, efficiency and effectiveness in the management of operations. At a third level, the focus has been on the design and implementation of approaches to enhance performance and accountability in government.

The following chapters are organized around these three foci of the new public management. Chapters 2 and 3 examine the first. Chapter 2 considers the fundamental connection between the principles of responsible government and the justifications for a career public service. Chapter 3 outlines and assesses the ways by which political leaders in government have sought to reshape this connection and what is required to preserve and promote its essential foundations. Chapters 4 and 5 examine the second focus. Chapter 4 considers the structural deficiencies attributed to both the fragmentation of executive governance and the centralization of administration and their consequences for strategic leadership and productive management respectively. Chapter 5 outlines and assesses the efforts of governments to overcome these deficiencies. Chapters 6, 7 and 8 examine the third focus. Chapter 6 considers the critique of traditional public administration as bureaucratic management from the perspective of those who argue the need for a paradigm shift to go beyond bureaucracy in search of well-performing government organizations. Chapter 7 outlines and assesses the efforts of government to enhance performance and responsiveness. Chapter 8 considers ways to secure better accountability.

The range of matters encompassed by the new public management is obviously broad. This study, accordingly, had to be cast at a high level of generality to stay within the limits of what could be reasonably attempted in a single study. This requirement was made even more necessary by my decision to compare the Canadian experience with that of the experiences in the three other Westminster systems.

The comparative dimension of this study has two purposes. First, it helps to place the Canadian experience in a broader context. In this sense, it provides a perspective on the Canadian experience that is not confined to a consideration of the forces present within a single jurisdiction, several of which cannot but be idiosyncratic to a particular regime in a given place and at a given time. Second, and of greater interest given my related concern for addressing practical matters, a comparative perspective enabled me to search out a broader range of ideas about what constitute best practices in public management. Governance, including public management, has a practical intellectual dimension, and the more one studies what is attempted elsewhere, the greater the likelihood that knowledge of one's own political system is enhanced.

There is always the danger in comparative studies that the best practices of other countries may look better than our own simply because they are so different or novel to our own experience. Moreover, in assessing foreign experiences, one may too readily accept the assumed merits of foreign systems, especially if they are described or interpreted by the very people who have designed them. There are, of course, ways to check for such possible shortcomings in conducting comparative research. One is to expand the number of comparative experiences examined. Another is to pay careful attention to the works of scholars in foreign jurisdictions, who presumably are more attuned to the nuances and particular circumstances of each system. Such assessments are especially useful when they themselves have a comparative perspective. The increased number of comparative analyses of public management in recent years is an important development in advancing scholarship. At the same time, comparative studies of public management ideas are constrained by the limited number of cases that can be studied in relation to particular ideas in practice, especially the interaction of a set of practices. Comparative learning is a slow and uncertain exercise.

Australia, the United Kingdom and New Zealand were chosen as the comparative context for a number of obvious reasons. Each has pursued major public management reform initiatives across the full scope of the new public management. Along with Canada, they share common traditions with respect to their constitutional structures of representative and responsible government and their approach to a professional, nonpartisan career public service. At the same time, governments of different political persuasions have been involved; the new public management has not been the exclusive concern of neo-conservative governments. While a Conservative government has been in power in Great Britain since 1979, public management reforms began in both Australia and New Zealand under Labour governments, and in the latter were continued by a conservative National government elected in 1990.

Finally, I have not included the American experience in this study despite the traditional Canadian emphasis on comparing public management experiences in Canada to those in the United States, and the extent to which Ronald Reagan was an inspiration to the Mulroney Conservatives in Canada. This comparative dimension has been well documented by Savoie in his recent study of Thatcher, Reagan and Mulroney.[36] I did not include the American experience for two reasons. First, its institutional structures for governance and public administration are fundamentally different from those of the Westminster systems. Second, and more compelling when I began my research, its record with regard to the new public management has been so uninteresting. Notwithstanding the hype associated with "reinventing government" on the part of the Clinton administration, the United States has clearly been a laggard in this field.[37] Indeed, the leadership of the Westminster systems has been acknowledged by the numerous references to these systems in the American reform literature.

Notes

1. Colin Campbell, *Governments Under Stress* (Toronto: University of Toronto Press, 1983).

2. Peter Aucoin, "The Politics and Management of Restraint in Government: An Overview," in Peter Aucoin (ed.), *The Politics and Management of Restraint in Government* (Montreal: Institute for Research on Public Policy, 1981), pp. 1-23.

3. Christopher Hood, "A Public Management for All Seasons?", *Public Administration*, Vol. 69, no. 1 (Spring 1991), pp. 3-19.

4. Organisation for Economic Co-operation and Development, *Public Management Developments: Survey 1993* (Paris: OECD, 1993), pp. 9-19.

5. *Creating a Government that Works Better and Costs Less: Report of the National Performance Review* (Washington: US Government Printing Office, 1993).

6. Organisation for Economic Co-operation and Development, "Serving the Economy Better," Public Management Occasional Papers, Paris (1991).

7. Christopher Hood and Michael Jackson, *Administrative Argument* (Aldershot, England: Dartmouth Publishing Company, 1991), pp. 195-96.

8. Gerald Caiden, *Administrative Reform Comes of Age* (Berlin: Walter de Gruyter, 1991).

9. Peter Aucoin, "Administrative Reform in Public Management: Paradigms, Principles, Paradoxes and Pendulums," *Governance*, Vol. 3, no. 2 (April 1990), pp. 115-37.

10. Gregory Albo, David Langille and Leo Panitch (eds.), *A Different Kind of State? Popular Power and Democratic Administration* (Toronto: Oxford University Press, 1993).

11. Christopher Pollitt, *Managerialism and the Public Services: The Anglo-American Experience* (Oxford: Basil Blackwell, 1990).

12. Henry Parris, *Constitutional Bureaucracy* (London: George Allen and Unwin, 1969), pp. 40-42.

13. Tim Plumptre, "Reform at the crossroads: efforts to implement an integrated strategy for renewal in the Canadian federal government," mimeo, June 1994.

14. Campbell, *Governments Under Stress*, pp. 93-94.

15. Peter Aucoin, "Organizational Change in the Canadian Machinery of Government: From Rational Management to Brokerage Politics," *Canadian Journal of Political Science*, Vol. 19, no. 1 (March 1986), pp. 3-27.

16. Colin Campbell and George J. Szablowski, *The Super-Bureaucrats: Structure and Behaviour in Central Agencies* (Toronto: Macmillan Company of Canada Ltd., 1979).

17. Campbell, *Governments Under Stress*, pp. 77-99.

18. David Zussman, "Walking the Tightrope: the Mulroney Government and the Public Service," in Michael Prince (ed.), *How Ottawa Spends 1986-87: Tracking the Tories* (Toronto: Methuen, 1986), p. 255.

19. Zussman, "Walking the Tightrope," pp. 258-59.

20. Zussman, "Walking the Tightrope," p. 257.

21. Quoted in Peter Aucoin and Herman Bakvis, *The Centralization-Decentralization Conundrum: Organization and Management in the Canadian Government* (Halifax: Institute for Research on Public Policy, 1988), p. 1.

22. Ian Clark, "On re-engineering the public service of Canada," *Public Sector Management*, Vol. 4, no. 4 (1994), pp. 20-22.

23. Canada, Auditor General of Canada, *Report of the Auditor General of Canada to the House of Commons* (Ottawa: Minister of Supply and Services, 1993), pp. 159-85.

24. *Report of the Auditor General of Canada*, 1993, p. 178.

25. *Report of the Auditor General of Canada*, 1993, pp. 175-76.

26. *Report of the Auditor General of Canada*, 1993, p. 178.

27. Marcel Massé, "Getting Government Right," address to the Public Service Alliance of Canada, Longueuil, Quebec, September 12, 1993, p. 6.

28. Massé, "Getting Government Right," p. 4.

29. H.L. Laframboise, "Administrative reform in the federal public service: signs of a saturation psychosis," *Canadian Public Administration*, Vol. 14, no. 3 (Fall 1971), pp. 303-25.

30. S.L. Sutherland, "Responsible Government and Ministerial Responsibility: Every Reform has its Own Problem," *Canadian Journal of Political Science*, Vol. 24, no. 1 (March 1991), pp. 91-120; A.W. Johnson, "Reflections on administrative reform in the government of Canada 1962-1991," Discussion Paper, Ottawa, Office of the Auditor General of Canada, 1992.

31. Donald J. Savoie, *Thatcher, Reagan, Mulroney: In Search of a New Bureaucracy* (Toronto: University of Toronto Press, 1994), p. 322.

32. Paul M. Tellier, "No time for half-measures: the urgency of re-engineering the public service of Canada," remarks to the Canadian Institute, Ottawa, February 21, 1994 (an abridged version of Tellier's remarks is printed in *Canadian Speeches: Issues of the Day*, Vol. 8, issue 1 (April 1994), pp. 45-48).

33. Clark, "On re-engineering the public service of Canada."

34. Ian Clark, "Restraint, renewal, and the Treasury Board Secretariat," *Canadian Public Administration*, Vol. 37, no. 2 (Summer 1994), p. 247.

35. United Kingdom, Prime Minister, Chancellor of the Exchequer and Chancellor of the Duchy of Lancaster, *The Civil Service: Continuity and Change* (London: HMSO, July 1994); Australia, Task Force on Management Improvement, *The Australian Public Service Reformed: An Evaluation of a Decade of Management Reform* (Canberra: Australian Government Publishing Service, December 1992).

36. Savoie, *Thatcher, Reagan, Mulroney*.

37. John Halligan, "The Art of Reinvention: the United States National Performance Review," *Australian Journal of Public Administration*, Vol. 53, no. 2 (June 1994), pp. 135-43.

TWO

Responsible Government and
Career Public Service

The Westminster model of government, created in Great Britain and emulated in Australia, Canada and New Zealand, is predicated on two assumptions that co-exist in a constant state of tension. The first is that responsible government is best secured through the dynamics of party politics in order that government, including the state bureaucracy, be subject to democratic control.[1] The second is that good government is best secured through a professional, nonpartisan public service, or "constitutional bureaucracy," as Henry Parris calls it,[2] that serves government but nevertheless is staffed and managed as an institution independent of party politics. The tension inherent in these two assumptions has long been recognized but traditionally accepted as part and parcel of the public interest in securing effective democratic government, on the one hand, and competent public administration, on the other.

In the 1970s, however, the assumption that a professional, nonpartisan public service is a necessary condition to good government and can co-exist with responsible government as party government began to be questioned. In each of the four Westminster systems, such questioning struck at the very foundations of constitutional bureaucracy. These concerns were hardly novel in the experiences of these four political systems, especially insofar as they were voiced by opposition parties or newly elected governments. But the spectre of "politicization" that accompanied the questioning of the impartiality of these career public services was supported by the popularization of theories purporting to account for the dynamics and dysfunctions of bureaucratic power within representative government. Although the salience of these theories varied among the four systems, in every case the effect was to raise fundamental issues about the co-existence of representative government and career public service.

In this chapter, these challenges to the traditional assumption of the contribution that a career public service makes to good government within the Westminster model are outlined and assessed. First, however, it is necessary to identify the reasons for the relationship between representative government and a career public service.

Responsible Government and Good Government

The four Westminster systems share a common set of traditions with regard to parliamentary government. There are variations in the design of political representation among the four: Great Britain and Canada have non-elected second chambers (the House of Lords and Senate respectively) and an elected House of Commons; Australia has an elected second chamber (Senate) in addition to its elected House of Representatives; and New Zealand has only one legislative assembly, its elected House of Representatives. In each case, however, a "government" is formed by and is responsible to the legislative assembly that is elected on the basis of representation by population – the House of Commons or Representatives. Responsible government is thus embedded within a system of representative government.

Within parliamentary government, formal executive authority is vested in the Crown but exercised by the prime minister and the ministers of her or his Cabinet who constitute the government. This executive authority is exercised by ministers, individually and collectively. Ministers, in turn, are accountable to the House of Commons or Representatives for their exercise of executive authority, encompassing responsibilities both for initiating legislation and for administering public affairs. While individual ministers cannot be formally impeached by Parliament, a government that loses the confidence of the House of Commons or Representatives must either resign or call a general election.

Legislative authority, on the other hand, resides in Parliament. But Parliament includes the government: in formal terms, the Crown-in-Parliament. Aside from officials in the judicial branch of government, certain quasi-judicial institutions and a number of parliamentary agencies, and with the exception of those who head or are employed by agencies that operate at arm's length from direct government control, state officials are subordinate, directly or indirectly, to the executive authority of ministers. Although public servants in those Westminster systems where appointment is governed by statute – as opposed to royal prerogative, as is still the case in Great Britain – may no longer be considered "servants of the Crown,"[3] in practice, their subordination to the government remains a fundamental feature of responsible government.

Responsible Government as Party Government

The political dynamic that underpins the operation of this constitutional system of responsible government is partisan politics as organized by parliamentary political parties. Parties not only recruit and nominate candidates for election to legislative bodies, and thereby structure the electoral choices of voters, but also provide the means whereby a government is formed by and is held responsible to the House of Commons or Representatives. They also thereby enable voters to hold a government to account at the time of general elections. Responsible government within this system is thus "party government"; its politics are party politics.

This partisan dynamic makes possible the practice of a constitutional politics that simultaneously provides for responsible government and allows for a "loyal opposition". Because political parties constitute the organizational mechanism to achieve these constitutional ideals, the prime minister and ministers who exercise the executive authority of the state are partisans. In the exercise of their executive responsibilities, they are meant both to propose laws to Parliament that advance their partisan agenda for governance and to oversee the execution of these laws as well as all others on the statute books. In the discharge of these executive responsibilities, however, partisanship is not meant to rule out good government.

Good Government and Career Public Service

Securing good government in the Westminster system has entailed the acceptance of the idea of a public service staffed on the basis of merit. This nonpartisan approach to staffing rests upon the assumption that an independently staffed, and thereby neutral, public service is superior to a public service staffed on a partisan basis. This approach has led to the conception of the public service as a "service," and not merely "a collection of job-holders."[4] On this basis, the management of the public service is organized as a separate, yet subordinate, institution of government.

With partisan politics as the basic dynamic of responsible government, a nonpartisan public service entails two critical conditions. First, appointments and promotions respecting the public service are to be made by an authority or authorities independent of the government of the day. Such staffing decisions are to be based on the merits of the individuals in question (or, in the case of the most senior officials appointed by the prime minister or Cabinet, on the advice of senior public servants). The criteria of merit, however defined (or redefined over time), are meant to exclude partisan considerations. Second, dismissals from the public service are to be governed by the same criteria and independent process. Therefore, they can happen only for reasons related to individual performance or behaviour in the discharge of prescribed duties as governed by statutes, government regulations or formal codes of conduct.

Within this regime, changes in government should not affect the composition of the public service. The public service, as an institution, is to be insulated from the ebb and flow of partisan politics. In this context of a nonpartisan public service, a "permanent" or "career" public service is required. This implies a bargain between those who engage in the partisan political process and seek to form a government and those who serve government as nonpartisan public servants. This bargain restricts both the executive discretion of the ministers of government and the political rights of public servants.

The executive authority of ministers is restricted insofar as staffing is a critical function in the management of organizations. The limitation is accepted in the cause of good government: the nonpartisan character of the career public service should not be undermined by ministers seeking to advance their partisan interests by virtue of their executive authority. On the other hand, by accepting the conditions of a nonpartisan public service, individual public servants agree, while they hold office, to forego certain political rights. In particular, these include waiving the right to be a candidate for elected office and accepting limits on the right to free speech respecting matters of public policy and administration. Such conditions are necessary in order that public servants, in carrying out their assigned duties, conduct themselves in ways that do not undermine their capacity to serve government in a nonpartisan manner.

The acceptance of the concept of a nonpartisan career public service emerged only gradually. The British experience constituted the precedent, although here it took much longer to be established in all its dimensions than is often supposed.[5] While the acceptance of it in the other Westminster systems occurred later and took somewhat different forms, at least four factors were common in all four systems.

First, staffing the appointed offices of the state on the basis of either party- or personal-partisan patronage meant that ministers were invariably caught in situations where there were more supplicants than positions, however bloated the state apparatus. The number not given posts inevitably exceeded the number appointed, with the perverse result that the disappointed outnumbered the grateful.

Second, the partisan utility of patronage appointments diminished considerably as the franchise expanded. Although party supporters continued to claim that appointments on this basis were crucial to the health of their local party associations, party leaders in all four political systems became increasingly dubious, at least insofar as important offices of the state were concerned.

Third, as the functions of the state inexorably expanded in scope and complexity, the one dimension of government that did not change was the time available to ministers to administer the affairs of state. The management of patronage appointments took time away from managing the business of government. Adding to ministers' burden were the increasing responsibilities of managing the political side of government, that is, attending to the demands of Parliament for new or revised legislation and for an accounting of the government's administration of public affairs.

As the business of government became more time-consuming, senior ministers (secretaries of state) began to rely on the assistance of a growing number of junior ministers (under-secretaries). But this offered only a partial solution; junior ministers had their own political tasks. Moreover, as the business of government became increasingly complex and more technical, it required a measure of knowledge and experience that junior ministers did not always have or were able to develop while in office. Required, therefore, were "men of business"[6] who could attend to the administration of public affairs free from the political demands and functions of government.

Thus was conceived the position of the "permanent secretary" in British government – an official immediately below the rank of secretary of state who, unlike junior ministers, would be permanent in his or her position. As Parris notes, permanent secretaries "were administrators of a new kind, as permanent as the clerks [as the practice had evolved], yet competent to handle business at the ministerial level [that is, to make decisions on behalf of their ministers]."[7]

The fourth factor that influenced the development of a permanent public service arose as a consequence of the third. If permanent secretaries were to be "men of business," they had to be experienced in and knowledgeable about this business; they had to be men whose careers were based in public service. Hence, the establishment of a career public service was deemed to be a functional prerequisite of good government.

In addition to the positive advantages a permanent public service provided for ministers, there was a second driving force behind the adoption of a nonpartisan public service in Canada, Australia and New Zealand. In these countries, a neutral public service was viewed as a necessary requisite for the elimination of, as it was called in Canada, the "patronage evil."[8] Although the practice of partisan-party patronage to fill appointments to the public service in these systems was not as extensive as its opponents usually claimed, it was sufficiently prominent to lead reformers to demand its demise. Campaigns to eradicate patronage in staffing the public service thus had all the characteristics of a moral crusade that overwhelmed its defenders, including at times party leaders, who claimed that patronage was simply an extension of responsible government as a form of democratic government predicated on party government.

In part, of course, the challenge to patronage struck a responsive chord within the body politic for it meant that positions in the public service would not be restricted to partisan adherents of the government of the day, or, more generally, those willing to adopt a partisan commitment to any party. Eventually, the right of citizens to compete for public service appointments became a major principle of the merit system. More important then, however, given the limited number of positions in the public services of the time, was the claim that a nonpartisan public service would enhance good government, particularly "efficiency in government."[9] In the Canadian case: "It was the simple equation of patronage with inefficiency – laying all the ills of bureaucratic structures at the door of the 'patronage evil' – that proved the clinching argument."[10]

In Canada especially, the equating of patronage with inefficiency was predicated on the assumption, explicit or not, that responsible government could co-exist with a neutral public service because "politics" could be separated from "administration" in the management of the state. Canadian reformers were influenced in this regard by the American reform movement that sought to achieve good government by asserting the separation of politics and administration. What was, and remains, significant is that this particular understanding of governance and public management derives from a conception of the "neutrality" of the career public service that is subtly different from that advanced by those British reformers who saw how good government would benefit from a permanent public service. They saw that the advance of efficiency was important – the "men of business" would see to that – but it was equally understood that a permanent public service, recruited on the basis of merit, would bring to office those who could assist in governance, that is, in the design of public policy.[11] The permanent bureaucracy, in short, was *not* to be confined merely to the administration of public policies formulated and decided upon by a political process from which bureaucrats were excluded.

Whatever the rationale for the acceptance that a career public service was essential to good government, responsible government now assumed the obligation to attend to the state of the public service. The good government that a career public service was meant to promote assumed that the public interest would be protected by a nonpartisan and, therefore, independently staffed public service. The public interest in good government, accordingly, required more than the effective operation of responsible government within a parliamentary democracy. It also demanded that ministers respect and promote the public interest in a career public service.

Career Public Service and the Administrative State

The career public service was instituted and developed in each of the four Westminster systems in a variety of ways, but, in each case, its subsequent growth was accompanied by a continual expansion of government intervention in the societies and economies of these political systems. With this expansion, particularly over the last half century, both the scope and the complexity of government business gave rise to a class of public service mandarins at the central core of government with significant influence in governance. Even though career public servants eventually removed themselves from the partisan arenas of party politics, they had by no means been excluded from the inner sanctums of governance.

Appointments to the most senior public service positions in Canada, Australia and Great Britain were subject to prime ministerial prerogative and thus not encompassed by the provisions pertaining to the independent staffing of the public service proper. However, this did little to alter the complexion of the career public service in any of these systems. With very few exceptions, these officials – deputy ministers in Canada and permanent heads in Australia and Britain – were promoted from the ranks of the career public service. In New Zealand, the independence of the most senior positions was even stronger, as permanent heads were recommended to Cabinet for appointment by the independent public service staffing agency, the State Services Commission – a process that virtually guaranteed the selection of career public servants for these top positions.

Regulations and procedures for the nonpartisan staffing of public services, coupled with ever-increasing demands on the time of ministers to manage the political dimensions of governance, meant that the public services became essentially self-governing. In addition, as with the emergence of managerial elites in the private sector following the creation of the corporate form of ownership, the public service was able, even required, to exercise considerable influence. The result was the "administrative state."

While remaining constitutionally subordinate to its political masters, the public service, especially its elite mandarins, could not but constitute a challenge to the supremacy of ministers. This state of affairs was tolerated so long as the dominant policy perspectives of the public service accommodated, and thereby were seen to serve, the partisan political objectives and priorities of governing parties. To this extent, ministers could accept not only their limited control over the career public service as an institution of government but also the significant role of public servants, both in administering the law and in the formulation of public policy.

There were ministers who occasionally doubted the nonpartisanship of their career public services. This was especially the case following change in the governing party. In these circumstances, some ministers voiced concerns, sometimes publicly, that the preceding government, particularly if it had been in power for a long time, had influenced the complexion of the senior ranks of the public service and thus the policy orientations of the service. Others worried that the public service had become an independent power in its own right. In such cases, it was not so much the loyalty of the public service to the policies and programs of past governments that was at issue. Rather, the public service in question was viewed as an institution that sought to perpetuate its own policy preferences, even at times in opposition to those of its political masters. Until the 1970s, however, governments, including newly elected governments, invariably accepted the established order of ministerial-public service relations, even in those instances where ministers suspected that they were not being well served.

By the 1960s, the career public services in these four systems had reached the zenith of their status and power. Government expansion in the post-war period, with the full flowering of the economic interventionist and social welfare state, had resulted in a practice of governance in which expertise in matters of public policy and administration was viewed as paramount. This was an era characterized by a diminished relevance of the traditional ideological dispositions of governing parties. The fundamental challenges and essential tasks of government were increasingly considered beyond partisan ideology. Partisan ideology was replaced by public policy technocracy.

This "end of ideology" proved to be exceedingly short-lived. Throughout the 1970s, economic malaise was compounded by an "overload on government" brought about by ever-expanding political demands for government services, with their attendant fiscal implications. An emerging "crisis of democracy" was proclaimed.[12] The prevailing public policy of simultaneously securing economic growth, high levels of employment, increases in personal incomes and continuous improvements in social services began to be questioned. Neo-conservatism had been conceived. Soon after, neoliberalism emerged. "Governability" demanded restraint in government.

Challenging the Administrative State

Although economic factors were the primary driving forces of the emerging politics of restraint, there were also newly energized ideological and intellectual attacks on the policy foundations of the modern state. But more than the foundations were under attack; fundamental questions were also being raised about the structures and processes of policy formation and management. Although not restricted to the role of the career public service, the focus of this assault first centred on the permanent bureaucracies in these four Westminster systems.

Public Choice Theory

The principal intellectual challenge to the idea of career public service as a condition of good government came from public choice theory. Although there are numerous articulations of this theory, the common point of reference with respect to relations between politicians and public servants is the assumption that career public servants are not primarily motivated by the public interest in good government but by the promotion of their own individual or collective self-interests. Public choice theory assumes, moreover, that these self-interests will often be at odds with those of elected representatives, as well as those whom they represent. And, furthermore, the interests of the bureaucracy too often win out over those of its political masters and/or their constituents.

Public choice theory also assumes that elected representatives invariably will deviate from the interests of their constituents in order to secure their primary self-interest, namely re-election. Further, it assumes that citizens, as voters and members of interest groups, are also motivated by self-interest. It thereby questions a basic assumption underlying representative government as such – namely, that political behaviour can transcend the mere pursuit of self-interest. This view of politicians, however, has not deterred some political leaders from adopting the understanding of representative government put forward by public choice theory.

Although developed as an account of political and bureaucratic behaviour within the American system of divided government, with its separation of powers between executive and legislative branches of government, public choice theory has been applied to the Westminster systems of parliamentary government. In particular, the assumptions of the theory were popularized, and thus given political salience, initially in Britain, by the "Yes, Minister" television series. More than any academic scribbling could, "Yes, Minister" did much to propagate an extreme form of cynicism respecting the contribution of a career public service to good government.[13]

Public cynicism fuelled by this mythology was reinforced by the declining capacity of the state to respond to public demands for quality public services while still managing public resources economically and efficiently. Dissatisfaction with government generally was fostered by increasingly aggressive mass media, legislatures, legislative committees and legislative auditing agencies, each of which sought to expose shortcomings within governance and public administration. Public knowledge of government waste and inefficiency and of the failure of many government socio-economic undertakings grew. In addition, an increasingly well-educated citizenry became less deferential to authority. Demands for more opportunities for public consultation and participation in governance, as well as greater transparency in government and public accountability, reflected a widespread distrust of the closed character of the modern administrative state, particularly on the part of political activists and pressure groups.

Budget-Maximizing Bureaucrats
The closed character of the administrative state in each of the four Westminster systems could not but invite suspicions about self-serving bureaucrats and bureaucratic abuses of power. In the context of the newly

arrived fiscal crisis, the most widely publicized thesis of public choice theory was that advanced by William Niskanen. His "budget-maximizing bureaucrat" thesis thus became a central theme in the challenge to the administrative state. There were two obvious reasons for its appeal.

First, for politicians, it provided a simple and convenient explanation for the significant growth in public expenditures. Bureaucrats, Niskanen argued, not only seek to "maximize" the growth of the budgets of their organizations, but succeed in doing so. They seek to do so because budget increases are presumed to be in their personal interest. They succeed, he stated, because their political masters have neither sufficient incentive to restrain them nor sufficient knowledge to determine what levels of resources are required for the public service programs that politicians are willing to provide citizens in response to their political demands. Since the incentives of governing politicians are geared, first and foremost, to re-election, responding to demands for expenditure programs, it is assumed, is what politicians in office do to get re-elected. In any event, politicians cannot counter the information possessed by their bureaucrats; the state constitutes a regime in which there is only one supplier for each of the required public services. The monopolistic character of public services, accordingly, renders politicians victims of bureaucratic manipulation and exploitation.

Second, for voters, Niskanen's thesis provides an account of bloated bureaucracy and the proverbial waste in government: bureaucrats not only press for and receive maximum budgets, they also build into their demands for resources considerable room for discretionary spending.[14] This element of discretionary spending, or resource slack, allows them to spend surplus resources not essential to the provision of services at levels demanded by either politicians or their constituents. They use these dis-cretionary resources in ways that enhance their personal power and status in their organizations as well as their own personal perks and privileges, including their salaries.

The appeal of this thesis of budget-maximizing bureaucrats to a politi-cian such as Thatcher was obvious; little wonder that she deemed Niskanen required reading for her senior public service.[15] Although Niskanen is not the most acclaimed public choice theorist (James Buchanan won the Nobel Prize in Economic Science in 1986 for his work in this area, and Anthony Downs may arguably have had a better claim to the same), it has been his focus on the bureaucracy, rather than politicians or voters, that has appealed most to those who see bureaucracy as the culprit. In "Yes, Minister," it should be noted, Minister (later Prime Minister) Jim Hacker was, at least initially, portrayed as the hapless victim of Sir Humphrey Appleby, his permanent secretary. Thatcher was determined not to suffer such a fate; the "iron lady" would prevail against the bureaucratic resistance and obstructionism that, in her view, previous governments had failed to overcome.

In contrast to public choice theory generally, Niskanen's thesis appears to place the blame for public expenditure growth primarily on the bureaucracy. It thereby absolved politicians, as well as voters. In so doing, it conveniently enabled political leaders, such as Thatcher and later Brian Mulroney, both to deflect criticism of the basic arrangements of responsible government, with its concentration of power in the executive structures of parliamentary government, and to avoid criticism of the voting public, with its propensity to demand more in the way of public services while simultaneously opposing increased taxation. The voting public could thus also be portrayed as hapless victims of bureaucratic power.

Notwithstanding the appeal of the budget-maximizing bureaucrat thesis, the empirical evidence to support its principal claims is limited, especially in the Westminster systems. André Blais and Stéphane Dion, the editors of a major volume on Niskanen's thesis, conclude that "the idea of a passive sponsor [that is, politicians] has to be rejected. The evidence that public spending is related to the partisan composition of government...and is affected by the electoral cycle...shows that politicians do exert substantial control on budgetary matters."[16] While public servants may pursue budget-maximizing strategies, they do not monopolize the expenditure decision-making process. The absence of restraint in public spending, in short, has more to do with the dynamics of the broader political arena than with bureaucrats conning politicians into spending.

Agency Theory

The bureaucracy bashing exhibited at the outset of the Thatcher regime and subsequently by the Mulroney regime was less pronounced elsewhere, except, of course, in the United States where it reached even greater heights. However, concerns about the independence of permanent public services were not confined to conservative regimes intent on rolling back the social welfare and interventionist state. In both Australia and New Zealand, Labour governments came to power in the early 1980s against a backdrop of increasing bipartisan concern that their permanent bureaucracies were not abiding by the principles of responsible government. An Australian royal commission in the mid-1970s expressed this worry as follows:

[T]he administration, especially in its higher echelons, has an exaggerated conception of its proper role in the processes of government...
[I]t believes, consciously or unconsciously, that, independently of Parliament or the government, it is the guardian of the 'public interest' as opposed to sectional or vested interest, of continuity and stability in government administration, and of assumed social consensus about certain basic 'supra-political' values.[17]

In New Zealand, a similar concern was voiced in 1983 by then Opposition leader David Lange; in too many instances, he claimed, "departments were run by their civil servants rather than their Ministers."[18] In both Great Britain and Canada, similar criticisms have been voiced. Indeed, the perceived hubris of bureaucracy in all four systems has been a major irritant to many political leaders, particularly those ill-disposed to public policy activism.

In several respects, agency theory is more useful than public choice theory in understanding ministerial-public service relations. While ministers and their public servants function in a formal structure with prescribed superior-subordinate status, the nature of this hierarchical arrangement masks an important reality. Ministers possess constitutional executive authority, but in the performance of their executive functions they depend on their subordinate officials for policy advice and administrative assistance for the two reasons that give rise to all "principal-agent" relations: limits on the time a principal can devote to making decisions, and the principal's lack of expertise on the matters for which decisions are required.

The multiple roles of ministers within the governmental-political process prevent them from functioning as full-time chief executive officers of their portfolios. As a result, they must delegate some considerable measure of authority for the development of policy proposals and the administration of the public services provided by their departments and agencies. More important, however, their lack of expertise results in a dependence on the policy and management advice of those who assist them. Relationships between ministers and their public servants are thus essentially relationships between principals and agents. Ministers are principals who are obliged to rely on agents, a fact that gives rise to the requirement that ministers trust their public service advisers if good government is to be achieved.

Agency theory is as equally persuasive as public choice theory in explaining why agents are so powerful in relation to their principals. In all principal-agent relations, the latter invariably has significant influence over the former. Agents have an inherent advantage over their principals due to their knowledge and practical experience in the application of knowledge. They have a second advantage in determining possible courses of action and in taking action: their behaviour often cannot be observed by their principals.[19]

Although an agent's first and foremost duty is to secure the interests of her or his principal, the discretion that constitutes the essential rationale for this kind of relationship affords the agent considerable, if not unlimited, scope to decide what is in the principal's interest. It is this dimension that often gives rise to the claims of public choice theorists that the agent is pursuing her or his own interests. However, agency theory recognizes that the agent's conception of what is in the principal's interest is not always self-serving. In this case, conflict between the principal and agent is not a conflict between two competing sets of self-interests; rather it is a conflict between differing perceptions of what is in the principal's interests.

Agency theory, in contrast to public choice theory, does not assume, therefore, that agents will necessarily pursue their own interests to the detriment of the interests of their principals. This is an empirical issue to be examined in each case. Moreover, it provides a better account of why agents may assume to know better than their political masters. Given that they are expected to apply their knowledge and experience to the management of public affairs, public servants inevitably develop policy preferences, and these may be at odds with those of their political masters. However, these are not necessarily preferences that advance the personal interests of public servants; they may derive from different conceptions of the public interest in various public policy options.

If political leaders are not able to provide clear policy direction and ministerial leadership, the policies pursued will often be those formulated by public servants. The result, in these cases, is that public servants, rather than ministers, will appear to be in charge of government. More often than not, where public servants exercise considerable influence in the design and implementation of public policy, it is as a consequence of the political leadership devolving discretion to them. Bureaucrats thus seek to secure or preserve the autonomy of their organizations against efforts to coordinate them, to protect their turf against encroachment and to advance the interests of their clients when changes are proposed to the allocation of resources or regulatory policies. In doing so, they will seek to obtain, or retain, the budgetary resources and statutory authority necessary to achieve these organizational goals and/or to resist initiatives that run counter to these goals.[20] They will do so either because they are implicitly doing the bidding of their ministers in inter-ministerial politics, in which case "bureaucratic politics" is merely ministerial politics played out in the bureaucratic arena, or because ministers have yet to reach a definitive consensus on what precisely must be done, in which case "bureaucratic politics" is merely the ongoing intra-organizational politics to be expected in any complex organization that pursues a multiplicity of goals.[21]

The common existence of these two conditions gives rise to the appearance of "bureaucratic power." This can be deceptive, however. The exercise of bureaucratic power *per se* is first and foremost a function of delegated authority: bureaucrats do the bidding of their ministers. The exercise of bureaucratic "influence," on the other hand, is what is required of public servants in the performance of their advisory duties: bureaucrats press for what they consider to be in the best interests of their respective organizations as embodied in ministerial mandates. That this may lead to conflict is hardly surprising. Individual ministers have different mandates.

Public choice theory and agency theory have illuminated several dimensions of these inherent conflicts within governance. At the same time, much, if not most, of what has been posited by these theoretical accounts is hardly new knowledge. A long tradition of Western political science and public administration scholarship, some of it emanating from experienced politicians and public service practitioners, has addressed these matters in detail. What is new, of course, is the salience that public choice and agency theories has obtained in political and bureaucratic circles. It is in this sense that one can speak of new paradigms gaining ascendancy. The fact that there is little evidence on which to build a case for a runaway public service confiscating the public purse in its own self-interest is thus beside the point; ministers have been given reason to believe that they cannot trust their bureaucracies.

Ministers, Public Servants and the New Politics

Ministerial trust in career public servants has been eroded by recent developments in modern governance that suggest bureaucracies are self-serving. In addition to what are now traditional concerns of ministers that the career public service, at least at the senior echelons, has been politicized by the outgoing governing party, and whose loyalty is thus suspect, several developments have caused stresses and strains in ministerial-public service relations.

One of these results from the changing character of partisan politics, namely the decline of political parties as mechanisms of public participation and the proliferation of interest groups in the political arena. Interest groups are hardly a new phenomenon in representative democracies. But their increase in number has profoundly affected the governance of parliamentary democracies, in particular the capacity of political parties to structure political interests and thus to manage the state.

This development has not transformed the Westminster model of party government into an American-style form of divided government. Interest groups are powerful in the American system for at least two reasons. First, they are able to exploit divisions between those in the legislative, executive and bureaucratic arenas. Second, they are able to exercise influence over legislators given that they, and not political parties, are the major source of funding for electoral campaigns in a system where campaign spending is largely unregulated. In contrast, parties still form governments in the Westminster system. Nonetheless, governing parties are subject to expressions of organized demands that they increasingly cannot accommodate in traditional ways, particularly in a period of budgetary restraint and a growing global economic order.

Political parties have experienced difficulty in accommodating the increasing diversity of organized constituencies effectively, primarily because their political demands do not match the configurations of partisan coalitions upon which the major political parties have been constructed. This is true even in the more brokerage-styled Canadian party system. Precious few of these groups are interested in establishing close relationships with traditional governing parties, let alone being absorbed by them. They developed, and seek to maintain themselves, as independent political forces. Their leaders derive their political influence, particularly their access to the mass media, by virtue of their autonomy from partisan-based party politics.[22]

The institutional dynamics of political representation within parliamentary government are thus altered in important ways. The leaders of interest groups and social movements claim status within the political order of representative government, even though they are not elected by the voting public. They demand access to the executive-administrative apparatus of the state, recognizing that policy formulation in Westminster systems is still primarily undertaken in that arena, although increasing attention is now given to the legislative arena, given the new assertiveness of legislative bodies in parliamentary systems.[23]

A second development has been the new aggressiveness with which the mass media scrutinize government. Their focus is primarily on the actions of government and individual ministers. However, increased formal access to government information, as well as the perceived need of government to communicate with its various publics, including the general public, have given the media greater opportunity to expose the influence of public servants on government policy and to demand that they explain government policy and decisions.

In part, of course, the perceived need of governments to "communicate" with a mass public that is increasingly less partisan is also driven by the fact that the mass media are more than willing to give their own interpretations of the merits and shortcomings of government policies and actions. While there are cases of publishers who have reverted to the traditional mode of the "partisan press," in most cases the new aggressiveness of the fourth estate has taken the form of an "opposition" to the governmental establishment, whatever its partisan stripe.[24] Given the traditions of confidentiality, let alone secrecy, that pervade ministerial-public service relations, these media have an obvious inclination to mount a continual investigation of the citadels of power. Exposures of governmental shortcomings, real or perceived, attract readers and audiences in an era of increasing competition in the media business.

A third development in this regard has been the more assertive demands of parliamentarians for an enhanced role in governance. Under the Westminster system, the government must account to Parliament for its exercise of executive power. But the government is formed and maintained on the basis of party government, and this requires disciplined political parties. Many parliamentarians have now begun to challenge this state of affairs.

Given the aforementioned decrease in voter attachment to parties, growing numbers of citizens do not accord legitimacy to a politics dominated by the partisanship traditionally practised by political parties within Parliament. The result has been the demand that members of Parliament act independently to advance the interests of their constituents. Combined with more aggressive mass media and more assertive interest groups, this has also led to demands for greater public accountability on the part of government. These demands have been extended to parliamentarians' demands for direct public service accountability.

Public servants have thus had to accustom themselves to heightened scrutiny by parliamentary committees – the principal forums whereby public servants must encounter parliamentarians – even though the traditional principle of ministerial responsibility for policy *and* administration remains the official doctrine. But many parliamentarians demand more. A 1985 report of the Special Committee on Reform of the House of Commons in Canada (McGrath Report), for instance, went so far as to state:

> The idea of a minister being responsible for everything that goes on in a department may once have been realistic, but it has long ceased to be so. A minister cannot know everything that is going on in a department. The doctrine of ministerial accountability undermines the potential for genuine accountability on the part of the person that ought to be accountable – the senior officer [that is, the deputy minister] of the department.[25]

Finally, relations between ministers and public servants have been affected by the increasingly comprehensive mandates assigned to, or assumed by, parliamentary audit agencies, especially those that audit government finances and financial management. There is precious little that is not formally audited by this burgeoning array of auditors who function at arm's length from government in the service of Parliament, in some cases, as in Canada, with considerable independence from the Parliaments they serve.[26] While the scope of these audits varies from system to system, their scope has expanded to include almost every dimension of public management. While much of this work is conducted according to professionally recognized auditing standards, the findings and conclusions are seldom either communicated by the mass media or used by parliamentarians in ways that adhere to these standards. In these circumstances, auditing agencies, however professional they may be in their work, cannot but contribute to an increased politicization of public management.

The political management of the state in securing the consent of the governed in this new order has important implications for ministerial-public service relations. For their part, ministers find that political management assumes an even greater proportion of their time, in much the same way that the advent of responsible government in Britain led to a decrease in the time ministers could spend on administering their departments and attending to the execution of public business. Discussion and debate extend to new public venues, as ministers consult and enter into dialogue with a wide variety of interests. In Canada, even the finance minister's budget has been subject to this new political imperative.[27]

Demands for public consultation take ministers outside the executive-bureaucratic arena, where government-interest group relations have traditionally been managed in ways that afford ministers considerable discretion in responding to a limited range of groups with access to them. More generally, in this new order of nonpartisan public consultations, ministers are increasingly deprived of the support of their partisan followers in the public dialogue that these consultations require. When a consensus between ministers and these groups is not forthcoming – and consensus is exceedingly difficult to achieve given the variety of demands made by the great diversity of such groups, their general disinclination to compromise and the public character of these consultations – ministers confront an "opposition" that, however divided it may be, undermines confidence in the responsiveness of the institutions of democratic governance. Within Parliament, ministers are increasingly confronted by challenges from parliamentary committees as well as by auditing agencies that augment the partisan claims of the opposition – challenges that cannot be as easily met by the traditional partisan responses of parliamentary debate.

For their part, nonpartisan public servants are awkwardly positioned to assist ministers in these new contexts. Although public servants have long given advice to ministers on the political implications of policy alternatives, the public character of these new modes of political discourse and communication runs counter to the expectation that public service advice be confidential to ministers and that public servants, including those providing service on the front lines, not comment publicly on the merits or shortcomings of government policy. Confidential advice cannot be paraded in public, subjected to public negotiations or defended against the claims of opposing groups or opposition parties, without appearing to be subservient to the government of the day or disloyal to ministers. The first of these results would suggest that the public service had ceased to be neutral and impartial; the second, that it had failed in its duty as a subordinate institution within parliamentary government. Either way, public servants at all levels are caught between a rock and a hard place. The logic of a career public service as a nonpartisan institution does not easily admit of a role for public servants in this new order of political representation, public discourse and open government.

The Neutrality of the Public Service

This new order accounts in some large measure for the perceptions, both inside and outside government, that career public servants have become politicized, at least at the most senior levels. In this order, senior public servants cannot but be drawn into the political fray: ministers expect them to participate in various consultative and parliamentary forums. Going public not only eliminates the traditional anonymity of public servants; it often exposes their views on matters of public policy, however much they attempt to restrict their commentaries to approved government policy. It is exceedingly difficult to address complex matters of public policy without being perceived as advocates of particular policy alternatives.

If public servants are perceived as advancing, as opposed to merely explaining, the government's point of view, their neutrality is undermined. However, if public servants do not appear to be sufficiently aggressive in promoting or defending government policy, their loyalty is likely to be questioned by ministers. Ministers may not be much troubled by whether the neutrality or impartiality of the public service appears to be compromised; on the other hand, they will probably be concerned by indications that public servants are less than enthusiastic about their policy preferences.

It is not surprising, in the context of this new politics, that ministers are inclined to want public servants who share their policy preferences or, at the least, assurance that public servants will be responsive to them. This is the most elementary basis of trust in a principal-agent relationship. When a government, or individual ministers, has explicit policy preferences, it is not difficult to ascertain the extent to which public servants support them. In cases where they have not developed explicit policy directives, trust can only be established over time, if and when ministers come to value the advice they receive. If this is not achieved, ministers are likely to perceive attempts on the part of public servants to question ministerial preferences as merely disguised efforts to make them captives of the public service's preferences. That such ministers may possess no coherent sense of policy direction will be irrelevant. The claim will be made that public servants are obstructing ministers.

The tension in these circumstances goes to the essential character of the relationship between responsible government and a neutral public service. There are two views of this relationship that are difficult to reconcile. On the one hand, as Graham Wilson reminds us with respect to the tradition that began in Great Britain:

[A] paradox lies at the heart of the British senior civil service...[T]he civil service is not expected to be neutral, but partisan for whatever government the electorate has returned...The professional skill of the senior bureaucrat lies in being able to perform...[their management and advisory] functions for any duly constituted government; their professional skill lies not in being politically chaster but in being sufficiently *promiscuous* to accommodate to changes in the party in power.[28]

It is only on the basis of this willingness to be promiscuously partisan that the public service is made a permanent public service, with ministers not interfering in public service staffing. This view accords well with the idea of the public service as a "profession," given that the members of a profession, as agents, can serve different principals at different times and thus avoid conflicts of interest. It assumes, moreover, that ministers make policy decisions: the career public service is at their "service" while they remain in office. They are loyal to the government of the day, dutifully implement the partisan agenda of the government regardless of their personal views and provide "*impartial* advice to ministers."[29]

A second view of neutrality, however, is often implicit in the defence of a career public service. In this view, a professional, nonpartisan public service pursues neutrality by providing advice, as Joel Aberbach and Bert Rockman describe it, albeit without endorsing the concept, that also speaks to "the long-term, broader interests of the country and the government [as an institution]."[30] As they note: "Some assumptions obviously lurk behind these noble words." They point out that this assumption lies at the heart of the politics-administration dichotomy, the very idea upon which the idea of a neutral public service, freed from the "patronage evil" of partisan appointments, was developed in the United States. The politics-administration dichotomy assumes a public service with an obligation to render advice that addresses the merits of government policy preferences or proposals against the broader public interest, whether requested or not: it must fearlessly "speak truth to power."[31]

This assumed obligation of a neutral public service, especially in the context of the Westminster system of responsible government and in contrast to the American model, raises the spectre of a public service that sees itself (or is assumed by others as required to see itself), in the words of the previously quoted Australian Royal Commission, as "the guardian of 'the public interest'...independently of Parliament or the government." This understanding of a neutral public service can easily fail to distinguish between: (1) the public interest as independently conceived by a nonpartisan public service; and (2) the public interest that is served by the creation and maintenance of a nonpartisan public service in the service of a partisan government.

The former understanding implies a separation of politics and administration that simply does not obtain in the Westminster model. It also depends on the requirement that politics not intervene in the administration of the state, a situation that simply cannot be sustained in a context where public policy infuses public administration. The latter understanding does not deny that ministers are to observe and uphold the law in the administration of public affairs and thereby adhere to the principles of impartiality, or non-partisanship, in public administration. But it conceives of the public interest in a nonpartisan public service on essentially empirical grounds. The public service serves ministers who have constitutional *and* political responsibilities for policy and administration, but it is staffed according to criteria that do not include party partisanship. The public interest that is thereby secured is the technical superiority of a public service constituted in this manner. This assumes, however, as John Martin puts it, that there can be developed a "profession of statecraft,"[32] which not only would not result in "government of bureaucrats"[33] and thus undermine democratic control over the management of the state, but also would secure the highest possible degree of competence on the part of those who advise on public policy and manage the business of government. As discussed in the next chapter, governments in each of the four Westminster systems seriously questioned their career public services over the past decade on each of these two counts.

Conclusion

There is clearly a tension between the twin pillars of the modern Westminster model: responsible government and a career public service. While responsible government requires that authority be vested in ministers, good government requires more than political direction and decision. It demands that the state possess a professional public service in order that ministers be served by those with the requisite knowledge and experience not only to administer large-scale technical operations but, even more important, to advise on complex and often intractable policy issues. This idea of a professional public service cannot be implemented with the desired effect without an explicit bargain between ministers and their public servants: the public service will be loyal and responsive in its service to ministers; in return, ministers will accept political responsibility in Parliament for the administration of public affairs. Public service accountability is thereby internal to government; it does not engulf the public service in the partisan politics of public accountability as secured through the dynamics of responsible parliamentary government.

Public services within the Westminster systems considered here have assumed significant influence in governance. But this influence is subordinate to political authority. Where public servants have behaved in ways that raise questions about either their loyalty or their responsiveness, the issue is often one of inadequate, incompetent or corrupt political leadership. Where public servants have exercised great power in the design and implementation of public policy, it is invariably as a consequence of the political leadership devolving authority to them and usually because a consensus exists between ministers and public servants as to the general direction of public policy: a policy paradigm prevails within government. Moreover, when one party is in office for a long period, it is not uncommon for relations between ministers and their senior public servants to become "close and congenial." The charge of politicization in this circumstance is next to inevitable.

Discounting the traditional suspicions held by new governing parties of the public service they inherit on assuming office – as evidenced in the four Westminster systems over the last decade – it is striking to what extent the malaise in modern government has been blamed on the professional public service. Of course, a professional public service does not guarantee good government, any more than the Westminster system necessarily secures responsible government. Whether it flows from constitutional authority or administrative discretion, power can be abused and misused in any institutional setting. The idea of a professional public service, in short, does not presuppose that all "men [and women] of [public] business" are virtuous and motivated purely by the public interest. Nor, for that matter, does the creation or maintenance of a nonpartisan, professional public service automatically secure, or preserve over time, the policy or management competence required to achieve good government. But there is no evidence to indicate that good government can be established and maintained without a professional public service underpinning a democratic political system.

Notes

1. S.L. Sutherland, "Responsible Government and Ministerial Responsibility: Every Reform has its Own Problem," *Canadian Journal of Political Science*, Vol. 24, no. 1 (March 1991), p. 120.

2. Henry Parris, *Constitutional Bureaucracy* (London: George Allen and Unwin, 1969).

3. John Martin, *A Profession of Statecraft?* (Wellington, New Zealand: Victoria University Press, 1988), pp. 18-19.

4. F.F. Ridley, "Career service: a comparative perspective on civil service promotion," *Public Administration*, Vol. 61 (Summer 1983), p. 179.

5. Parris, *Constitutional Bureaucracy*, pp. 50-79; Gavin Drewry and Tony Butcher, *The Civil Service Today* (Oxford: Basil Blackwell, 1988), pp. 31-48.

6. Parris, *Constitutional Bureaucracy*, p. 40.

7. Parris, *Constitutional Bureaucracy*, p. 42.

8. J.E. Hodgetts, William McCloskey, Reginald Whitaker and V. Seymour Wilson, *The Biography of an Institution* (Montreal: McGill-Queen's University Press, 1972), p. 8.

9. Hodgetts, McCloskey, Whitaker and Wilson, *The Biography of an Institution*, pp. 16-19.

10. Hodgetts, McCloskey, Whitaker and Wilson, *The Biography of an Institution*, p. 16.

11. Graham K. Wilson, "Prospects for the public service in Britain. Major to the rescue?", *International Review of Administrative Sciences*, Vol. 57, no. 3 (September 1991), p. 328.

12. Michel Crozier, *The Crisis of Democracy* (New York: New York University Press, 1975).

13. Sandford Borins, "Public Choice: 'Yes Minister' Made it Popular, But Does Winning the Nobel Prize Make it True?", *Canadian Public Administration*, Vol. 31 (1988), pp. 12-26.

14. William Niskanen, "A reflection on *Bureaucracy and Representative Government*," in André Blais and Stéphane Dion (eds.), *The Budget-Maximizing Bureaucrat: Appraisals and Evidence* (Pittsburgh: University of Pittsburgh Press, 1991), pp. 13-31. See also Mark Sproule-Jones, "Science as art and art as science: a response to Professor Borins' paper," *Canadian Public Administration*, Vol. 31, no. 1 (1988), pp. 34-41.

15. André Blais and Stéphane Dion, "Introduction," in Blais and Dion (eds.), *The Budget-Maximizing Bureaucrat*, p. 4.

16. André Blais and Stéphane Dion, "Conclusion: Are Bureaucrats Budget Maximizers?", in Blais and Dion (eds.), *The Budget-Maximizing Bureaucrat*, p. 358.

17. Quoted in John Halligan, "The career public service and administrative reform in Australia," *International Review of Administrative Studies*, Vol. 57, no. 3 (1991), p. 352.

18. John Roberts, "Ministers, the Cabinet and Public Servants," in Jonathan Boston and Martin Holland (eds.), *The Fourth Labour Government: Radical Politics in New Zealand* (Auckland: Oxford University Press, 1987), p. 100.

19. Jonathan Boston, "The Theoretical Underpinnings of Public Sector Restructuring in New Zealand," in Jonathan Boston, John Martin, June Pallot and Pat Walsh (eds.), *Reshaping the State: New Zealand's Bureaucratic Revolution* (Auckland: Oxford University Press, 1991), pp. 1-26.

20. James Q. Wilson, *Bureaucracy: What Government Agencies Do and Why They Do It* (New York: Basic Books, 1989); Stephen Brooks, *Public Policy in Canada: An Introduction* (Toronto: McClelland and Stewart, 1993).

21. Michael M. Atkinson and William D. Coleman, "Bureaucrats and politicians in Canada: an examination of the political administration model," *Comparative Political Studies*, Vol. 18, no. 1 (April 1985), pp. 58-80.

22. A. Paul Pross, "The pressure group conundrum," in James P. Bickerton and Alain-G. Gagnon (eds.), *Canadian Politics*, 2nd ed. (Peterborough: Broadview Press, 1994), pp. 173-87.

23. F. Leslie Seidle, "Interest Advocacy through Parliamentary Channels: Representation and Accommodation," in F. Leslie Seidle (ed.), *Equity and Community: the Charter, Interest Advocacy and Representation* (Montreal: Institute for Research on Public Policy, 1993), pp. 189-225.

24. Peter Self, *Government by the Market? The Politics of Public Choice* (Boulder: Westview Press, 1993).

25. Canada, House of Commons, Special Committee on the Reform of the House of Commons, *Third Report* (Ottawa: Queen's Printer, June 1985), p. 21.

26. S.L. Sutherland and G.B. Doern, *Bureaucracy in Canada: Control and Reform*, Vol. 43 of the Research Studies of the Royal Commission on the Economic Union and Development Prospects for Canada (Toronto: University of Toronto Press, 1985).

27. Evert Lindquist, "Citizens, Experts and Budgets: Evaluating Ottawa's Budget Process," in Susan D. Phillips (ed.), *How Ottawa Spends 1994-95: Making Change* (Ottawa: Carleton University Press, 1994), pp. 91-128.

28. Wilson, "Prospects for the public service in Britain," p. 328; emphasis added.

29. Kenneth Kernaghan, "Career Public Service 2000: road to renewal or impractical vision?", *Canadian Public Administration*, Vol. 34, no. 4 (1991), p. 560; emphasis added.

30. Joel Aberbach and Bert Rockman, "Civil Servants and Policymakers: Neutral or Responsive Competence?", *Governance*, Vol. 7, no. 4 (October 1994), p. 461.

31. Aaron Wildavsky, *Speaking Truth to Power: The Art and Craft of Policy Analysis* (Boston: Little, Brown and Company, 1979).

32. Martin, *A Profession of Statecraft?.*

33. Sutherland, "Responsible Government and Ministerial Responsibility," p. 92.

THREE

Renewing the Profession of Statecraft

In her first report as Head of the Public Service to the Prime Minister of Canada in August 1995, Jocelyne Bourgon, Clerk of the Privy Council and Secretary to the Cabinet, concluded that: "Public attitudes and political institutions evolve, but our tradition of a professional, nonpartisan public service transcends any specific reform or restructuring."[1] In her covering letter to the Prime Minister, she characterized the public service as "a national institution of great importance," which, she argued in her report, provides government with "frank and honest policy advice – not for ideological reasons but because history has taught us that is the best way to serve Canadians and their elected representatives."[2]

That the Head of the Public Service of Canada should consider it necessary in 1995 to draw attention to the importance of a professional, nonpartisan public service in the governance of Canada is indicative of the extent to which the value of this institution to good government has been questioned in recent years. The Canadian experience in this regard has not been unique. In all four Westminster systems, the fundamental premise of a professional, nonpartisan public service as a necessary condition of good government has been placed in doubt over the last decade.

By 1995, however, there were some indications that the tide may have begun to turn. For instance, the British government has rediscovered, at least rhetorically, the contribution that a permanent public service makes to good government. Its 1994 White Paper on the Public Service stated:

> This Government, like its predecessors, believes that a permanent Civil Service, up to and including the highest levels, has considerable advantages for effective and efficient administration. It provides continuity through changes in government; and the Government believes that the need for Ministers to test proposals and prospective initiatives with a permanent Civil Service committed to providing politically impartial, objective advice is likely to produce better government.[3]

The prospects of a rediscovery of the value of a permanent public service in the 1990s follow a decade or more of bureaucracy bashing. Not only the responsiveness of the permanent public service has been challenged but, more important, various efforts were made to check, counter and even supplant this institution at the core of the executive structures of government. Some of these measures were undoubtedly a necessary corrective to the monopoly position of the permanent public service in the provision of advice to ministers; others were required to ensure greater responsiveness on the part of public servants to the political direction and policy priorities of government.

In pursuing some of these measures, however, governments, including the Canadian government, have come dangerously close to undermining the core values of a professional, nonpartisan public service – particularly, as the Australian Management Advisory Board put it, the value of "frank and fearless advice."[4] Indeed, Colin Campbell and Graham Wilson titled their recent book on the British civil service *The End of Whitehall: Death of a Paradigm?*. They claimed they could find little evidence to be optimistic about the prospects of a reaffirmation of the former virtues of the civil service. They concluded that "the Whitehall model has reached a condition such that even if it survives, it will no longer seem an attractive model of governance to the rest of the world."[5]

This chapter considers the experiences of the four governments over the last decade and more in reining in the permanent public service, on the one hand, and to make the public service more responsive to the executive, on the other. Subsequent chapters examine how governments have tried to engage the permanent public service in the pursuit of improved public management. The experiences outlined below illustrate the dilemma inherent in seeking to make the public service responsive to political direction without eroding its nonpartisan integrity. Finally, a reaffirmation of the value of a professional, nonpartisan public service requires an explicit and nonpartisan political commitment from politicians. It also needs effective leadership from within the public service to ensure public service support for good government.

Strengthening the Political Arm of Government

The permanent public service in Westminster systems has traditionally possessed significant influence within governance because of its position in affecting public policy – the decisions of government about what the government will do, or not do, in its efforts to manage the state. By the late 1970s, political leaders appeared willing to curtail the influence of the career public service in ways that went well beyond anything previously attempted. The spectre of "politicization" of the state apparatus was clearly present.

Pursuing the American Approach?

The Conservatives who came to power in Canada in 1984 viewed the leadership of the federal public service as closely, indeed too closely, aligned with the departing Liberal government. They would have agreed with Colin Campbell's assessment that there had developed a "symbiosis [of the senior public service] with the dominant party, the Liberals."[6] This was not a new claim by the Conservative party in Canada; it had been a constant since the emergence of a professional bureaucracy in the late 1930s. With the Liberal party in power from 1935 to 1957, it was inevitable that there would be a perception that the senior mandarins were attached to the Liberal agenda, if not the Liberal party. Indeed, John Meisel has described how extensively the federal bureaucracy was involved in preparing the Liberal party platform for the 1957 election, which, ironically, brought to an end this long period of Liberal rule.[7]

Moreover, by 1984, the Conservatives had experienced the strained, to say the least,[8] ministerial-public service relations of the Diefenbaker Conservative government (1957-63) and the short-lived Clark Conservative government (1979-80). There were now many in the Conservative party who advocated the adoption of the American approach to staffing the state apparatus. As J.L. Manion, a former top mandarin, noted: "There was some talk of opening up the public service to outside appointment, to extending political appointments down into the hierarchy, and to appointing 'political commissars' within departments."[9]

A principal means of giving ministers control over the state apparatus was the 1984 Conservative transition team's plan to upgrade ministers' offices (these are the personal offices of ministers that are separate from their departmental bureaucracies and thus the public service proper). Staff in these offices are ministerial appointees and thereby exempt from the staffing regime of the public service. Since at least the late 1960s when the size of ministers' offices began to increase beyond a handful of personal assistants, ministerial office staff have come primarily – in several cases exclusively – from outside the public service. While a few ministers during the lengthy Trudeau regime deployed their personal staff to pursue projects independent of their departmental bureaucracies,[10] the basic tone of relying on the professional public service for policy advice was set by the Prime Minister himself. Trudeau expanded the Prime Minister's Office (PMO) in terms of numbers, but throughout his tenure it never achieved a substantial policy advisory capacity. His willingness to depend on his public service department, the Privy Council Office (PCO), as a countervail to mandarins in the line departments of government made this unnecessary.

The upgrading of ministerial offices during the Mulroney regime took two forms. First, the most senior position in each minister's political office was elevated from "executive assistant" to "chief of staff." The explicit intention was to have these "political commissars," as Manion described them, provide "strategic political advice in relation to [a minister's] departmental responsibilities and to balance the advice from [departmental] public servants."[11] As a former member of Mulroney's PMO described it: "The chief of staff position was in large measure created to act as a check on bureaucratic power...to ensure that ministerial directives are being carried out within the department."[12]

The second form of upgrading was the increase in the number of staff appointed to ministerial offices, including the PMO. This move was to enhance ministers' control over the influence of the bureaucracy. The "political arm of government," as Gordon Osbaldeston, a former Clerk of the Privy Council and Secretary to the Cabinet, called these offices, was to be strengthened to counter the bureaucratic arm of government.[13]

Strengthening the political arm of government proved not to be as effective as expected even though the PMO in particular, and ministerial offices in general, assumed greater power and influence throughout the

Mulroney era than had been the Canadian experience.[14] But with precious few exceptions, even in the PMO itself, the government failed to recruit well, particularly for chief of staff positions. At best, the vast majority of chiefs of staff performed at a level of competence no higher than good executive assistants under the former system.[15] At worst, they merely contributed to a general deterioration in good government by providing a new avenue of access to ministers for a rapidly expanding coterie of lobbyists with partisan ties to the governing party.

Equally detrimental was that, in too many instances, the plethora of political aides combined with the large number of ministers merely served to convolute the process of decision making. Without a doubt, the greatest irony in all this was the need for Mulroney himself to turn to a career public servant – Derek Burney from the Department of External Affairs – to assume control of the PMO to give it some semblance of good management, discipline and direction.[16]

Putting Partisan Politics in its Place?

On assuming office, the Chrétien government both eliminated the post of chief of staff – reverting to the traditional post of executive assistant as head of the minister's office – and reduced the size of ministers' offices, including that of the Prime Minister. It did so for several reasons. First, it was responding to a public dissatisfied with the size and cost of government. Second, it acknowledged that capable ministerial staff able to provide competent policy advice were a rare commodity if they were recruited from outside the career public service. Third, the Liberal government accepted that the roles of political staff were best confined to the function of "minding" ministers, to use James Walter's term.[17] Among other things, this meant managing their time; controlling access to them; handling the media; preparing them for their parliamentary and political party duties; and alerting them to the partisan implications of the decisions required of them by their departmental mandates and their participation in cabinet decision making. Given the frequency with which the Canadian government has ministers with neither ministerial nor parliamentary experience,[18] the function of ministerial "minders" is especially critical. And finally, it wished to send a signal to the career public service that its primacy in advising ministers on public policy would be restored.

This approach, however, has not met with favour in all quarters of the Liberal party. There are those who feel that Prime Minister Chrétien went too far in seeking to restore the influence of the career public service – a service that some Liberals consider to have been politicized by the outgoing Conservative regime, at least in its acceptance of the Conservative agenda. These Liberals include some ministers, many members of the parliamentary caucus and a good number of partisan ministerial aides. They also claim that public service opposition to certain ministerial initiatives accounts for a number of major leaks to the media of internal government reports.

To date, however, there is no hard evidence that public servants have sought to obstruct ministerial objectives on grounds other than their traditional resistance to policy changes they deem not to be in the interests of good government. Even so, the Chrétien government's efforts to erase the legacy of the Mulroney government in enhancing the partisan dynamic in public management has been resisted by some Liberals. There are, as a consequence, internal pressures to increase the number of partisan staff in ministers' offices.

Comparative Experiences

The experience of the other three Westminster systems in enhancing the political arm of government is similar to that of Canada in some ways but different in two critical respects. These are the degree to which governments have recruited party-partisans with policy expertise and private-sector personnel with public-sector experience on the one hand, and the secondment of public servants to ministerial offices on the other.

In Britain, Margaret Thatcher was obviously keen to ensure that her advisers and those of her ministers were committed to her political agenda. Her regime was to be characterized by "conviction politics."[19] At the outset, however, she was forced to eschew an expansion of both her personal office and those of ministers because "she could not convincingly preach economy in government if she permitted her political bureaucracy to increase. In addition to allowing only half as many special advisers to ministers as provided under Callaghan (10 instead of 20), Thatcher initially eliminated the No. 10 policy unit [that is, the policy unit in her personal office]."[20]

It was clear from the outset, nevertheless, that however few their number, personal advisers were to have a crucial role in the Thatcher government. Eventually she re-established the policy unit in her office and, thereafter, its role was critical in the various initiatives she pursued as personal priorities.[21] Unlike the experience of the PMO in Canada, however, in staffing her office she continued the British tradition of employing career public servants in considerable numbers and often in critical roles.

Some of these officials were to provide a link to the bureaucracy, but others functioned as key policy advisers in their own right. Fully one-quarter of the advisers in her policy unit were career public servants.[22] Although some of these seconded officials became so identified with her prime ministership that they did not return to the public service at the conclusion of their terms in her office, most were able to do so. Equally significant, she appointed Derek Rayner, a senior private-sector executive with experience in government, as her personal "efficiency adviser" with responsibility to effect major changes in public management.

In Australia, the Hawke government also chose to upgrade ministerial offices, thus continuing a practice begun on a major scale in the 1970s. But it also created a new position of "ministerial consultant" and allowed each minister to appoint two such senior staff to his or her office. These consultants were "to provide ministers with the assistance of persons who shared the party's values and objectives and/or offered special skills and who were to be engaged by a different process from that of the public servant."[23]

While it was accepted that staffing these offices from outside the public service could be increased, the Australian government continued a prior tradition as in Britain of seconding public servants to the prime minister's and ministers' offices. In recruiting outsiders, however, emphasis was placed on finding "party operatives with policy backgrounds."[24] After an initial emphasis on recruiting such party operatives, the balance shifted to "roughly even proportions" between them and career public servants and eventually tipped in favour of the latter. As Campbell notes, "the Prime Minister's Private Office has become a proving ground for high flyers marked for key secretary and deputy secretary posts [the two highest levels in the Australian public service]."[25]

Not surprisingly, the role of these ministerial offices, especially that of the prime minister, has been significant in managing the political agenda of the government while maintaining critical linkages with the state bureaucracy. As Colin Campbell and John Halligan note, during the Hawke government, "all ministers – not just the prime minister...tended to rely upon their political staff much more than would their Canadian or British opposite numbers."[26] In the Keating government, reliance on personal advisers has increased, at least on the part of the Prime Minister, although in his personal office "the upper echelons...are dominated by trusted former Treasury advisers."[27]

In New Zealand, the Labour government elected in 1984 also increased the opportunities for ministers to obtain political assistance from other than public servants, although appointing public servants to ministers' offices, as in Britain and Australia, was still maintained. But now, ministers were given the authority to appoint "outside consultants,"[28] an especially critical development since in New Zealand, unlike in the other Westminster systems, the appointment of permanent heads of departments was not the prime minister's prerogative. As a result, the permanent bureaucracy had been able to practise a significant degree of *de facto* self-government in staffing even at the most senior levels.

Comparative Perspectives

Enhancing the political arm of government cannot but create a measure of tension between those employed in ministerial offices and those employed in public service departments, including central agencies. Other things being equal, however, the longer a government is in office, the more likely ministers will develop close relations with their senior public servants, particularly if they themselves are able to have some say in their appointment. Moreover, the experience in Britain, Australia and New Zealand demonstrates that a more effective political arm of government is possible when the party-partisans in these offices can claim expertise in the arts of government as opposed to electoral and party politics, and when public servants are among those who staff ministerial offices.

A few notable exceptions aside, the Canadian experience has been marked since the late 1960s by "two solitudes" – political and bureaucratic. The continued practice in Canada of recruiting ministerial staff almost exclusively from outside the public service, with scant experience in public policy or public management, does not serve ministers well. The perpetuation of the two solitudes, moreover, invites an exaggerated suspicion of the bureaucracy on the part of ministers and their political aides. Deputy ministers and other senior public servants welcome competent ministerial aides who can address the partisan dimensions of their ministers' responsibilities. However, unless the respect is mutual – that ministerial staff appreciate the responsibilities of senior public servants for good government – interaction between the two is unlikely to be productive. Finally, the two solitudes mean that too few public servants become well versed in the full range of political imperatives facing ministers *before* reaching senior positions in the bureaucracy.

Chrétien's efforts to cleanse government of some of the worst excesses of partisanship in the administration of public affairs contributed to an unprecedented measure of public approval for his leadership that went well beyond a traditional honeymoon period. As noted, however, not all of this has gone down well with some Liberal partisans. This continuing tension within Liberal circles illustrates how difficult Canadian partisan elites and their advisers find it to accept the realities of managing the state in the current context. A partial explanation of this is that many federal politicians and their aides question the contribution that good public administration makes to good politics.

Staffing the Public Service

To manage the state, ministers need different kinds of assistance and advice, not just in relation to partisan politics. They also need advice on policy decisions. However, what constitutes a policy decision, and thus policy advice, is not always straightforward. Ministers make a multitude of policy decisions, covering the spectrum of developing new policy, adjusting existing policy and implementing policy. All of this is political, but not all is explicitly, even implicitly, partisan. The nature of advice can thus vary from decision to decision. In all cases, nonetheless, ministers need to be served by an apparatus that is both responsive and competent.

Securing Responsiveness in the State Apparatus

Efforts by governments in the Westminster systems over the last decade or more to secure responsiveness in the state apparatus have clearly diminished the influence of the career public service. Responsiveness has been winning over competence in part because the Westminster systems have not been willing to move to the approach found in several other Western democracies where career public servants with party affiliations may be appointed to the top levels of the public service at the discretion of ministers. In Germany, for instance, following a change of government, officials in the top two levels may be temporarily retired or redeployed to make way for new appointments.[29] However, competence is not meant to take a back seat to responsiveness. Rather, those appointed are expected to meet the criteria for such positions and to function as professionals. The German experience indicates that these people see themselves as having distinct roles from those who hold political office or serve in ministerial offices.

Without such a tradition and culture to secure responsiveness and competence, ministers in the Westminster systems will be well served only to the extent that their public service advisers are able to speak out effectively on the political dimensions of strategic decisions. This need

not mean that they must take part in partisan affairs; they need not dupli-
cate the work done by political assistants. Nor does it mean that they
must promote the partisan interests of the governing party in the implementation of policy, as might be the case in regional or constituency
pork-barrelling, for instance. And it certainly need not mean that public
servants must forego giving advice that runs counter to what the government or individual ministers may wish to do.

Good political advice does not necessarily mean telling ministers simply what they want to hear. Saying "No, Minister," or "Yes, but, Minister,"
rather than "Yes, Minister," may equally indicate that a public servant
adviser has fully considered a minister's wishes or best interests. There is,
in short, nothing inherent in the provision of advice that need eliminate
professional integrity. However, this integrity is forthcoming only if the
leadership of the public service is willing and able to maintain a measure
of distance from the political leadership.

Canada: Changing the Guard

Although the Mulroney government was committed to strengthening the
political arm of government, it did not pursue an explicit partisan-politicization of the ranks of the senior public service. In a handful of cases,
Mulroney did appoint deputy ministers from outside the public service, as
had prime ministers before him. He had originally intended to appoint
more people from outside government but was unable to attract capable
persons to assume the public service offices at the prerogative of the
prime minister, namely deputy and associate deputy positions.[30]

Several factors account for this. The pay and associated perks were clearly
unattractive to senior private-sector executives. Those who might otherwise
have been tempted knew that, as subordinates of ministers and given the
centralized management systems of the federal bureaucracy, the scope for
exercising authority was much more limited than in the private sector.
Furthermore, they were aware of the Conservatives' intention to minimize
the influence of senior officials in favour of partisan-political advisers.

However, several deputies left shortly after the arrival of the Conservatives
in 1984, and, as a result of deputy minister shuffles and new appointments,
a new team was in place within two years, with a change in "virtually all
deputy ministers."[31] This development was not in any way unique to the
Mulroney government; as Jacques Bourgault and Stéphane Dion have
shown, changes had occurred with new Liberal prime ministers in the
past.[32] Frequent turnover of deputy ministers, moreover, had become the

norm well before 1984. But Mulroney's changes were unprecedented, with 32 transfers in the first two years. As Bourgault and Dion point out: "This series of transfers was seen as a way of quickly establishing political control of the bureaucracy. Administrative officials judged too imbued with the thinking of the previous government or too compromised by some of the government's policies were expelled from their lairs."[33] At the same time, Mulroney did not immediately replace Gordon Osbaldeston as Clerk of the Privy Council and Secretary to the Cabinet, and when Osbaldeston retired in 1986, the Prime Minister selected not only a career bureaucrat, Paul Tellier, but one whom Conservatives, among others, had identified with the Trudeau regime.

The Mulroney government's distrust of the senior public service did not disappear simply because there had been extensive changes at the top. The government was still unwilling to engage the senior public service in the management of public affairs, particularly in providing collective deputy ministerial advice to cabinet committees. This, combined with the minimal capacity of its political aides, goes a long way to explain the government's shortcomings. Even though the government's political arm had to be rescued by a senior public servant on secondment to the PMO, both the Prime Minister and many of his colleagues continued to rely primarily on partisan and external advice in their efforts to manage the state. Staffing the leadership of the federal public service was thus a priority of the Prime Minister only in that it ensured that those appointed were willing to accept their largely passive role in the formulation of the government's agenda.

Turning to the Public Service?

On assuming office in 1993, the Chrétien government went out of its way to reassure deputy ministers that their ministers would be expected to turn to them for professional advice on policy and operations. Continuity in the senior ranks was also maintained. The massive turnover following Mulroney's election in 1984 was not replicated, in part because the major restructuring that preceded the 1993 general election had already led to substantial changes at the top of the public service as a result of the consolidation of a number of departments. Within a year, however, a new Clerk of the Privy Council and Secretary to the Cabinet, Jocelyne Bourgon, had been appointed. She replaced Glen Shortliffe, the second of two Clerks appointed by Mulroney (the other being Tellier). Each of the latter two had come to be closely identified with the Mulroney regime.

Equally important, the Liberal government's management of its major policy and program review processes differed substantially from the Conservatives' 1984 program review in the contribution expected of the professional bureaucracy. Since the Liberal government did not assume that bureaucratic waste was the reason for such exercises, it did not feel it necessary to involve outsiders as a check on the bureaucracy. Outsiders were used as consultants and advisers to ministers *and* public servants. More important, the public service was asked to do more than tinker; it was to think seriously about the future role of the state.[34]

Comparative Experience

In Great Britain, Thatcher was explicit from the outset about her intention to ensure that appointments to senior public service positions would promote both her agenda and her conception of good public management. She used the prerogative power of the British prime minister to appoint permanent secretaries in ways that caused more than a little consternation in bureaucratic as well as political circles. Thatcher was able to appoint more permanent secretaries than any other prime minister in British history because of the number of normal retirements during her tenure. Also, as Savoie noted, "[s]he took a direct hand in who was being promoted as permanent secretaries, often looking to less obvious or less senior candidates, favouring those who appeared impatient with the status quo and who demonstrated a capacity 'to manage'."[35] By going outside the permanent public service to fill the post of chief economic adviser in the Treasury, Thatcher confirmed the fears of those who saw the public service coming under her direct control.[36]

Thatcher's generally negative attitude to the British public service, especially its senior ranks, was further confirmed by the adoption of open competitions to fill the chief executive posts of the newly designed "executive agencies." The latter began to be established in the late 1980s to separate the operational units responsible for the delivery of government programs from the policy advisory structures of ministerial departments. There was a clear intention to promote the recruitment of executives from the private sector. Although the plan was not totally successful, a number of chief executives have come from outside the central public service, but most of these had experience in the broader public sector, that is, in public-sector organizations other than the central public service. More recently, the Major government, while re-committing itself to a career public service, announced it would promote a greater use of open competitions in staffing the senior public service in central departments.[37]

In Australia, before the election of Labor in 1983, a partisan politicization of the senior public service had been proposed in the party's election platform. This would have entailed "a political tier within the senior ranks of the public service that would comprise all department heads (who made up the first division) and up to five percent of the second division. The appointment would be made by Cabinet on the recommendation of individual ministers."[38] On assuming office, however, the Hawke government declined to implement this scheme, thus avoiding the "appearance of politicization."[39]

Nevertheless, changes were made in the appointment process and terms of appointment for the most senior public service posts, that is, departmental secretary (the title of these most senior positions having been changed from "permanent head"). Responsibility for advising the Prime Minister on these appointments shifted in 1987 from the Chairman of the Public Service Board (at the same time it was abolished) to the Secretary of the Department of Prime Minister and Cabinet (PMC), the equivalent of the Clerk of the Privy Council and Secretary to the Cabinet in Canada. According to Patrick Weller, however, "since 1975 the secretary of PMC has always been the most influential adviser. The new arrangements legitimized what had long been the practice."[40] The policy of five-year terms, first introduced in 1987 for those appointed from outside the public service, was made a statutory requirement in 1994. The idea of "permanent" heads, however, had for some time become a thing of the past as successive prime ministers, as in Canada and Britain, had become increasingly active in the use of their prerogative power.

In New Zealand, the Labour government elected in 1984 also declined to politicize the senior bureaucracy with partisan appointments to the public service, notwithstanding the musing of its leader (subsequently Prime Minister) while in opposition.[41] However, two major changes were effected in 1988. First, in the reorganization of the machinery of government, departmental permanent heads became "chief executives," appointed following open competitions and on the basis of contracts for fixed terms – up to five years, subject to a reappointment in the same position not to exceed three years. Second, while the State Services Commissioner (the head of the public service) makes a single recommendation to Cabinet for each appointment, ministers have "an opportunity to inform the Commission about any matters they believe ought to be considered in making an appointment...[and] can suggest people who might be useful to include on the interview panel and can encourage people who they think would be suitable candidates for appointments to apply for the job."[42] Furthermore, the Cabinet can reject a recommended candidate and make its own appointment, providing it makes public its use of this reserve power.

This new appointment process was designed to provide ministers with an opportunity to influence the staffing of the most senior posts in the public service. This was to reduce the extent to which appointments to these posts had been the preserve of "a self-perpetuating elite" (or an "old boys' club") of permanent heads who previously had essentially controlled who would be brought into their ranks when vacancies occurred.[43] Given this tradition, the new system was viewed by some as inviting partisan politicization of the senior mandarinate. These fears proved to be unfounded. Indeed, as the 1990 review undertaken by the new National government stated, the New Zealand appointment process continues to be "less political than in any other Westminster system."[44]

Even with the much more open competitive process, most chief executives have been selected from the public sector, although more broadly defined than in the past when it was confined essentially to the central public service. Indeed, some persons from foreign public services have been appointed as chief executives. As the same report noted: "[Q]ualified private-sector executives are reluctant to take on Public Service chief executive positions because of the perceived high level of political intervention, public scrutiny, the bureaucratic nature of the work and the inadequate remuneration package. A lack of Public Service experience is also seen as a handicap."[45]

Comparative Perspectives

Experience in all four systems has demonstrated that political executives can take steps to exert greater authority over the staffing of the senior public service. Partisan-politicization of the public service has not been pursued overtly, or formally, in any of the four Westminster systems. This does not mean, however, that there has not been a politicization of the senior ranks of their public services. In Canada, Britain and Australia, prime ministers have demonstrated their willingness to appoint those who, while they have no partisan ties to the governing party, are nevertheless perceived by the prime minister, and her or his advisers, as fully in support of a government's agenda or its management philosophy. In this nonpartisan sense of politicization, they are considered to be, as Margaret Thatcher was wont to put it, "one of us."

This "personalization" of senior appointments, as the Royal Institute of Public Administration in Britain described developments during the Thatcher regime,[46] has not required prime ministers to be intimately involved in every decision where the prerogative power is exercised. But their choice of who assumes the very top positions defines the type of personnel desired by the character of the regime. It is a clear signal to the senior bureaucracy to use the same criteria in selecting or recommending others. And no explicit change is required to the formal procedures of the merit system as applied to staffing positions immediately below those appointed by prime ministerial prerogative.

There has been a transformation in the staffing of the senior public service that falls within the prerogative powers of the prime minister. As Campbell notes, this requires "that we cast around for new terms to capture the 'politicization' of bureaucracy. All traditional public services at their highest levels operate in extremely political – though mostly covert and reactive – ways...Yet, they remain formally nonpartisan."[47] He goes on to suggest that there are "two seemingly conflicting forces in the battleground. On the one side the advocates of partisan responsiveness seek the institutionalization of a party-political thrust to governance. On the other side, more cautious voices see value in safeguarding the prerogatives of a permanent bureaucracy, in order to secure continuity in great affairs of state."[48]

The personalization that has characterized the staffing of senior positions in Canada, Great Britain and Australia is perhaps little more than an inevitable reaction to the traditional approach in which the prime minister deferred to the senior mandarinate to ensure professional competence in staffing top positions. While various norms, values and practices served to provide these respective national governments with first-class public services in the development of the modern administrative state, there were precious few institutional constraints to guard against the emergence of cronyism among the senior mandarin class.

By the 1960s, the senior public service in Britain and to a lesser extent in Australia, had provided political leaders with a great deal of ammunition to support their claims that hubris was the defining characteristic of these two bureaucracies. In Canada, this was not quite the case for three reasons. First, the norms, traditions and values of public service had stayed strong, and effective leadership had been provided by senior public servants. Second, the system was not as closed as it was in Britain or Australia. Third, the political leadership had been able to engage the public service effectively; in part this was because several key ministers, including three prime ministers in the Liberal governments of the 1950s and 1960s, had themselves been professional public servants.

However, when prime ministers began to assert their authority, there were only traditions, norms and values to restrain a politicization in the form of personalization. In the Canadian context, this personalization is generally considered to have begun in the mid-1970s when Trudeau appointed Michael Pitfield, a relatively young career public servant and a close associate of the Prime Minister, to the position of Clerk of the Privy Council and Secretary to the Cabinet. At the time, Trudeau acknowledged senior public service fears respecting Pitfield's role in advising on senior public service appointments. Trudeau thus retained the outgoing and highly regarded Clerk, Gordon Robertson, in the newly created post of Secretary to the Cabinet for Federal-Provincial Relations. For some time, Robertson continued to have responsibility for advising the Prime Minister on senior appointments.[49]

Pitfield's association with Trudeau was perhaps an exceptional case in this regard, but it is not unique in the Westminster systems; the close relationship between British Prime Minister Edward Heath and his head of the public service, William Armstrong, led to the latter being commonly referred to as Heath's "deputy prime minister."[50]

This kind of politicization, which Bourgault and Dion label "functional politicalization,"[51] need not necessarily result in a corruption of the permanent bureaucracy. In any event, there are bound to be variations over time and across systems. However, the Canadian case over the last two decades, as well as the British case at least since the Thatcher era, illustrate what can go wrong. In each of these systems, top officials focused their efforts more on serving the interests of ministers to the detriment of their leadership of the public service. At times, little or no leadership was forthcoming; and worse, on occasion the public service was abused, even publicly, as in the Al-Mashat affair in Canada.[52]

The chilling effect of "managing with power," as described (in part, even endorsed) by Jeffrey Pfeffer,[53] an American scholar of organizational politics, meant that the norms, values and traditions of the public service in the cause of good government were not only left undefended, but were contradicted by the practices of those meant to be the role models for the public service. The study of the Canadian management cadre by David Zussman and Jak Jabes in the mid-1980s confirmed the scant regard held by the lower ranks of the senior public service for their top leaders, including those appointed *via* the prerogative power.

Public Service in Transition

Given the challenges that have confronted political executives over the last two decades in managing the state, it is not surprising that the value of a professional public service should have been cast in doubt at this point in the evolution of these Westminster systems. However, while political change and public management reform have been evident in almost all industrialized democracies, the bureaucracy bashing directed at career public services has been confined largely to the Anglo-American democracies. At least part of the explanation for this must centre on the particular shortcomings that emerged in the career public services in each of these systems.

The case for a career public service, as previously noted, rests on the assumption that its men and women have the required skills and experience to manage the operations of government on behalf of their ministers and the necessary knowledge and expertise to advise ministers on their policy responsibilities. Beginning in the 1960s and continuing into the 1970s, there was growing concern in each of the Westminster systems that the conditions required for competence in one or both of these tasks no longer existed to the extent necessary for good government.

It was argued that the most senior career public servants had too little in the way of line management experience to provide the managerial leadership required by the public service complex that was put in place in the two decades following the Second World War. Doubts also began to surface as to the quality of policy advice emanating from the senior echelons of the career public service. At issue was not whether there existed a cadre of senior officials able to move proposals through the decision-making process. Rather, it was whether those senior officials had the depth of knowledge to address the increasing complex policy issues present in modern governance.

Getting to the Top

In Britain, where it has long been assumed that the primary responsibility of the senior public service is advising on public policy, the tradition has been to have a "generalist" caste of public servants to assist ministers in the administration of public affairs. The management of public services as government operations did not take high priority; this was left essentially to lower orders in the state bureaucracy or delegated to a variety of non-departmental organizations and local governments. At the same time, the generalists who occupied the senior posts were not expected to be specialists in the technical dimensions of public policy. They were administrators – practitioners of the liberal arts of governance. The norm, accordingly, has been an Oxford or Cambridge degree in the liberal arts, followed by an apprenticeship in a minister's office, then a stint in a central agency and more than one department with increasingly significant policy-related assignments. As late as the mid-1980s, this was the normal career experience of permanent secretaries.[54]

This state of affairs came under increasing criticism beginning in the 1960s, especially after the scathing condemnation of what the Fulton Committee Report on the civil service termed the amateurism of the British administrative elite.[55] Members of this elite were not formally educated in the modern social, economic or management sciences. Their careers consisted of constant movement between short assignments that meant even their practical experiences could not provide them with much depth of knowledge of the business of government. While their general intellectual abilities were perhaps not beyond doubt, their capacity to assist ministers in steering the British state, beyond controlling the bureaucratic machinery of government and facilitating or constraining the passage of ministerial initiatives in the labyrinth of the executive's decision-making processes, was increasingly suspect. A measure of their ability to manipulate the system, however, was their success in scuttling, at least for some time, the general thrust of the Fulton Committee Report.

In Canada, Australia and New Zealand, the British approach to the career public service was not emulated in every respect in the early development of their professional bureaucracies. In each case, a more vertically integrated and departmentally based public service responsible for both policy advice and the management of operations was the norm. However, in more recent decades, especially in Canada and Australia, the top public service posts increasingly came to be staffed by those who had spent their careers largely in policy-related, rather than operational, positions. As well documented in the Canadian case by Frank Swift, a former senior public servant, a significant proportion of deputies and associate deputies had little or no experience in program management, as compared to policy or process management assignments in line departments and central agencies.[56] Except for the continued importance in Britain of serving in a minister's office at some point, the route to the top in these two systems began to mirror the British practice. While those who reached the top tended, in contrast to Britain, to have postgraduate degrees in the social and natural sciences, and later the management sciences, their careers were marked by relatively short assignments in a variety of departments and central agencies.

The result in Canada, claims Barbara Wake Carroll,[57] was a decline "in the proportion of senior managers who are knowledgeable about the substantive aspects of the policy areas in which they are expected to provide policy advice."[58] This situation was exacerbated by the increase in deputy and associate deputy ministers with no experience in the line departments to which they were appointed as the top public service executives.[59] The rationale for this development, which began in earnest during the Trudeau regime, was to minimize the degree to which ministers were captured by departmental bureaucrats.[60] The actual effect, suggests Carroll, was a swing too far in the opposite direction. The consequence of deputies not having prior experience in the departments they head, she suggests:

> may help to partly explain the steady decline in the influence or importance of policy planning units. If the decision makers cannot understand something they are unlikely to consider it important. It may also explain the perceived isolation of ministers from their departments – ministers are concerned with legitimation, and legitimation also implies solving problems.[61]

The failure to recognize the importance of technical expertise and experience in the provision of policy advice, and thus in problem solving, meant that those with such attributes and experience were overtaken by those perceived to have better skills at managing the policy process. This, argues Carroll, meant that there were too few senior departmental managers who "understand what it is the[ir] organization is supposed to do";[62] and this is "one of the causes of nonadaptiveness and the inability of public bureaucracies to resolve policy problems."[63]

The question of the competencies required of the senior echelons of a public service is not a simple matter. What is required at any one time is necessarily partly contextual: much depends on what are perceived to be the central challenges facing a government. The rapid growth of the senior federal public service during the late 1960s and 1970s, combined with the increasing specialization in ministerial portfolios resulting from a continual expansion in the size of the Cabinet, contributed to the perceived need to strengthen central coordination and control in the face of the increasing fragmentation of the state apparatus.

When restraint began to take effect in the late 1970s and became even more urgent in the 1980s, a new priority was given to the management of government. In the absence of a major effort to redefine the role of government, however, the Trudeau and Mulroney governments, especially the latter after the failure of the 1984-85 ministerial task force on program review, paid less and less attention to the development of policy alternatives. The order of the day was simply to do the same, or even more, with less. It did not entail a substantial reconsideration of government policies. Moreover, the prevailing view in the federal bureaucracy as late as 1989 was that managerial economies and efficiencies were sufficient to cope with the fiscal situation.[64] Given the limited managerial experience of the senior public service, however, its capacities to manage government better, beyond simply implementing budget cuts, was questionable. Aside perhaps from the quasi-profession of management consulting, no serious profession would have tolerated the dilettantism represented in the frequent shuffling of deputies and others in the senior ranks.

Applying Knowledge in Governance

Managing the state, even in times of great change in the environment of government, requires a good deal of "disjointed incrementalism."[65] Disjointed incrementalism is the most rational approach to governance because it recognizes the "bounded rationality" of the knowledge upon which public policy, as social engineering, is predicated.[66] Public bureaucracies are central to governing to the degree that they constitute the principal institutional repository of knowledge on public policy.[67]

When those at the top insist on major changes across the full spectrum of public policy, they must have ideas about what is to be done.[68] Political conviction may not be a sufficient condition for policy innovations, but it is a necessary condition. It is the force that drives change in the management of the state. In Australia, Great Britain and New Zealand, political conviction was evident throughout the 1980s and into the 1990s. In all three, and especially in Australia and New Zealand, the bureaucratic leadership has thus been able to respond to a political agenda that was coherent and consistent enough to link the management of the state to the management of government and public services. In Britain, the political leadership has been more ideological, and it has paid the price that comes from an excessive reliance on ideology, namely the fostering of cynicism, if not opposition, on the part of those whose cooperation is essential to change.

In Canada under Mulroney, political conviction was too often absent.[69] His practice of brokerage politics invariably led to inconsistent decisions and a lack of coherence in the effort to bring about change. On too many occasions he ignored the knowledge present in the public service, particularly as this applied to the management of the economy, and relied instead on centrally managed bureaucratic subservience to maintain a semblance of political control over the state apparatus.

The Chrétien government has been able to draw on the experience of the Mulroney government as well as that of the other Westminster systems. In seeking to reaffirm the policy advisory role of the bureaucracy in the management of the state, however, it has had to cope with the diminished capacity of the bureaucracy to perform this role, a legacy of the Conservatives. Even as late as 1993, the major restructuring of departments involved, among other things, a downsizing of policy development and evaluation staff in departments.

If governments are to be served well by their public services in the management of the state, the policy advisory capacities of the public service must be restored.[70] Shifting the focus is not something done overnight, however, even with political conviction. It requires both a mindset and commitment to what is now styled as continuous learning in pursuit of concrete results.[71] There is, of course, nothing new in this. The value of a career public service, beyond the simple eradication of partisan patronage in public service staffing, has always been its capacity to add value to governance on the basis of knowledge applied to the management of the state.

Without the knowledge that emanates from rigorous evaluation and analyses of present and past policy initiatives, both in one's own government and in other jurisdictions, public servants cannot add value to the policy-making process beyond what can be contributed either by partisan aides or outsiders, such as politically sympathetic think tanks. The fact that knowledge must always be incomplete when brought to bear on complex policy issues is not a valid reason for ignoring the empirical evidence that can be applied; political conviction by itself does not necessarily produce good government, as certain initiatives in Britain have amply demonstrated.

However, in their efforts to justify the distinctiveness of public administration, too many bureaucrats have succumbed to the temptation to see policy making as too complex to be subject to rational analysis. Such an attitude inadvertently invites political leaders and their partisan assistants to weaken the policy advisory role of the public service and to rely extensively on their own personal policy advisers as in Britain under

Thatcher or, worse, on partisan advisers as in Canada under Mulroney. If public servants cannot add value by way of expertise and experience related to policy knowledge, their role is reduced to one of managing the policy process. When the senior bureaucracy is in favour with the political leadership, as under Trudeau, for example, it exercises considerable influence; when it is not, as under Thatcher or Mulroney, it is overridden and shunted to the sidelines. By failing to recognize that the critical role of the public service in providing policy advice must go beyond manipulating the machinations of the decision-making process, the senior public service does a great disservice to its profession.

The fact that the public service is required to be loyal to the government of the day once decisions are made need not, indeed should not, restrict the obligation or opportunities of public servants to advise on different policy options as they relate to good government, including the several ways in which the ends and means of governance interact. Ministers may reject this advice for any number of reasons, including their reading of either political support from important interest groups or general public support as measured by public opinion polls. This is their prerogative and, at some point, they will be held accountable.

Policy planning and evaluation were designed to be central in the increasingly elaborate decision-making schemes that emerged in the 1960s, but in an era of expansion, insufficient attention was given to these elements as the foundations of organizational learning. The Achilles heel of the "policy science" movement that flourished briefly in the 1960s was twofold: not only, in its rush to "plan," did it downplay, even ignore, the practical knowledge of those with experience in administering public affairs, it also failed to adhere to the dictates of science itself, particularly the requirement to engage in empirical study.[72] As applied to governance as public management, this requirement can only be met to the extent that proposed policies are informed by objective research and critical analysis, and that existing policies and programs are systematically evaluated in terms of their actual results.

The Canadian government was the first of the four Westminster systems to apply a formal system of evaluation to public management. But this approach soon languished and had to be resurrected in the late 1970s. Even then, as the Nielsen Task Force discovered to its dismay in 1984-85, evaluations seldom focused on the central questions of public policy. Rather, they had been used, at best, as a device to improve program management. The organizational knowledge generated by the use of program evaluation was thus limited. Despite the criticisms by the Nielsen Task Force in this regard, little was done throughout the Mulroney era to address the critical importance of evaluation to governance.

In relation to program evaluation, the conundrum is how can the public service apply knowledge to policy making and still avoid the "partisan pitfalls" – to use A.W. Johnson's succinct term – inherent in having such knowledge become public. Ministers are unlikely to welcome the invitation to "commit a form of political hara-kiri"[73] that the public disclosure of program evaluations, or policy research generally, entails. The absence of a commitment to program evaluation in Britain is testimony to this partisan dynamic. It also explains the Canadian record, notwithstanding a formal process for program evaluation.

Restricting effectiveness evaluations *within* government to "the middle and lower level programs, where the political ingredient is small – because the policy ingredient is small and the administrative ingredient is large,"[74] as Johnson suggests, and leaving "the higher-level policies and programs" to a more public process (e.g., royal commissions, parliamentary enquiries or the Auditor General) would avoid the "partisan pitfalls" to a certain extent. This would, however, leave the professional bureaucracy with purely managerial evaluations. This is hardly a prescription to enhance the capacity of the professional bureaucracy in the management of the state.

The stated commitment of the Chrétien government to enhance the policy development and evaluative capacity of the federal government constitutes at least a formal recognition of the need to develop the professional capacity of its public service to assist in the management of the state. This mirrors the efforts of the Australian government to give priority to corporate planning and evaluation in its public management reforms. Such an approach goes beyond questions of economy and efficiency to focus on both what the state should do and the effectiveness of what it does, that is, the outcomes of public policy.[75]

Reaffirming Career Public Service

Notwithstanding the shortcomings of the career public services in each of the four Westminster systems, the consequences, intended and otherwise, of the various initiatives to counter, check and supplant them have demonstrated, in ways that appeals to tradition could not, that a professional public service is critical to good government. At the same time, the collective experiences of these systems have confirmed that good government also requires that political leaders engage the state apparatus. A public service left unengaged will either pursue its own conception of the public interest in governance (which may or may not be a rationalization of its own interests), or it will be underused as political leaders look elsewhere for advice. The former condition will not be tolerated by governments intent on change, for whatever reasons. The latter condition, however, is not a recipe for good governance. The public service is too intimately involved in the business of government to be shunted aside without perverse consequences.

In these four systems, the monopoly position of career public services in the provision of advice to ministers and in determining appointments to its top positions is now clearly a thing of the distant past. At the same time, the need for frank and fearless advice by public servants is even more critical, given the proliferation of external sources of advice, public policy commentary and special interest pleading by advocacy groups. Frank and fearless advice, however, is of little use to ministers if it is not based on knowledge, research and evaluation, informed by practical experience in the administration of public affairs and directed at the results ministers seek in order to realize their political agendas.

Political Leadership

Political leadership is central in the pursuit of these conditions. Without a sustained political commitment to the application of objective knowledge in governance, mere conviction politics, or various forms of partisan brokerage politics, can only diminish the commitment to quality public service of those who must implement public policies in the provision of public services. This, in turn, will reinforce the need for command and control systems that inevitably run counter to best practices in the management of financial and personnel resources and public service programs. While contracting out the provision of public services to the private sector can offset these failings in certain cases, it brings with it its own challenges of managing contracts in ways that secure strategic direction, control and evaluation, and public accountability.

Equally critical, the diminution of professional public service does not eliminate the need for a critical core of public policy and public management advisers. A politicized state apparatus highly dependent on private-sector contracts for the provision of policy advice and public services runs the risk of transforming whatever remains of a career public service into little more than a collection of public-sector employees. In this circumstance, the capacity to recruit the quality of personnel who can provide frank and fearless policy advice is diminished. The experiences of several provincial governments in Canada in politicizing and/or overriding their career public services ought to be cause for grave concern on the part of the national political elites of Canada. The trashing of career public services, while it may serve the purposes of partisan aggrandizement, has brought few benefits to citizens in the form of good government.

At the same time, political leaders who are committed to political change but also wish to promote good government face a dilemma. On the one hand, effective political change requires that ministerial initiatives not only be implemented in ways that secure the outcomes desired by ministers, but that those responsible for the design of implementation schemes fully adhere to objectives of ministers in advising on ways to best meet these objectives. The public service must thus be responsive to a minister's or, more generally, the government's agenda in developing and recommending options, including those developed by nonpublic service advisers. This requires, of course, that ministers engage the public service in designing and assessing options. While ministers have every right to test public service advice against external advice, and indeed should provide as much contestability as feasible, they must also take the risk of trusting their public servants, especially when their advice runs counter to what ministers originally had in mind or what external advisers have recommended. Ministerial trust, in this sense, does not imply, let alone require, that ministers always follow such advice. Rather, it means that ministers keep public servants fully involved in the process.

On the other hand, a professional, nonpartisan public service requires a certain distance or independence from ministers if it is to be able to serve governments of different political stripes. It must also have a measure of institutional security to ensure that its advice to whatever party is in government is objective and professional. In this sense, those who deliver frank and fearless advice also take a risk by trusting that ministers will receive such advice in the spirit in which it is offered. A career public service does not mean that ministers should not have some say over who their public service advisers should be. But it does require that they respect the professional integrity of the process whereby recommendations on appointments are made and performance subsequently appraised.

The Independence of the Public Service

While the career public service is a subordinate institution in governance, it is also meant to be an institution separate from the ministry or government.

This is most clearly reflected in the independent staffing process for initial appointments and promotions in which the principle of merit is applied. This process also ensures that decisions on discipline or dismissal are subject to criteria and procedures that remove ministers from these aspects of personnel administration. While each of these matters has been subject to alterations over the last decade in the four Westminster systems, in no case have the basic principles been altered.

Governments' deviation from tradition has taken the form of prime ministers personalizing the top positions in their public services. Given the prerogative powers of prime ministers, or Cabinet in the case of New Zealand, these deviations have not required a departure from formal procedures. The adoption in Australia and New Zealand of term contracts, moreover, enables these prerogative powers to be exercised more frequently. A 1993 joint report of the Australian Management Advisory Board and its Management Improvement Advisory Committee (the former with statutory responsibility to advise government on the management of the public service) proposed that "two people at Secretary level (or equivalents, which includes the Public Service Commissioner) should join the Secretary of the Department of Prime Minister and Cabinet in preparing recommendations to the Prime Minister."[76]

Although the Report did not make any explicit commentary on the Australian experience in the selection of secretaries, its recommendation was preceded by a reference to the positive development whereby the Public Service Commission (PSC) had been given effective powers to select senior executives below the level of departmental secretaries, thus providing "an important check to ensure that [these] senior appointments are based on the merit principle."[77] The inference was clear: broadening the participation of departmental secretaries in the process whereby secretaries are selected might diminish the potential for a personalization of appointments by the prime minister directly or indirectly by her or his own departmental secretary. It would be a check similar to that provided by the PSC in selecting members of the executive below this level: the role of the PSC constitutes an important restraint on bureaucratic personalization by departmental secretaries in selecting their own executive subordinates.

The process in Britain is more inclusive, with the head of the public service making recommendations to the prime minister with the support of a Senior Appointments Selection Committee (SACO). While the tradition was for prime ministers to "invariably rubberstamp SACO proposals" for appointment at the permanent secretary and deputy secretary level,[78]

Thatcher, as noted, decided to depart from this tradition. In Canada, there is also a provision whereby the Clerk of the Privy Council in making recommendations to the prime minister is advised by a committee of senior deputy ministers. A more broadly based structure for recommending on such appointments, in short, is obviously not a guarantee that prime ministers will abide by the preferences of senior mandarins. Moreover, a prime minister's responsibilities in these regards include, among other things, ensuring that cronyism among senior mandarins does not in itself undermine merit considerations and that merit is not defined in ways that are prejudicial to women or members of minority groups.

The New Zealand model offers an institutional corrective to the practices of the other three Westminster systems. It protects the merit principle while retaining the advantages that flow from the exercise of the executive prerogative. As previously noted, it requires that, if Cabinet rejects a recommendation from the State Services Commissioner for a chief executive appointment and appoints some other person, it must make public its decision. This has proven to be a largely successful approach.[79] It does, of course, build on a tradition that did not admit of a prime ministerial prerogative power of appointment; but the actual practice in Canada, as in Australia and Great Britain, before the last two decades was not radically dissimilar. The development of a world-class public service in the Canadian government was due, in no small measure, to prime ministerial deference to the senior mandarin class in the exercise of the prerogative power.

Adopting this dimension of the New Zealand approach might well combine the advantages of a tradition that worked to produce a highly professional, nonpartisan public service in the past, while adapting it to contemporary realities. In particular, such an approach might go a long way to address at least one critical element in the current malaise in the public service, namely the need to provide the measure of distance between the political and bureaucratic arms of government necessary to diminish what Mulroney before assuming office criticized as the "commingling that has gone on with the Liberal party and the upper reaches of the civil service."[80] This was a phenomenon that, as Prime Minister, he not only did not eradicate but, some claim, took to a higher level, albeit to a different purpose – to diminish the influence of the career public service. While no institutional change in and of itself can guarantee the desired results, such a measure could help to confirm that the principle of merit is the basis for a professional, nonpartisan public service, including its top positions.

The Chrétien government, with its avowed commitment to a neutral, merit-based and professional public service, is well positioned politically and publicly to institute such a reform. Public confidence in government, also a stated concern of the Chrétien government, might be bolstered even further if such an approach were extended to the appointment of all positions that fall within the prime ministerial prerogative, in particular the appointment of chief executives and directors of Crown corporations and other government agencies, as well as diplomats. These are widely viewed as partisan-patronage appointments, and especially to the extent that retiring public servants are among those appointed as chief executive officers of these corporations or agencies, these appointments do not reflect well on the public service, whatever the merits in individual cases.

The adoption of this approach to staff top positions in the public service, it might be argued, would diminish the role of the public service in the provision of policy advice because prime ministers and ministers would turn to other sources for strategic advice. However, this has already occurred under the current approach. Even in Australia where, of the other three systems, there has been perhaps the most restraint in personalizing the senior bureaucracy, personal advisers in ministerial offices have played a crucial role in assisting ministers to pursue their agendas. Such a development ought not to be regarded as a negation of good government. Indeed, in the conjunction between responsible government and good government, the more that strategic policy advice is subject to contestation, the more likely that ministers will turn to their professional bureaucracies for their knowledge and administrative experience, and with less concern of being captured by them.

Public Service Leadership

While political commitment to a professional, nonpartisan public service is critical to a reaffirmation of good government, the leadership of the public service must also promote measures to institute what the Public Service Commissioner of Australia, Denis Ives, calls a "new professionalism."[81] This challenge will be met only by a forthcoming and sustained corporate leadership.

Leadership in the public service is now too transient for one person, as head of the public service, to secure the necessary institutional commitment to corporate leadership. Further, responsibility for the health of the public service as an institution is already, and must invariably be, shared by more than the official designated as head of the public service. This is evident in Canada given the respective responsibilities, among others, of the Clerk, the Chair of the Public Service Commission and the Secretary of the Treasury Board.

In each of the four systems, the need for an institutionalization of corporate leadership is acknowledged in various ways. In Canada, a Committee of Senior Officials on Executive Personnel is chaired by the Clerk and includes the Chair of the Public Service Commission, the Secretary of the Treasury Board and a number of senior deputy ministers. This Committee plays a critical role in bringing a corporate perspective to the appraisal of the performance of deputy ministers. Over the last decade especially, successive Clerks have sought to institute a greater sense of collegial participation and corporate responsibility among the deputy minister community. This is now being extended downward to encompass the assistant deputy minister cadre. The present Clerk, for instance, has formed a number of task forces and working groups to address issues facing the public service in the longer term as well as issues that extend horizontally across the public service. Equally important, the Clerk is now designated as the Head of the Public Service and has a statutory responsibility to prepare and publish an annual report to the prime minister on the public service.

Australia has taken the institutionalization of the public service leadership even further, with the statutory creation of a Management Advisory Board. As noted, this board is chaired by the Secretary to the Prime Minister and Cabinet, who is designated Head of the Public Service. Its membership includes the Public Service Commissioner, the Secretary of the Department of Finance (the equivalent of the Treasury Board Secretariat in Canada), the Secretary of the Department of Industrial Relations, three other departmental secretaries, a senior union representative and a senior private-sector executive. It is advised by a Management Improvement Advisory Committee whose members come from the senior executive service (that is, the ranks immediately below the departmental secretary level) and senior regional officials.

The Management Advisory Board is not an executive body. In its advisory capacity, however, it has the responsibility to address the major issues facing the public service in carrying out its functions under the direction of ministers and departmental secretaries and to provide performance assessments of the public service for the prime minister and government. To this end, it has commissioned and published several reports, as well as an unprecedented evaluation study, released in 1992, of the public management reforms undertaken since 1983. The commissioning of these studies and, equally important, their publication, have required the Board itself to pay careful attention to major issues of public management facing the public service and government. These activities have also focused the ongoing attention of the senior public service on its corporate responsibilities. Perhaps the most significant contribution of these efforts, accordingly, has been the extent to which the Board and its activities have required the leadership of the public service to bring coherence and consistency to public management designs and practices. In so doing, the Board promotes a broader corporate perspective on the part of those who have specific responsibilities for the health and performance of the public service. However, the Board's own evaluation in 1992 of public service reforms noted that more needs to be done to increase the visibility of its work and to enhance its credibility by ensuring that critical perspectives are fully and publicly addressed, as opposed to adherence to a "party line."[82]

The Canadian public service would be well served by a greater institutionalization along the lines of this Australian model. This would build on recent developments, including the aforementioned task forces and working groups established by the Clerk, the designation of the Clerk as the Head of the Public Service and the statutory requirement for the Clerk to report annually on the public service. These last two developments themselves were products of a corporate public service undertaking, namely the 1989 establishment of the Public Service 2000 initiative, which entailed extensive participation across the leadership of the public service and down the ranks, with reports published on a wide range of public management issues.

Regular studies, evaluations and advisory reports would help to ensure that major issues are addressed in ways that entail greater transparency. Confidentiality is required of the public service in the performance of several of its functions, including advice to ministers. But a professional public service, whose contribution to good government is based on knowledge and its application, diminishes its pursuit of competence as well as its credibility if confidentiality is used as a cover to keep matters secret that ought to be examined and discussed by the profession at large and by those whom its serves.

Parliament and the Public Service
The state of the public service as "an institution of national importance," as the present Clerk has put it, has not been a subject of much interest or concern

on the part of the Canadian Parliament. In fact, on the few occasions over the last decade when parliamentarians have turned their attention explicitly to the public service as an institution, the exercises have invariably had a negative flavour. This was most clearly evident in the 1985 report of a major committee on the reform of the House of Commons which demanded that deputy ministers be directly accountable to the House of Commons. The assumption was that deputy ministers, rather than ministers, were the persons who were "responsible" for what "goes on in a department" and ought to be accountable for administration, including "policy implementation."[83] Little or no support was forthcoming for the constitutional position of the public service as a subordinate institution with respect to the principle of responsible government; no recognition was given to the inability of Parliament and its committees to ensure due process and fairness in parliamentarians' treatment of subordinate officials in seeking direct accountability.[84] In this latter respect, several incidents have demonstrated that the importance of a professional, nonpartisan public service is not something that parliamentarians judge to be a priority in the political system.[85]

For the most part, however, Parliament has simply ignored the question of the state of the public service as an institution in the service of good government. The operative assumption has been that the public service is a powerful institution that needs no defence, least not by those whose primary responsibility is to scrutinize the administration of public affairs. Indeed, if anything, it must be brought to heel by Parliament and its committees, supported by its parliamentary agencies, including the Office of the Auditor General and the Public Service Commission. Here, however, neglect has been the norm. With precious few exceptions, even the reports of the Auditor General that have explicitly addressed major matters of administrative reforms, undertaken or proposed, have fallen on deaf ears.

The Canadian experience stands in contrast to the relatively greater interest in the public service as an institution and the reform of public management on the part of parliamentarians in Britain and Australia. There is no comparable experience in Canada, for instance, to the interest shown and work done by the Treasury and Civil Service Committee in the British House of Commons or the Australian House of Representatives Standing Committee on Finance and Public Administration or its Senate committee with the same mandate. In each of these systems, both the value of a professional, nonpartisan public service and the need for reform have been highlighted by the attention given these matters. At the same time, there has been support for public management reforms from opposition as well as backbench government members in both countries. Even in New Zealand, where the House of Representatives is a less effective institution in large part because of its size and limited pool of capable members who are not part of the ministry itself, there has been support for reforms across partisan lines.

The continuing demands of parliamentarians in the Canadian House of Commons for a greater role in governance are fuelled by the inevitable tendency of Canadian parliamentarians to compare their roles and influence unfavourably to those of their American counterparts. And since Canadian members of Parliament (MPs) are full-time politicians, they are focused almost exclusively on enhancing the role of MPs in the legislative process. The functions of parliamentarians in scrutinizing the work of government is not accorded high priority. In part, this is clearly a function of the degree of parliamentary inexperience of members of the House, given the instability of parliamentary careers in Canada, both absolutely and in comparison to the other Westminster systems. Short of a change in the electoral system that might produce greater stability, there is little that can be done beyond exhorting Canadian MPs to take a greater interest in the work of government and the place of the public service in public administration. New Zealand's adoption of a new electoral system of proportional representation is to take effect at the next general election. The consequences of this action on the performance of its House of Representatives bear close attention and assessment.

Greater attention might be given to the public service if Parliament were provided more comprehensive reports on the major challenges it faces in performing its critical functions. A joint Commons and Senate standing committee on the public service would help, especially if something along the lines of the Australian Management Advisory Board were created. The committee could review and report on studies published by such a management advisory board. The studies need not supplant but rather could complement parliamentary attention to the reports of the Public Service Commission and of the Auditor General (on public management reforms).

Given the record of the Canadian Parliament with respect to parliamentary reform, one has to be exceedingly optimistic to think that there is much prospect for change. Yet, the health, vitality and quality of the federal public service as an institution require both support and attention across the partisan political divide. In the Westminster model, this is best secured in Parliament, the single institution that brings together partisans in governance.

Conclusion

A decade and more of bureaucracy bashing has taken its toll on the institution of the public service. In part, the assault on the public service has been ideologically driven by those who see in it an institutional force for state aggrandizement in the socio-economic order. In part, it has been driven by politicians' concern that state bureaucracies have insulated themselves from political direction, either as self-proclaimed guardians of the public interest beyond partisan politics or in pursuit of their own self-serving interests. In all of this, the actual performance of governments both in managing their economies and in providing quality public services has led to a general public decline of confidence, not only in government generally but in the career public service in particular.

The efforts of political executives to assert their authority have resulted in a much greater reliance on advisers separate from the career public service and a more assertive role by ministers, especially prime ministers, in determining who occupies the top positions in the public service. Such practices of political leaders over the last 15 years began to emerge in the 1960s and 1970s, but they were extended considerably. Whether these changes have brought about "the death of a paradigm," as Campbell and Wilson put it, is open to debate. The monopoly position of the career public service as agents to ministers is now clearly a thing of the past, even if one does not exaggerate the extent to which there had been a monopoly. The closed character of public services is also a thing of the past although here too, some systems, in particular the Canadian public service, have been more open than others.

The fundamental idea of a professional, nonpartisan public service as a subordinate but separate institution within the Westminster system of responsible government is obviously not a sufficient condition to good government; but history confirms that it is a necessary condition. If well engaged by ministers and well led and managed by those senior public servants responsible for the health of the institution, it provides the best guarantee that ministers receive the quality of impartial and objective advice that knowledge and experience can provide, however limited and incomplete these must always be when applied to matters of governance. This requires a critical measure of continuity and corporate memory in the institutions of government. Good government also requires that, at a minimum, those who manage the delivery of public services, whether the delivery be undertaken by public servants or contracted out to the private sector, do so in ways that are in the public interest and that promote the highest standards of public service values and ethics. The knowledge and experience necessary to achieve these goals of good government require a public service characterized by institutional and personal commitments to a career public service.

Notes

1. Canada, Clerk of the Privy Council and Secretary to the Cabinet, *Third Annual Report to the Prime Minister on the Public Service of Canada* (Ottawa: Minister of Supply and Services, 1995), p. 47.

2. *Third Annual Report to the Prime Minister on the Public Service of Canada*, p. 37.

3. United Kingdom, Prime Minister, Chancellor of the Exchequer and Chancellor of the Duchy of Lancaster, *The Civil Service: Continuity and Change* (London: HMSO, July 1994), p. 6.

4. Australia, Management Advisory Board, *Building a Better Public Service* (Canberra: Australian Government Publishing Service, 1993), p. 4.

5. Colin Campbell and Graham K. Wilson, *The End of Whitehall: Death of a Paradigm?* (Oxford: Blackwell, 1995), p. 314.

6. Colin Campbell, "The Political Roles of Senior Government Officials in Advanced Democracies," *British Journal of Political Science*, Vol. 18 (April 1988), p. 261.

7. John Meisel, *The Canadian General Election of 1957* (Toronto: University of Toronto Press, 1962), pp. 37-38.

8. G. Bruce Doern, "The development of policy organizations," in G. Bruce Doern and Peter Aucoin (eds.), *The Structures of Policy Making in Canada* (Toronto: Macmillan Company, 1971), pp. 42-46; Flora MacDonald, "The Minister and the Mandarins," *Policy Options*, Vol. 1, no. 3 (September-October 1980), pp. 29-31.

9. J.L. Manion, "Career public service in Canada: reflections and predictions," *International Review of Administrative Sciences*, Vol. 57, no. 3 (September 1991), p. 362.

10. Herman Bakvis, *Regional Ministers: Power and Influence in the Canadian Cabinet* (Toronto: University of Toronto Press, 1991).

11. John L. Manion and Cynthia Williams, "Transition Planning at the Federal Level in Canada," in Donald J. Savoie (ed.), *Taking Power Managing Government Transitions* (Toronto: Institute of Public Administration of Canada, 1993), p. 107.

12. Loretta J. O'Connor, "Chief of Staff," *Policy Options*, Vol. 12, no. 3 (April 1991), p. 24.

13. Gordon F. Osbaldeston, "How Deputies are Accountable," *Policy Options*, Vol. 8, no. 7 (September 1987), pp. 10-13.

14. S.L. Sutherland, "The Public Service and Policy Development," in Michael M. Atkinson (ed.), *Governing Canada: Institutions and Public Policy* (Toronto: Harcourt Brace Jovanovich Canada, 1993), p. 100.

15. Micheline Plasse, "Ministerial Chiefs of Staff in the Federal Government in 1990: Profiles, Recruitment, Duties and Relations with Senior Public Servants," paper prepared for the Canadian Centre for Management Development, Ottawa, April 1994, pp. 33-34.

16. Peter Aucoin, "The Mulroney Government, 1984-1988: Priorities, Positional Policy and Power," in Andrew Gollner and Daniel Salée (eds.), *Canada Under Mulroney: An End-of-Term Report* (Montreal: Vehicule Press, 1988), pp. 348-49; Colin Campbell, "Mulroney's Broker Politics: The Ultimate in Politicized Incompetence," in Gollner and Salée (eds.), *Canada Under Mulroney*, pp. 331-32.

17. James Walter, *The Ministers' Minders* (Melbourne: Oxford University Press, 1986).

18. S.L. Sutherland, "The Consequences of Electoral Volatility: Inexperienced Ministers 1949-90," in Herman Bakvis (ed.), *Representation, Integration and Political Parties in Canada* (Toronto: Dundurn Press, 1991), pp. 303-54.

19. Les Metcalfe, "Conviction Politics and Dynamic Conservatism: Mrs. Thatcher's Managerial Revolution," *International Political Science Review*, Vol. 14, no. 4 (October 1993), pp. 351-71.

20. Colin Campbell, "I've Never Met a Transition I Didn't Like: Some Reflections on Sixteen Years of Comparative Research," in Savoie (ed.), *Taking Power*, p. 80.

21. Campbell and Wilson, *The End of Whitehall*, p. 67.

22. J. Burnham and G.W. Jones, "Advising Margaret Thatcher: the Prime Minister's Office and the Cabinet Office Compared," *Political Studies*, Vol. 41, no. 2 (1993), p. 302.

23. John Halligan, "The career public service and administrative reform in Australia," *International Review of Administrative Studies*, Vol. 57, no. 3 (1991), p. 353.

24. Colin Campbell, "The search for coordination and control revisited: for machinery of government, ten lost years?", paper prepared for the Ten-Year Reunion, Structure and Organization of Government Research Committee, International Political Science Association, Manchester, England, September 22-24, 1994, p. 36.

25. Campbell, "The search for coordination and control revisited."

26. Colin Campbell and John Halligan, *Political Leadership in an Age of Constraint: Bureaucratic Politics Under Hawke and Keating* (St. Leonards, Australia: Allen and Unwin, 1992), p. 8.

27. Campbell and Halligan, *Political Leadership in an Age of Constraint*, p. 234.

28. Bernard Galvin, *Policy Co-ordination, Public Sector and Government* (Wellington: Victoria University Press, 1991), p. 27.

29. Hans-Ulrich Derlien, "Historical legacy and recent developments in the German higher civil service," *International Review of Administrative Sciences*, Vol. 57, no. 3 (September 1991), pp. 385-401.

30. David Zussman, "Walking the Tightrope: the Mulroney Government and the Public Service," in Michael Prince (ed.), *How Ottawa Spends 1986-87: Tracking the Tories* (Toronto: Methuen, 1986), p. 279.

31. J.L. Manion, "Career public service in Canada: reflections and predictions," *International Review of Administrative Studies*, Vol. 57, no. 3 (September 1991), p. 363.

32. Jacques Bourgault and Stéphane Dion, "Brian Mulroney a-t-il politisé les sous-ministres?", *Canadian Public Administration*, Vol. 32, no. 1 (1989), pp. 63-83; Jacques Bourgault and Stéphane Dion, "Canadian senior civil servants and transitions of government: the Whitehall model seen from Ottawa," *International Journal of Administrative Science*, Vol. 56, no. 1 (1990), pp. 149-69.

33. Jacques Bourgault and Stéphane Dion, "Governments come and go, but what of senior civil servants? Canadian Deputy Ministers and Transitions in Power (1867-1987)," *Governance*, Vol. 2, no. 2 (1989), p. 144.

34. Sutherland, "The Public Service and Policy Development."

35. Donald J. Savoie, *Thatcher, Reagan, Mulroney: In Search of a New Bureaucracy* (Toronto: University of Toronto Press, 1994), p. 99; see also Gavin Drewry and Tony Butcher, *The Civil Service Today* (Oxford: Basil Blackwell, 1988), pp. 169-70.

36. Campbell and Wilson, *The End of Whitehall*, pp. 220-22.

37. *The Civil Service: Continuity and Change*, pp. 38-42.

38. Campbell and Halligan, *Political Leadership in an Age of Constraint*, p. 202.

39. Halligan, "The career public service and administrative reform in Australia," p. 353.

40. Patrick Weller, "Politicization and the Australian public service," *Australian Journal of Public Administration*, Vol. 48, no. 4 (December 1989), p. 375.

41. John Roberts, "Ministers, the Cabinet and Public Servants," in Jonathan Boston and Martin Holland (eds.), *The Fourth Labour Government: Radical Politics in New Zealand* (Auckland: Oxford University Press, 1987), pp. 100-01.

42. Jonathan Boston, "The Theoretical Underpinnings of Public Sector Restructuring in New Zealand," in Jonathan Boston, John Martin, June Pallot and Pat Walsh (eds.), *Reshaping the State: New Zealand's Bureaucratic Revolution* (Auckland: Oxford University Press, 1991), p. 83.

43. Boston, "The Theoretical Underpinnings of Public Sector Restructuring in New Zealand," p. 82.

44. New Zealand, State Services Commission Steering Group, *Review of State Sector Reforms* (Wellington: State Services Commission, November 29, 1991), p. 79.

45. *Review of State Sector Reforms*, p. 79.

46. *Top Jobs in Whitehall: Report of a Working Group* (London: Royal Institute of Public Administration, 1987), p. 43.

47. Campbell, "The Political Roles of Senior Government Officials," p. 271.

48. Campbell, "The Political Roles of Senior Government Officials," p. 271.

49. Colin Campbell and George J. Szablowski, *The Super-Bureaucrats: Structure and Behaviour in Central Agencies* (Toronto: Macmillan Company of Canada Ltd., 1979), p. 80.

50. Peter Hennessey, *Cabinet* (Oxford: Basil Blackwell, 1986), p. 80.

51. Jacques Bourgault and Stéphane Dion, *The Changing Profiles of Federal Deputy Ministers: 1968 to 1988* (Ottawa: Minister of Supply and Services and Canadian Centre for Management Development, 1991), p. 43.

52. S.L. Sutherland, "The Al-Mashat affair: administrative responsibility in parliamentary institutions," *Canadian Public Administration*, Vol. 34, no. 4 (Winter 1991), pp. 573-603.

53. Jeffrey Pfeffer, *Managing With Power: Politics and Influence in Organizations* (Boston: Harvard Business School Press, 1992).

54. Kevin Theakston and Geoffrey K. Fry, "Britain's administrative elite: permanent secretaries 1900-1986," *Public Administration*, Vol. 67 (Summer 1989), pp. 129-47.

55. Drewry and Butcher, *The Civil Service Today*, pp. 51-54.

56. Frank Swift, *Strategic Management in the Public Service: The Changing Role of the Deputy Minister* (Ottawa: Minister of Supply and Services and Canadian Centre for Management Development, 1993), Appendix, pp. 49-63.

57. Barbara Wake Carroll, "The structure of the Canadian bureaucratic elite: some evidence of change," *Canadian Public Administration*, Vol. 34, no. 2 (Summer 1991), pp. 359-72.

58. Carroll, "The structure of the Canadian bureaucratic elite," p. 353.

59. Swift, *Strategic Management in the Public Service*, pp. 58-61.

60. Richard D. French, *How Ottawa Decides* (Toronto: Canadian Institute for Economic Policy, 1980), pp. 3-4.

61. Carroll, "The structure of the Canadian bureaucratic elite," p. 359.

62. Barbara Wake Carroll, "Politics and Administration: A Trichotomy?", *Governance*, Vol. 3, no. 4 (October 1990), p. 362.

63. Carroll, "Politics and Administration," p. 361.

64. Ian Clark, "On re-engineering the public service of Canada," *Public Sector Management*, Vol. 4, no. 4 (1994), pp. 20-22.

65. David Braybrooke and Charles Lindblom, *A Strategy of Decision* (London: Free Press, 1963), pp. 81-110.

66. John J. Jr. DiIulio, Gerald Garvey and Donald F. Kettl, *Improving Government Performance: An Owner's Manual* (Washington: Brookings Institution, 1993), p. 2.

67. Henry Mintzberg and Jan Jorgensen, "Emergent strategy for public policy," *Canadian Public Administration*, Vol. 30, no. 2 (Summer 1987), pp. 214-29.

68. Keith Banting, "The Way Beavers Build Dams: Social Policy Change in Canada," in Keith Banting and Ken Battle (eds.), *A New Social Vision for Canada?* (Kingston: Queen's University School of Policy Studies, 1994), pp. 131-33.

69. Savoie, *Thatcher, Reagan, Mulroney*, p. 326.

70. B. Guy Peters and Donald J. Savoie, "Civil Service Reform: Misdiagnosing the Patient," *Public Administration Review*, Vol. 54, no. 5 (September-October 1994), pp. 418-25.

71. Canadian Centre for Management Development, *Continuous Learning* (Ottawa: Minister of Supply and Services and Canadian Centre for Management Development, 1994).

72. French, *How Ottawa Decides*; Evert Lindquist, "Think tanks or clubs? Assessing the influence and roles of Canadian policy institutes," *Canadian Public Administration*, Vol. 36, no. 4 (Winter 1993), pp. 547-79.

73. A.W. Johnson, "Reflections on administrative reform in the government of Canada 1962-1991," Discussion Paper, Ottawa, Office of the Auditor General of Canada, 1992, p. 27.

74. Johnson, "Reflections on administrative reform," p. 27.

75. Australia, Task Force on Management Improvement, *The Australian Public Service Reformed: An Evaluation of a Decade of Management Reform* (Canberra: Australian Government Publishing Service, December 1992), pp. 471-73.

76. *Building a Better Public Service*, p. 20.

77. *Building a Better Public Service*, p. 20.

78. Drewry and Butcher, *The Civil Service Today*, p. 169.

79. Jonathan Boston, "Assessing the performance of departmental chief executives: perspectives from New Zealand," *Public Administration*, Vol. 70, no. 3 (Autumn 1992), pp. 424-25.

80. Quoted in Zussman, "Walking the Tightrope," p. 256.

81. Denis Ives, "Next Steps in Public Management," *Australian Journal of Public Administration*, Vol. 53, no. 3 (1994), pp. 335-40.

82. *The Australian Public Service Reformed*, pp. 532-33.

83. Canada, House of Commons, Special Committee on the Reform of the House of Commons, *Third Report* (Ottawa: Queen's Printer, June 1985), p. 20.

84. Sutherland, "Responsible Government and Ministerial Responsibility," pp. 91-120.

85. Sutherland, "The Al-Mashat affair," pp. 573-603.

FOUR

Fragmented Government and Administrative Centralization

The expansion of the state in the three decades following the Second World War was characterized, in varying degrees in each of the four Westminster systems, by an increasing fragmentation of the core executive structures of cabinet government on the one hand, and an increasing centralization of the management dimensions of public administration on the other. The fragmentation occurred as governments assumed new functions, addressed a range of new policy problems and, in some cases, responded to the demands of particular policy sectors or segments of society for ministerial representation within government. The centralization occurred as governments introduced new procedures and processes to modernize their administrative systems across the public service. At the same time they brought in new statutory requirements and/or executive regulations in pursuit of a range of policy objectives for administrative practices.

The institutional fragmentation resulting from the enlarged responsibilities of the state led each of the four governments to adopt increasingly complex executive structures in an effort to provide coherence and discipline in decision making. Coordinating the policy process within such structures became a critical function of those central agencies serving the prime minister as government leader and Cabinet as the collective executive. At the same time, changes to administrative processes and practices brought a greater role and more power to central agencies in relation to the operating departments of government.

By the late 1970s, however, the executive and administrative designs of government were increasingly regarded as impediments to both effective cabinet government and effective public administration. The new executive designs had not arrested the fragmentation of government at the apex of power. In particular, the capacities of Cabinet to "steer the state"[1] and restrain public spending had not been substantially improved. In every case, Cabinet could cope neither with the overload on government nor the fiscal crises that had developed by the end of the 1970s. The new administrative systems and structures had either failed to achieve the expectations of governments or had resulted in unintended and dysfunctional consequences.

In the late 1970s, governments began to address what were perceived to be the major deficiencies in the institutional architecture of their executive and administrative structures. While these efforts were not uniform across all four Westminster systems, they had similar objectives: to consolidate and centralize decision-making power within the executive structures while fostering a greater devolution of administrative authority, responsibility and accountability for the management of government operations.

Although economic and political circumstances were the primary forces of change, governments gleaned intellectual support and practical experience by what were considered to be comparable developments in the private sector. Large corporations in the Western world had also succumbed to excessive executive fragmentation and administrative centralization in the post-war period. This situation arose in response to the growing scope of their operations and to the canons of the organizational and managerial sciences of modern business administration. Executive fragmentation led to increasingly complex mechanisms for horizontal coordination. These in turn demanded that decision makers at the strategic apex of organizations be supported by elaborate technostructures and support staff. Finally, corporate management systems with highly uniform processes and standardized procedures were necessary to compensate for the fact that senior executives no longer directly supervised the labyrinth their organizations had become.[2] The putative eclipse of this model in the world of private sector management, it was argued, had unleashed an entrepreneurial spirit, allowing organizations to innovate and excel and thus compete in the marketplace of the new global economy.[3]

This chapter outlines the basic dynamics of cabinet government and public administration that account for the fragmentation and centralization of the machinery of government in the four Westminster systems. It provides an analysis, within the context of the Westminster tradition, of the limitations of government in overcoming fragmentation and centralization.

Cabinet Government as Party Government

With the advent of responsible government in the last century came the principle that a government must function as a unified body. This meant that ministers constituted a collective executive that would stand or fall together. In the constitutional evolution toward responsible government, legislative political parties became not only the mechanism whereby political leadership in government was determined, but also the organizing dynamic for cabinet solidarity. Responsible government meant "party government." The Cabinet could act as a unified collective entity because disciplined parties provided the political basis on which a government would be both formed and maintained, at least for as long as the governing party, as government, retained the confidence of the legislature.

In seeking to realize its political objectives, including the overriding objective of maintaining the confidence of the legislature, the design and staffing of the Cabinet are much more than administrative functions of the executive. They constitute a fundamental test of political leadership. A prime minister's first and foremost political challenge is to construct a Cabinet (and a ministry, in cases where some ministers are not in the Cabinet) in ways that secure the support of the political leadership of her or his party and thereby represent the interests that a government considers critical to the maintenance of its standing with the electorate.

Although cabinet government involves a collective executive, how this executive is organized and operates in practice is dictated, in several critical respects, neither by constitutional law nor by constitutional convention. Prime ministers possess significant discretion with regard to the executive machinery of government. A prime minister's personal paradigm of political leadership, management style and strategic policy objectives determines both the formal and informal structure and management of the collective executive that is Cabinet.[4] At the same time, the prerogative powers of a prime minister, as first minister, are constrained in various ways. In Canada, there are strong norms arising from what Campbell calls the "representational imperative" that dictate close attention to the representative character of the Cabinet, both in the construction of portfolios and in the appointment of ministers.[5]

In New Zealand, prime ministers from the Labour party must form their Cabinet from those selected by their party caucus. The same is true for the Labor party in Australia. However, they do retain the right to assign portfolios as well as to design the system of portfolios. In contrast to the practice in the other three systems, Canadian prime ministers are first selected as party leaders by conventions of their party associations at large at which the legislative party caucus has minimal influence. It follows, of course, that Canadian prime ministers cannot be removed from office by the legislative caucus as can happen in the other three systems, most recently to Margaret Thatcher in Britain and Robert Hawke in Australia.[6]

Within cabinet government, moreover, neither constitutional law nor convention requires that the members of the Cabinet be considered equal in their authority or influence in decision making. The fact that all members are bound by the convention of cabinet solidarity as well as the principle of collective responsibility does not require that they be given an equal voice in determining government policy. And, while there are variations in the extent to which the four systems adhere to a principle of collective governance, in none is there an expectation that the Cabinet be involved in each and every decision. In these instances, collective responsibility simply means that when decisions are made, ministers either support them, at least in public, or resign.

There are, of course, reasons for Cabinet to function as a collectivity. When two or more ministers with overlapping responsibilities cannot resolve disputes among themselves, decisions tend to be pushed onto the Cabinet agenda. The political sensitivity of some decisions even on relatively minor items provides ministers with an incentive to consult with their cabinet colleagues. Insecure and/or inexperienced ministers are especially likely to see Cabinet and its committees as mechanisms to protect themselves from public embarrassment.

At the same time, individual ministers are responsible for the management of public affairs within their respective portfolios[7] and do not bring all matters requiring decision to Cabinet. Even where formal or informal conventions obtain, it is impossible to apply a general rule to what kind of issues are cabinet material. In short, ministers must make many decisions on their own on behalf of the government of which they are a member. For many ministers, of course, it is not necessary to make this point; they are more than willing to act independently. Given the choice, most ministers want to be the one in control of coordinating the policy interdependencies that affect their portfolios.

In each of the four Westminster systems, the complexities of cabinet government became more pronounced in the post-war period. During the 1960s and early 1970s especially, the decision-making processes of governments everywhere were overloaded as they sought to cope with the combined effects of the expansion of the role of the state and the emerging realities of restraint. These developments had a major effect beyond the simple increase in the volume of business to be conducted by government.

First, the interdependencies of public policy became increasingly difficult to manage as the ever-expanding role of the state led to overlap and inter-relation between different policy initiatives. Second, many new policy objectives intentionally cut horizontally across policy sectors. These initiatives, in areas such as science and technology, urban affairs and regional economic development, to name but a few examples, required increased attention to "program bending,"[8] as Laframboise graphically puts it. Horizontal coordination and program bending blurred the clarity of the missions of government operations undertaken by line departments and agencies and thus the responsibility and accountability of individual ministers. As ministers attempted to take charge of the expanding state apparatus, the highly departmentalized Cabinet that had predominated in the development of the administrative state started to give way to efforts to enhance the collegial mode of cabinet government.[9] Because of the high policy content in efforts to coordinate policy interdependencies and bend programs, ministers were not content to have that coordination effected through interdepartmental committees of officials as had been the practice of the administrative state.

In Search of Rational Governance
The policy activism of the 1960s and early 1970s had two principal consequences for the management of government in Canada. First, Cabinet expanded by almost 50 percent, from 21 ministers in the 1958 Conservative Cabinet of John Diefenbaker to 30 by the mid-1970s. When Trudeau became Prime Minister in 1968, serious consideration was given to a two-tiered ministry, with portfolio ministers in the Cabinet and junior ministers outside the Cabinet, as in Britain. However, the tradition of including all ministers in the Cabinet for reasons of provincial representation was too strong to overcome.[10]

The second consequence flowed from the first: new structures were put in place to provide for the coordination demanded by the growing differentiation of ministerial responsibilities, even though many of the new posts were formally designated "ministers of state to assist" senior portfolio ministers. The result was a complicated cabinet committee system whereby cabinet government increasingly meant not a single governing body but rather a "matrix" with multiple decision points.

To buttress collegial decision making, the Liberal governments of Lester Pearson and Pierre Trudeau, particularly the latter, expanded the size and strengthened the roles of central agencies, most notably the Prime Minister's Office, the Privy Council Office and the Treasury Board Secretariat (the office that supports the Treasury Board as the cabinet committee with responsibility for the expenditure budget and most aspects of administrative policy). These latter two central agencies were enhanced to serve ministers in the exercise of their collective responsibilities; they acted as bureaucratic counterweights to the public service mandarins serving ministers in their individual departments. This, it was hoped, would diminish the extent to which ministers became captives of their departmental interests, as was perceived to have been the case during the era of the administrative state with its "departmentalized cabinet."[11] Throughout the 1960s and 1970s, the central agency apparatus of the Canadian government was itself subject to further differentiation that went beyond comparable developments in the other three Westminster systems.[12]

This new design of cabinet government was initially structured to incorporate a new decision-making process, the Planning, Programming and Budgeting System (PPBS), as recommended by the 1962 Glassco Royal Commission to strengthen the "central direction of government."[13] A decade or so later, the PPBS was reorganized to conform to an even more elaborate Policy and Expenditure Management System (PEMS). In each case, decision making was meant to be coordinated by ministers both horizontally and vertically. As practised by the Trudeau government in the first half of the 1980s, the system became incredibly complex.

Under PEMS, for example, provision was made for the ministers of two new portfolios – social development and economic development (later economic and regional development) – to chair the major sectoral policy cabinet committees related to these areas. Each of these "superministers" was assisted by newly created agencies to provide policy coordination and expenditure management support for each committee. Each committee was responsible for decisions on policy proposals from the ministers whose programs fell within its sector. They also allocated budgetary resources to existing and newly approved programs of these ministers from a budget "envelope" established for each particular sector. Thus, with its super-minister as chairperson, its own specialized central agency and its policy and budgetary authority, each committee became a mini-Cabinet for its policy sector.

This matrix structure for cabinet decision making also required central direction. The result was a Priorities and Planning Committee, established in 1968 and chaired by the Prime Minister. Under PPBS, the Priorities and Planning Committee was meant to establish the general plans and priorities of the government to guide the work of each of the various committees. In the case of PEMS, this central executive committee also established the levels of the budget envelopes for each sectoral committee. Under PPBS, policy and expenditure decision making were thus separated. Policy committees decided on programs, using the strategic plans of government as set by the Priorities and Planning Committee. The Treasury Board decided on expenditures in light of government priorities as also set by the Priorities and Planning Committee. Decisions in all cases were subject to the final approval of the Priorities and Planning Committee and, in principle, by full Cabinet. Under PEMS, on the other hand, policy and expenditure decisions were meant to be integrated, at the macro level by Priorities and Planning, with input from the various corporate policy committees, and at the micro level by the policy sector committees with their budgetary envelopes.[14]

Each of these systems reflected the rational management paradigm of the Trudeau regime as applied to the Canadian imperatives of a highly "confederal cabinet," representing the 10 provinces, regions within provinces and assorted economic sectors and segments of the community.[15] When Trudeau was willing to engage the system, it conformed to his intentions. At other times, however, it was either overcome by its own processes, or by ministers who sought to "end run" its processes. On occasion, these breakdowns led Trudeau to adopt a command mode of decision making; assisted by a coterie of senior ministers and advisers, he simply overrode the formal process.[16]

Equally important, neither PPBS nor PEMS was able to secure the kind of ministerial discipline necessary to effect budgetary restraint. It was not without some justification that Trudeau's successor as Liberal Prime Minister, John Turner, in 1984, portrayed the PEMS design he inherited as "too elaborate, too complex, too slow, and too expensive."[17] Although he quickly took some steps to simplify the system during his brief tenure as Prime Minister, he lost the opportunity to institute a new approach when his government went down to defeat at the hands of the Mulroney Conservatives that autumn.

Comparative Experiences

In none of the other three Westminster systems throughout the 1960s and 1970s was there the same degree of adherence to the "canons...[of] institutionalized executive leadership"[18] that characterized the Canadian regime under Pierre Trudeau (or, for that matter, under the short-lived Conservative government of Joe Clark in 1979-80). Yet, the governments in all three systems faced the same challenge of steering the state in response to ever-diminishing resources. For reasons specific to each, their efforts were no more successful than Canada's in finding the right balance in organizing cabinet government.

In Britain, beginning with the Conservative government of Edward Heath in 1970, a conscious effort was made to redesign the executive machinery of government in order to cope with what was perceived to be an increasing "overload" on the decision-making system. Heath, a "rational managerialist" and former bureaucrat like Trudeau, had "scoured North America for business methods adaptable to Whitehall's needs."[19] He studied the Canadian experience, in part because it constituted a "blend" of the parliamentary system and "a great extensive application of American methods to the organization of...decision-making in central government."[20] Like Trudeau, he wished to have "Cabinet...be in a position to take strategic decisions."[21] A Central Policy Review Staff was established in the Cabinet Office, a new budgetary system called Programme Analysis and Review was introduced and new portfolios were established. These brought together in "giant super-ministries" (most notably, the Department of the Environment and the Department of Trade and Industry) functions that had become excessively fragmented by the departmentalized structure of the earlier ministries.

Heath's technocratic approach may well have been a contributing factor to his defeat in 1974 insofar as it was not well suited to manage the severe political and economic crises that beset his government after a year or so in office. The demise of Heath's attempt to provide for a greater strategic role for Cabinet, an unravelling that began even before his electoral defeat, was partly a function of Cabinet's inability to cope with political crises. Heath's plan also ran too much against the grain of British practice.

The dominance of a decentralized structure of cabinet government in Britain was due to several factors. First was the compact size of the British

Cabinet. By the 1950s, all major departments were represented in the Cabinet by a cabinet minister, who was in turn supported by one or more junior ministers not in the Cabinet. The scope for intra-portfolio coordination was thus significant. Second, the cohesive character of the mandarin class enabled a great deal of interdepartmental coordination to occur at the level of officials. Third, the coordinating capacity of the Treasury for expenditure budgeting was also significant, thus minimizing the need for elaborate cabinet mechanisms. In this context, the cabinet committee system had become, as Brian Hogwood and Thomas Mackie describe it, "highly ramified."[22] While this largely secret maze of cabinet standing committees, subcommittees and *ad hoc* committees could serve various purposes at different times, its most general effect was to diffuse power from Cabinet as a forum for strategic decision making. As Colin Seymour-Ure observed in 1971, "the Cabinet is becoming a principle of government and barely an institution at all."[23] This "principle of government," however, was hardly any less complicated for its absence of formal institutionalization. The maze was as complex as anything found in Canada. Collegial decision making had simply been pushed further down the line to a bewildering array of committees.

In Australia, the cabinet structure had a representative character that, while perhaps not as extreme as in Canada, nonetheless induced a collegial approach. From 1955 to 1983, excepting the 1972-75 Labor government, there existed a two-tiered cabinet/ministry system, with Cabinet having a dozen or so ministers. But because not all departments were headed by cabinet ministers, the Cabinet had to process a large volume of business. During the one-term Labor government of Prime Minister Gough Whitlam, the government was not constructed on the cabinet/ministry distinction. "From the outset," as Patrick Weller notes, "Labor used cabinet committees more extensively and more openly than the...[previous] government," and the system adopted was "explicitly based on federal Canadian experience."[24] This model did not prove to be effective, however, and Whitlam increasingly "relied on ad hoc committees and informal gatherings of ministers of his own choosing."[25]

The Liberal government of Malcolm Fraser, elected in 1975 and in office until 1983, reverted to the cabinet/ministry distinction, but instituted a formal system of cabinet committees with Fraser chairing most of the important committees himself. Given his prime ministerial style of government, he also strengthened the role of his public service department, the Department of Prime Minister and Cabinet, in the strategic management of government. However, this failed to reduce the overload on the cabinet system or the fragmentation extant in the system.[26] Indeed, it intensified the overload, precisely because it diminished the willingness of the Prime Minister to allow departmental ministers to make decisions on their own, without resolving the need for strategic direction and budgetary discipline.

The New Zealand Cabinet has long had two characteristics that, taken together, have enhanced collective decision making. First, the pool of potential cabinet ministers has been limited by the comparatively small size of the single legislative body, with fewer than 100 members in total. This has meant a Cabinet in the order of 20 members, a number that has enabled it to function as a decision-making body although, as in Australia and Britain, some ministers were not in the Cabinet. Second, as Weller noted before the election of the New Zealand Labour government in 1984, Cabinet remained an important decision-making body because the "comparative lack of talent in the New Zealand Parliament" meant that "many of the ministers...[were] weak and...require[d] the consistent support of their colleagues."[27] The fact that all ministers have their offices in one building also reinforced a collegial approach.

In 1972, the Labour government of John Kirk introduced a reorganized and streamlined cabinet committee system complete with a committee on policy and priorities. The latter, however, was soon transformed into an "expenditure review" committee, but "was still learning when the oil shock of 1973 turned it into a fire brigade."[28]

With the return of the National party to power in 1975, Prime Minister Robert Muldoon did away with the policy and priorities committee and appointed himself Minister of Finance, a portfolio he maintained throughout his entire term in office (1975 to 1984). While he thus "aggregated a tremendous amount of personal power within the Cabinet,"[29] "even...[this] most autocratic modern PM," as Matthew Palmer notes "could not subvert...a highly developed system of collective Cabinet decision making."[30] This collective approach, however, did little to address the fact that ministers were required to provide direction to a very large number of government departments, with most ministers responsible for two or more departments. To the opposition Labour party as well as Treasury officials at the time, this mix combined to provide neither the expenditure restraint nor the strategic policy direction in cabinet decision making necessary to cope with the deepening New Zealand crisis.

Comparative Perspectives

The search for an effective structure for collective decision making that would accommodate individual ministerial leadership in directing departments of government led governments in these four systems to continuous, and invariably disruptive, organizational changes throughout the 1960s and 1970s. Everywhere, the efforts to cope with the fragmentation resulting from the expansion of the state were subject to the stresses and strains brought about by the growing interdependencies of public policies and combined with increasing resource constraints. Cabinet committees appeared to offer an alternative to overloaded Cabinets by enhancing interministerial deliberation and decision making below the level of full Cabinet. But as Hogwood and Mackie concluded in their comparative analysis of cabinet committee systems: "the decisional arenas [of cabinet committees]...are *interrelated*...[but, at the same time] *fragmented*...[they are not] a fully integrated and coordinated system, with clearly defined criteria for delegation from the full cabinet."[31] As designed and re-designed in each of the four systems during the 1960s and 1970s, this form of collegial decision making enhanced policy coordination and program bending on the margins. However, it did little to secure either the strategic direction required by the expanded role of the state or the budgetary discipline demanded by increasing constraints on the public treasury.

The Corporate Management of Government

The corporate management of government is not a recent phenomenon in any of the four Westminster systems. Its genesis lay in the gradual acceptance of the need to ensure the nonpartisan character of the public service and to exert authority over the management of the public purse. Efforts on these fronts intensified, however, as governments sought to impose new standards on a broadening range of administrative matters. These included efforts to introduce new management systems applied to traditional corporate concerns as well as new initiatives to extend the corporate dimensions of public management across government. As in earlier periods of administrative reform, the basis for some of these new interventions was statutory. But even where it was not, the management of the means of public administration was increasingly subject to the ends of public policy. Moreover, central management agencies were given the authorities to ensure compliance with the rules and regulations deemed necessary to give effect to the public policies governing administrative practices.

Strengthening the Central Functions of Management

When the Canadian government finally agreed to end the patronage system for staffing the public service, the organizational instrument chosen was an independent Civil Service Commission. Although the merit system it was to operate developed in stages, by the end of the First World War, the Commission had evolved into "an all-powerful central personnel agency."[32] Its statutory powers to ensure independence from ministerial direction were significant. But by giving the Commission executive functions that previously belonged to ministers, including powers over "appointments, promotions, transfers, salary scales and classification,"[33] the management of the public service, in several important respects, passed from ministers to a parliamentary agency.

The depression that took hold at the end of the 1920s provided the impetus for financial management reforms. In 1930, an office of the Comptroller of the Treasury was created within the Finance portfolio to institute a centralized system of financial management and control. This was the first time that the administrative capacity existed to impose a uniform financial system throughout government. The Treasury Board, a cabinet committee chaired by the Minister of Finance, had been set up immediately following Confederation but its statutory authority covered only various aspects of government financial management.

By the end of the period that can be characterized as the era of the administrative state in Canada – from the 1930s to the late 1950s – the central apparatus of the government for corporate control over the management of government was firmly in place. By that time, the Canadian experience mirrored developments in the other three Westminster systems. Although the four systems differed in the degree to which, and precise ways by which, corporate controls were exerted over ministers and their public servants, a centralized system had come to dominate government in all four countries.

The debilitating effects of this system on the management of government did not go unnoticed, however. In Canada, this was perhaps best demonstrated by the extent to which "nondepartmental" government organizations were deployed to escape the strictures of the centralized system on managerial authority. Aptly entitled "structural heretics" by J.E. Hodgetts, these Crown corporations, regulatory commissions and other forms of nondepartmental agencies were established with varying degrees of independence from direct ministerial authority and central management controls. They were an inevitable reaction to the limitations of a centralized management regime for controlling management in the ministerial departments of government.[34]

It was clearly just a matter of time before a reaction against the complex system of rigid central controls would surface. By the mid-1960s, the Canadian government, acting on the advice of the Glassco Royal Commission on Government Organization,[35] sought to overcome the stifling effects caused by these controls over departmental managers. Some of the Glassco Commission's recommendations prefigured major tenets of the new public management almost two decades later, especially in its promotion of decentralization of management authority. "Let the managers manage" was one of its general prescriptions. Notwithstanding the removal of some controls, its principal effect, ironically, was the construction of an even more elaborate complex of central management systems. This occurred because a principal concern of the Commission was to elevate what it called "the task of departmental administration"[36] and "the functions of central direction."[37]

Departmental administration centred on what the Commission saw as "the more generalized functions of management" as distinct from the technical skills required in the management of public service operations. The general functions had to be performed "at the directing centre of each department" and were tasks "common to all departments," including planning, organizing, staffing, budgeting and evaluation.[38] The "functions of central direction" involved the same set of generalized functions of management except that they were to be performed for the government "as a whole," in recognition of the fact that the Government of Canada was "a single entity." With the exception of the "preparation of the budget," all the other functions of central direction, the Commission stated, were in "varying states of underdevelopment."[39]

The Commission's plan for the adoption of "a new concept of management"[40] prescribed that the mechanisms for the functions of central direction be lean in staff and limited in their regulatory capacities. However, it linked the general management functions to be performed both in departments and at the centre. In so doing, it paved the way for increased managerial specialization within departments as well as increased centralized control over these specialized management functions by central agencies, in particular the Public Service Commission and the Treasury Board Secretariat. This latter body was established as a separate agency following the Glassco Commission's report. Over a wide range of management functions, new standardized policies were applied by specialist managers in both central agencies and line departments. As central agencies expanded the scope of their management standards and controls, sub-specializations emerged to handle the increased burden of central rules and regulations.[41]

By the late 1970s, after extensive elaborations to the corporate management of government, the Canadian regime underwent a further strengthening of central control in response to the recommendations of the Lambert Commission on Financial Management and Accountability and the urging of the Auditor General. The result was a further extension of the corporate management of government, through the creation of a new central management agency, namely the Office of the Comptroller General operating under the authority of the Treasury Board, and the subsequent introduction of new financial management systems and a new system of program evaluation.

Comparative Experiences

The Canadian experience in these regards was hardly novel among the Westminster systems, although it arguably went further than in any of the other three. It drew on each successive wave of managerial fad and fashion in the North American private sector, as well as on various emulations of the same in the American federal government which, until the late 1970s, was very much a leader in public management innovations.

In Britain, the bureaucratization of public management was challenged from a managerial perspective in the 1968 report of the Committee on the Civil Service, the Fulton Report.[42] This highly controversial report attacked the "amateur" generalist administrators who populated the senior echelons of the British bureaucracy. It echoed many of the recommendations of the Glassco Commission in its call for a greater emphasis on management in government and the recruitment of management specialists. Like the Glassco Commission's recommendation that led to the creation of the Treasury Board Secretariat as the general management agency of government, the Fulton Report called for a separation of the central civil service management functions of the Treasury from its fiscal and expenditure management responsibilities. It also called for increased devolution of managerial authority by hiving off certain departmental functions to more autonomous agencies. In this, as well, it sounded much like the Glassco Commission with its call to "let the managers manage."

Although a Civil Service Department was subsequently created, and some measures were taken over the following decade to establish a more managerial approach to public administration, the response fell well short of what the Fulton Report had recommended. And the changes that were made did precious little to reverse the bureaucratization of management in government. If anything, as in Canada, the corporate management of government was strengthened over the following decade. When Thatcher came to power in 1979, this model as applied to management in government was still dominant.

In Australia in 1974, the Labor government of Prime Minister Gough Whitlam established a Royal Commission on Government Administration (the Coombs Commission) with a mandate similar to that given the Glassco Commission in Canada more than 10 years earlier. Its recommendations were not dissimilar, although were more up to date in reflecting what had become fashionable in the intervening decade. The Coombs Commission, as was the case with the Glassco Commission, reported to a government different from the one that had established it. In Australia, however, very little was done by the Liberal government of Prime Minister Malcolm Fraser in response to its recommendations. The Fraser government did create a separate Finance portfolio and department responsible for the expenditure budget and financial management, as had been done in Canada a decade earlier, thus ending Treasury's mandate in respect to these matters. Although some reforms were made to the Australian public administration, especially in the area of administrative law, by the early 1980s, public service reform was still prominent in the opposition Labor party's election preparations.

In New Zealand, a royal commission established in 1961 at the same time that the Glassco Commission was preparing its assault on the Canadian system, "found little evidence of bureaucratic ills." Its recommendations, in contrast to those of the Glassco Commission, "simply endorsed the existing system"[43] made up of a highly centralized structure for expenditure budgeting and financial administration provided by the Treasury department and an equally highly centralized structure for personnel administration provided by the State Services Commission. Indeed, these two agencies were understood to be, and in fact were referred to as, "control" agencies. Although this complacency was overtaken by a series of efforts at administrative reform over the next two decades, albeit within the existing management framework, a 1978 report of the Controller and Auditor General found major deficiencies and expressed the same kinds of concerns raised in Canada at the same time by the Auditor General and the Lambert Commission.[44]

Comparative Perspectives

The net result of various efforts to reform the corporate management of government in the Westminster systems during the 1960s and 1970s produced an increasingly professionalized cadre of management specialists within these governments, both at the centre and in line departments. While some attempts were made to reduce central control, for every gain in managerial authority in departments, further elements of central control were added. As a consequence, there was an increase in the numbers of staff in control agencies and, in all but New Zealand, the number of central agencies. This enhanced capacity for control, on the part of those whose mandates were to establish and enforce corporate management rules and regulations, resulted in professional management being equated with the design and implementation of "administrative systems."

Challenging Fragmentation and Centralization

The political and intellectual challenge to the designs of cabinet government and public administration by the late 1970s emanated from a variety of sources. In political and governmental circles, there was a developing consensus among political leaders and their advisers that firm leadership had to be imposed from the top if the fragmentation in cabinet government, and the resulting lack of strategic direction and collective discipline, were to be overcome. Public choice theory provided some inspiration in this respect, especially as it highlighted the consequences of fragmented authority in government decision making in pampering a multiplicity of interests.

Public choice theory has had an obvious appeal to "conviction politicians" intent on asserting their authority in the hierarchy of government. If political leaders are to overcome the overload created by the diffusion of power in fragmented government and thus rein in the state, they must engage in what Jeremy Moon calls "innovative leadership" and demonstrate both the necessary political will and the required policy capacity that come from an explicit agenda.[45] Armed with a strategic policy agenda and the political will to impose it, leaders do not need to seek a consensus at all costs, nor to accept the compromises that invariably weaken or even derail their agenda. In Westminster systems, of course, prime ministers are ideally positioned to provide this kind of leadership on their own or in concert with a coterie of key ministers and/or senior advisers. In any case, cabinet government will be characterized by an increasing concentration of power.

Agency theory has also provided inspiration in tackling the question of strategic policy in highly complex organizations. It makes clear the problems that arise when a multiplicity of principals seek to develop a coherent policy framework for dealing with issues of a horizontal character, without imposing inconsistent or conflicting objectives on one or more departments. At issue here is the need to address the number of decision points in the system from whence attempts are made to shape public policy. While agency theory may be considered simplistic in its insistence on a single focal point for a principal-agent relationship, its logic makes clear the degree to which missions and tasks may be undermined when multiple objectives are imposed by a variety of authorities.[46] The implication of agency theory here is not necessarily that a government should abandon the pursuit of horizontal policy objectives. Rather, agency theory would suggest that the authority structure be designed to consolidate as much as possible the major interdependencies of public policy within single organizations and thus reduce the extent of their dispersal across separate organizations. The objective should be to promote intra-organizational policy making on horizontal issues rather than relying on the complex coordinative and linking mechanisms required by interorganizational policy making.

Finally, further support for a concentration and consolidation of executive authority at the centre came from accounts of private sector experience in meeting the organizational challenges of an increasingly turbulent economic environment. This was best represented by *In Search of Excellence*,[47] by Thomas Peters and Robert Waterman, a work popularized internationally in ways that gave its basic ideas a profile as widespread as the story line of "Yes, Minister." Its critique of a corporate leadership model based on rational planning and complex matrix management structures, combined with its advocacy of a bias for action and engaged executive leadership, presumed to herald a new approach to organizational design. This design was characterized by "simultaneous loose-tight properties" whereby administrative centralization gives way to decentralization down the line to "the shop floor," decentralization being the "loose" part of the equation. But chief executives are "fanatic centralists" who insist on "the few core values they hold dear," the "tight" part of the equation.[48] The implications for political leadership were obvious: conviction politics was in line with the best practices of the private sector.

The challenge to the practice of administrative centralization, on the other hand, as Jonathan Boston notes, has been largely driven by "practitioners and private sector consultants rather than academics or theoreticians."[49]

Public service practitioners had experienced the shortcomings of the centralized corporate management of government first hand. For their part, nonetheless, private sector consultants brought with them the ideas current in private sector management, which promoted devolution – the "loose" properties proscribed by Peters and Waterman that "pushed autonomy down to the shop floor."[50] Not surprisingly, the focus of reforms thus centred primarily on how to improve public management in ways that would devolve management responsibilities from the central agencies to departments and within departments from corporate staff to line managers.

In some governments, moreover, agency theory was applied, explicitly or implicitly, to the issue of corporate management. In particular, agency theory took dead aim at the central premise of administrative centralization, namely that good public administration requires that all parts of the complex organization that is government should be treated as merely divisions of a unified whole. It follows from this premise that standardized rules and procedures are set by central management agencies for administrative practices across all departments. In government, this approach has been pursued with great vigour because personnel and financial administrative systems especially are deemed to be dedicated to avoiding partisan intervention or bureaucratic cronyism in staffing decisions on the one hand, and the political or administrative misuse of public funds on the other.

As a consequence, management authority is centralized, and corporate administrative functions take on a life of their own. Management authority is thereby restrained as central management agencies seek to micro-manage the administrative dimensions of management in government. To the extent that central management authority is itself subject to dispersal across two or more central agencies or across specialized divisions within one or more central agencies, those who seek to micro-manage will do so in ways that result in inconsistent or conflicting demands on line managers.

Agency theory is useful in considering the dysfunctions, even pathologies, that result from efforts to micro-manage line managers in respect to their deployment of the various resources, including personnel, used in the pursuit of organizational missions and the performance of organizational tasks. If those responsible for operational management do not have sufficient authority over the resources used, they cannot be held fully accountable to their superiors for the results achieved or not achieved. As agents, these public service managers are limited in their capacities to perform on behalf of their principals, namely their ministers. On the other hand, those who do have authority, namely the central management agencies of government, are not the agents of these individual ministers; they neither report nor are accountable to them except in their collective capacity as members of Cabinet or cabinet committees, such as the Canadian Treasury Board. In some cases, however, such as independent public service commissions or boards, they may not even be accountable to ministers.

The shortcomings inherent in this approach derive primarily from the fact that managers in operating departments are accountable not only to their own departmental ministers but also to the central agencies that exercise corporate management authority. And since central agencies have a greater capacity to hold departmental managers to account for their compliance with corporate management rules and regulations than ministers have to hold their managers to account for the implementation of departmental policies and programs, managers tend to pay closer attention to the dictates of central agencies than to their ministers. In organizational terms, administrative requirements will take precedence over the primary purposes of the organization.

In tackling this issue, agency theory is appealing because it provides the theoretical justification for delegated authority to government departments and operating agencies in order to promote productivity in the use of resources in pursuit of organizational missions. The barnacles of centralized control ought not to stand in the way of achieving the intended results of these missions. Public service managers, accordingly, must not be excessively regulated, beyond the core requirements of corporate policies and values of best management practices, if they are to fulfil their obligations as agents of ministers. In particular, they must have sufficient authority to deploy departmental resources in ways that secure results. This implies a reduction in interference from corporate management agencies.

Finally, agency theory is appealing because it emphasizes transparency in ministerial-public service relations: ministers decide what they want to see accomplished and then contract with their public service managers to deliver the results. The principal-agent relationship can thus produce a collaborative effort in which policy objectives, missions and tasks are closely aligned. To the degree that this alignment is achieved, ministers are better able to hold public service managers to account for their performance. Because these managers have been given delegated authority by their ministers to achieve explicit results, as specified in contracts, managers can be freed from an excess of centrally determined rules and regulations. Compliance with standardized rules and regulations is no longer an excuse for not realizing ministerial policy requirements.

Public Management as Governance

The various appeals of public choice theory, agency theory and the managerialist prescriptions of the private sector could not but strike a responsive chord in government, given the degree to which executive fragmentation and administrative centralization have hamstrung *both* political leaders and public administrators. The many examples of the dysfunctional consequences of these two developments in steering the state and managing the public purse and in securing best management practices in government and in delivering quality public services have provided much grist for the mill for public administration reformers. The media, government commissions and enquiries, parliamentary auditors and academic studies have issued case study after case study purporting to demonstrate that governmental and management designs with these features suffer from a serious and perhaps terminal pathology.

Just as the critique of career public service emanating from various academic theories contains an element of reality that cannot be discounted, the critique of fragmented executive structures and centralized administrative management cannot be dismissed as irrelevant to the intractable problems facing governments and their public services. These theoretical approaches have given rise to an impressive number of changes in governance and public management.

At the same time, the basic dynamic of responsible government as party government means that, notwithstanding the fact a government has an obvious incentive to act in a unified manner to preserve cabinet solidarity in the face of opposition in the legislature, all governments are characterized by conflict and competition within the governing party itself. Partisanship does not eliminate differences within a party. Indeed, any party with sufficient public appeal to form a government is essentially a coalition of political factions representing different socio-economic interests and political dispositions.

In Canadian federal politics, for instance, the only two parties that have formed governments, namely the Liberals and Progressive Conservatives, have always been essentially coalitions representing the numerous diversities of Canadian political life – regional, provincial, ethnic, religious, economic and ideological interests. It is not surprising that scholars have described these parties as "brokerage parties."[51] This has meant, at a minimum, that territorially based interests must be represented in the Canadian Cabinet. As Herman Bakvis' major study of this dimension of cabinet government makes abundantly clear, there has always existed within the Canadian Cabinet a distribution of power *and* responsibilities to a number of key "regional ministers" (also referred to as "political ministers") that overlays the formal assignments and authority of official ministerial portfolios.[52] The Canadian Cabinet, in short, has had to function as a "confederal executive."[53]

The Canadian experience in this regard is especially interesting but not unique. In the other three Westminster systems, territorially based interests are present although less pressing. This is the case even in Australia, a federal political system in which the states and territories of the Australian federation are represented in an elected Senate. Although some of the governing parties in these three systems have been at times relatively more ideologically programmatic in their partisanship, Cabinets in each of these three systems have still evinced the conflict and competition that reveal them as fundamentally coalitions of political factions.

The critical point of these political dynamics is not simply that politics pervades the practice of cabinet government, as is the case in all organizations, but that this politics has a representational character to it. Organizational politics within cabinet government certainly entails both interpersonal power struggles, wherein ministers pursue their political ambitions, and interministerial competition, wherein ministers protect their turf and fight for organizational resources for their respective portfolios. But organizational politics at the executive level also constitutes the "high politics" of governance: the interests of significant groups, constituencies and even whole communities are at stake in the exercise of power within the collective political leadership that is Cabinet. How a governing party accommodates these interests in formal cabinet design and informal practice cannot but affect its political fortunes.

For these reasons, a government that seeks to appear to be responsive to a wide range of policy constituencies is likely to become fragmented in either its formal structures or in its actual operations. The character of high politics entailed in executive governance, however, is all too often simply not understood by those who want to reform executive structures. This is especially true for those advisers from the private sector who ignore, or do not recognize, the particular kind of organizational politics inherent in the management of government. A Cabinet, for instance, cannot be equated with a board of directors as found in private sector corporations. The members of a board of directors do not exercise individual responsibilities for the different parts of the organization. Rather, they direct and oversee a chief executive officer, who then has general authority over those subordinate executives with responsibility for the various divisions of the organization.

Under ministerial government, in contrast, ministers of the Cabinet are themselves individually the chief executives of the various departments of government. In these individual capacities they seek to advance the particular interests of the various portfolio constituencies they represent. As members of the Cabinet, they also seek to influence what their colleagues do in order to advance the interests of the various territorially based constituencies they represent, including the constituents of their individual electoral districts. It is little wonder that many private sector executives are unable to make the transition from business administration to public administration, at least within the core institutions of ministerial government. Too many fail to appreciate the representational imperatives of executive leadership in government. By seeking to remove this kind of politics from the organizational designs and practices of public management, they become its victims.

For a different set of political reasons there are strong pressures to limit the authority of public service managers in ministerial departments. Because departmental public servants function as subordinates to ministers, and ministers are therefore required to accept responsibility for what their officials do or do not do, public servants are constrained in their management functions. These constraints are corporate in character and thus imposed from the centre, but they are reinforced by individual ministers insisting that their senior public servants establish whatever additional departmental controls ministers consider necessary for the particular circumstances of their individual departments.

In contrast to the private sector, governments' management of resources used in their operations are not simply administrative activities, that is, activities without public policy content or statutory requirement. This is most obvious in relation to personnel and financial management. With regard to these and numerous other dimensions of public management, public policy has come to encompass a wide range of the administrative means used to realize the ends of public policy: public policy pervades public administration.

Conclusion

In response to the overload on government, the imperatives of fiscal restraint, increasing demands for quality public services as well as the perverse consequences of excessive micro-management in government, political leaders must diminish both the fragmentation of their executive structures and the administrative centralization within public management. The first requirement was clearly not met by the highly complex and collegial decision-making cabinet structures developed during the 1960s and 1970s. The diffusion of power inherent in these systems did little to promote either policy coherence or expenditure discipline. The second requirement was not met by the increasing roles and powers of central management agencies or their corporate counterparts within departments. The complicated array of constraints issuing from these quarters served, in too many instances, to undermine the pursuit of productive management.

At the same time, it must be acknowledged that the political dynamics and pressures that lead to both executive fragmentation and administrative centralization are inherent in the Westminster model of government and public administration. Restructuring government, nonetheless, can affect the ways this model contributes to, rather than diminishes, a regime of executive governance and public administration that realizes both responsible and good government.

Notes

1. Martin Painter, *Steering the Modern State: Changes in Central Coordination in Three Australian State Governments* (Sydney: Sydney University Press, 1987).

2. Henry Mintzberg, *The Structuring of Organizations: A Synthesis of the Research* (Englewood Cliffs: Prentice-Hall, 1979), pp. 17-34.

3. Thomas Peters and Robert Waterman, *In Search of Excellence* (New York: Harper and Row, 1982), pp. 29-54.

4. Peter Aucoin, "Organizational Change in the Canadian Machinery of Government: From Rational Management to Brokerage Politics," *Canadian Journal of Political Science*, Vol. 19, no. 1 (March 1986), pp. 3-27.

5. Colin Campbell, "Cabinet committees in Canada: pressures and dysfunctions stemming from the representational imperative," in Thomas T. Mackie and Brian W. Hogwood (eds.), *Unlocking the Cabinet: Cabinet Structures in Comparative Perspective* (London: Sage, 1985), pp. 61-85.

6. Patrick Weller, "Party rules and the dismissal of prime ministers: comparative perspectives from Britain, Canada and Australia," *Parliamentary Affairs*, Vol. 47, no. 1 (January 1994), pp. 133-43; Martin Smith, "The core executive and the resignation of Mrs. Thatcher," *Public Administration*, Vol. 72 (Autumn 1994), pp. 341-63.

7. S.L. Sutherland, "Responsible Government and Ministerial Responsibility: Every Reform has its Own Problem," *Canadian Journal of Political Science*, Vol. 24, no. 1 (March 1991), pp. 96-100.

8. H.L. Laframboise, "Here come the program-benders!", *Optimum*, Vol. 7, no. 1 (1976), pp. 40-48.

9. Stefan Dupré, "The Workability of Executive Federalism in Canada," in Herman Bakvis and William Chandler (eds.), *Federalism and the Role of the State* (Toronto: University of Toronto Press, 1987), p. 239.

10. Gordon F. Osbaldeston, *Organizing to Govern*, Vols. 1 and 2 (Toronto: McGraw-Hill Ryerson, 1992), Vol. 1, p. 143.

11. Dupré, "The Workability of Executive Federalism in Canada," pp. 238-39.

12. Colin Campbell and George J. Szablowski, *The Super-Bureaucrats: Structure and Behaviour in Central Agencies* (Toronto: The Macmillan Company of Canada Ltd., 1979); Colin Campbell, *Governments Under Stress* (Toronto: University of Toronto Press, 1983).

13. Canada, Royal Commission on Government Organization, *Report*, Vol. 1 (*Management of the Public Service*), abr. ed. (Ottawa: The Queen's Printer, 1963).

14. Ian Clark, "Recent changes in the cabinet decision-making system in Ottawa," *Canadian Public Administration*, Vol. 28, no. 2 (Summer 1985), pp. 185-201.

15. Peter Aucoin, "Cabinet government in Canada: corporate management of a confederal executive," in Colin Campbell and Margaret Jane Wyszomirski (eds.), *Executive Leadership in Anglo-American Systems* (Pittsburgh: University of Pittsburgh Press, 1991), pp. 139-59.

16. Campbell, *Governments Under Stress*, pp. 91-93.

17. Canada, Office of the Prime Minister, "Release," September 17, 1984.

18. Campbell, *Governments Under Stress*, p. 351.

19. Peter Hennessey, *Cabinet* (Oxford: Basil Blackwell, 1986), p. 74.

20. Hennessey, *Cabinet*, p. 169.

21. Hennessey, *Cabinet*, p. 76.

22. Brian W. Hogwood and Thomas T. Mackie, "The United Kingdom: decision sifting in a secret garden," in Mackie and Hogwood (eds.), *Unlocking the Cabinet*, p. 38.

23. Quoted in Hennessey, *Cabinet*, p. 6.

24. Patrick Weller, "Cabinet committees in Australia and New Zealand," in Mackie and Hogwood (eds.), *Unlocking the Cabinet*, p. 93.

25. Weller, "Cabinet committees in Australia and New Zealand," p. 95.

26. Colin Campbell and John Halligan, *Political Leadership in an Age of Constraint: Bureaucratic Politics Under Hawke and Keating* (St. Leonards, Australia: Allen and Unwin, 1992), pp. 21-22.

27. Weller, "Cabinet committees in Australia and New Zealand," p. 103.

28. Weller, "Cabinet committees in Australia and New Zealand," p. 105.

29. Matthew S.R. Palmer, "Cabinet Ministers and Single Party Majority Government in New Zealand: the Collective Decision-Making Approach," paper presented to the Joint Sessions of Workshops on "The Political Role of Cabinet Ministers in the Process of Parliamentary Government," European Consortium for Political Research, University of Limerick, March 30-April 4, 1992, p. 20.

30. Palmer, "Cabinet Ministers and Single Party Majority Government in New Zealand," p. 21.

31. Thomas T. Mackie and Brian W. Hogwood, "Cabinet committees in context," in Mackie and Hogwood (eds.), *Unlocking the Cabinet*, pp. 32-33; emphasis in the original.

32. J.E. Hodgetts, *The Canadian Public Service* (Toronto: University of Toronto Press, 1973), p. 266.

33. Hodgetts, *The Canadian Public Service*, p. 268.

34. Hodgetts, *The Canadian Public Service*, pp. 138-56.

35. Royal Commission on Government Organization, *Report*.

36. Royal Commission on Government Organization, *Report*, p. 49.

37. Royal Commission on Government Organization, *Report*, p. 53.

38. Royal Commission on Government Organization, *Report*, pp. 49-51.

39. Royal Commission on Government Organization, *Report*, pp. 51-3.

40. Royal Commission on Government Organization, *Report*, p. 62.

41. Frank Swift, *Strategic Management in the Public Service: The Changing Role of the Deputy Minister* (Ottawa: Minister of Supply and Services and Canadian Centre for Management Development, 1993).

42. United Kingdom, Committee on the Civil Service, *Report* (London: HMSO, 1968).

43. J. Roberts, *Politicians, Public Servants and Public Enterprise* (Wellington: Victoria University Press, 1987), p. 34.

44. Canada, Office of the Auditor General, *Toward Better Governance: Public Service Reform in New Zealand (1984-94) and its Relevance to Canada* (Ottawa: Minister of Supply and Services, 1995), p. 17.

45. Jeremy Moon, "Innovative Leadership and Policy Change: Lessons from Thatcher," *Governance*, Vol. 8, no. 1 (January 1995), pp. 1-25.

46. James Q. Wilson, *Bureaucracy: What Government Agencies Do and Why They Do It* (New York: Basic Books, 1989), pp. 370-72.

47. Peters and Waterman, *In Search of Excellence*.

48. Peters and Waterman, *In Search of Excellence*, p. 15.

49. Jonathan Boston, "The Theoretical Underpinnings of Public Sector Restructuring in New Zealand," in Jonathan Boston, John Martin, June Pallot and Pat Walsh (eds.), *Reshaping the State: New Zealand's Bureaucratic Revolution* (Auckland: Oxford University Press, 1991), p. 9.

50. Peters and Waterman, *In Search of Excellence*, p. 15.

51. Janine Brodie and Jane Jenson, "Piercing the Smokescreen: Brokerage Parties and Class Politics," in Alain G. Gagnon and A. Brian Tanguay (eds.), *Canadian Parties in Transition* (Scarborough, Ontario: Nelson Canada, 1989), pp. 24-44.

52. Herman Bakvis, *Regional Ministers: Power and Influence in the Canadian Cabinet* (Toronto: University of Toronto Press, 1991).

53. Aucoin, "Cabinet government in Canada," pp. 140-46.

FIVE

Consolidating and Devolving Authority

Restructuring government has been a principal focus of public management reform in Canada and the other three Westminster systems over the last decade. Despite important differences in each case, two primary patterns of change are evident. On the one hand, authority has been consolidated at the centre of government to counter the fragmentation of power in cabinet decision making. The purpose here is to secure greater adherence to strategic priorities, particularly expenditure restraint. On the other hand, authority has devolved to operational departments and agencies in order to diminish constraints on productive management and require public servants to manage their operations in more economical, efficient and effective ways.

This chapter considers the restructuring of government as it has encompassed movement in each of these two directions. In each system, the practices of cabinet government and public administration have been altered to accommodate this simultaneous consolidation and devolution of authority. Modifications in the architecture of government have gone much further in Great Britain and New Zealand than in Australia or Canada in the devolution of authority, at least in separating policy and operational responsibilities. In the Canadian case, restructuring of government to accommodate both consolidation and devolution of authority has lagged behind changes in the other three systems.

Consolidating Authority

In the four Westminster systems, consolidating authority in executive governance did not require the same kind of initiatives in each case. While the basic principles of cabinet government were similar in each system, there were differences in formal designs as well as practices among the four systems. As a result, the changes required to consolidate authority and to concentrate power were also different.

Mulroney's Brokerage Politics

The conventions and practices of cabinet government in Canada, as noted in the previous chapter, had led to an ever-expanding Cabinet, buttressed by a consequent increase in its institutionalization. In at least one important respect, these conventions dovetailed both with Brian Mulroney's approach to political leadership and with the situation he faced in 1984. His brokerage style of executive leadership accepted the need to have important political interests represented within the government. These were the interests that had to be brokered in the determination of public policy. With 211 members of the House of Commons on the government benches and more than ample representation from every province, it is not surprising that he constructed the largest Canadian Cabinet ever.

At the same time, Mulroney's brokerage politics did not fit with the highly institutionalized collegial decision-making structures that had been developed over the previous two decades.[1] Mulroney preferred to lead by transacting government business with individual ministers in response to issues as they arose on the political agenda. Consensus within the Cabinet and caucus was not considered any less critical for this, but a collegial approach to decision making was not his preferred option for managing government, that is, brokering the interests at stake on any given issue. He questioned the willingness and capacity of the central bureaucratic apparatus that was meant to serve the Prime Minister and Cabinet to be responsive to the Conservative political agenda, especially as the agenda included the reduction of the interventionist role of the federal government and a greater inclination to meet provincial government demands.

By opting for a large Cabinet but not a collegial structure of leadership and management supported by the central executive bureaucracy, Mulroney depended greatly on two factors. The first was the extent to which he could establish the conditions for what Trudeau's former principal secretary,

Thomas Axworthy, entitled the "strategic prime ministership."[2] This was the central political and policy capacity that would enable him to pursue a select number of strategic initiatives that would define the major directions of his government. The second was the extent to which he could effect a more hierarchical structure to the cabinet system in order that an inner circle of senior ministers could provide the necessary control and discipline in what would otherwise be an unwieldy executive structure.[3]

Over the course of Mulroney's tenure, strategic prime ministerial leadership was present at times, for example, in the adoption of a goods and services tax, the successful pursuit of a free trade agreement with the United States and a well-orchestrated, though ultimately unsuccessful, approach to constitutional change. However, on a broad range of issues, especially those related to the fiscal position of the federal government and in a number of social and economic policy sectors, strategic prime ministerial leadership was absent more often than it was present.

While his brokerage style had its advantages, especially in maintaining Cabinet and caucus solidarity, it did little to secure a coherent approach to executive governance. Indeed, it led to a further fragmentation of the governmental system through the creation of a new set of ministerial portfolios and agencies for regional development. This made a more hierarchical decision-making system even more critical. Yet, Mulroney's refusal to involve himself sufficiently in the management of government limited the capacity of other ministers to provide the necessary leadership. This was the case even for the Minister of Finance, notwithstanding the extent to which this portfolio and department assumed a key role with respect to spending controls especially as the Policy and Expenditure Management System (PEMS) became less and less the actual system for expenditure decision making.

Although PEMS was retained for some time as the formal process, its capacity for enhancing budgetary discipline had long since been acknowledged as ineffectual. Indeed, on assuming office, the Mulroney government established a Ministerial Task Force on Program Review under the direction of the Deputy Prime Minister, Erik Nielsen, to subject the entire range of government programs, numbering approximately 1,000, to a critical assessment. Although this process may have highlighted the urgent need for expenditure restraint,[4] the political will to take the necessary action was absent. As a consequence, the government had to adopt what was perceived to be the only politically feasible option – a policy of continual across-the-board cuts to the operating costs of government.[5]

In Pursuit of Hierarchy

The inadequacy of the cabinet structure, especially when coupled with the Prime Minister's leadership style, was eventually acknowledged when, going into the 1988 election, an informal operations committee was created to manage the business of cabinet operations. This committee was chaired by the Deputy Prime Minister, Don Mazankowski who, on assuming the position of Deputy Prime Minister in 1986, had quickly established himself as the "general manager" of the government with the Prime Minister acting as "chairman of the board." More than anything else, the creation of this committee reflected a recognition that the Priorities and Planning Committee, then numbering just over 20 ministers, could not function as an effective steering committee for the Cabinet, particularly without a Prime Minister who would assume a strong leadership role in this collective setting.

The Operations Committee was given formal status following the re-election of the Conservative government in 1988. At the same time a new Expenditure Review Committee (ERC) was created. Chaired by the Prime Minister, the ERC drew on the experiences of Great Britain and Australia. These two committees signified Mulroney's willingness to accept a greater degree of hierarchy in the conduct of cabinet business.[6]

The addition of the Expenditure Review Committee to the cabinet structure, managed by the Operations Committee, enabled a handful of senior ministers to effect restraint better. This concentration of political power in the hands of a small number of ministers, several of whom served on both the Operations and Expenditure Review committees, did not take long to produce a backlash among the majority of ministers who were excluded from this inner circle. Because Mulroney did not assume his role as chair of the ERC but delegated this responsibility to Mazankowski, this new structure had an extremely short life as a significant factor in the management of public spending. Notwithstanding an initial measure of success in restraining expenditures, the ERC process fell into disuse when Mazankowski also assumed the Finance portfolio. By 1992, the Committee had been disbanded.

Although the Mulroney government began its tenure in 1984 with some effort to effect the restraint demanded by the government's financial situation, its term was marked by an unwillingness to mount a major assault on the increasing fiscal crisis. Continuing across-the-board cuts and a limited number of *ad hoc* reductions achieved through the budgetary process, as identified by the Department of Finance and the Treasury

Board Secretariat, were clearly insufficient. A bloated Cabinet and a highly fragmented set of portfolios and departments were increasingly recognized as major structural obstacles to expenditure restraint as well as to the kind of program review required for a strategic redefinition of the role of the federal government. Belatedly, the stage was set for a major restructuring that in several respects drew upon the comparative experience of the other three Westminster systems, particularly that of Australia.

Streamlining the Cabinet
By the early 1990s it was increasingly acknowledged that the structure of the executive, given its size, the absence of a distinction between Cabinet and ministry, and its inclusion of a number of ministers who represented highly specific regional and sectoral constituencies, clearly could not cope with the policy and expenditure exigencies confronting the federal government. The consequences of a fragmented decision-making system with multiple decision points was recognized within Cabinet, the central bureaucracy and, equally important, outside government.

Several factors forced a change of attitude toward what had traditionally been considered a virtue of the Canadian cabinet structure, namely its responsiveness to the representational imperatives in Canadian politics. First, the representational character of the Cabinet meant constant pressure on government expenditures. Too many ministers regarded their representational responsibilities as requiring them to seek as much as possible from the public purse for their regional or sectoral constituencies whatever their collective rhetoric on fiscal restraint. Second, opinion leaders, best represented perhaps by a former Clerk of the Privy Council and Secretary to Cabinet, Gordon Osbaldeston, began to campaign for a new approach to cabinet design.

A third factor was Reform party leader Preston Manning's support for reducing the number of ministers in Cabinet. Founded in 1987, the increasingly popular Western Canada-based populist Reform party was regarded as a serious electoral threat to the Conservatives by the early 1990s, especially in the Western provinces. And fourth, ministerial frustration with the excessive fragmentation of ministerial portfolios and the consequent complexities and rigidities of the cabinet decision-making process led Mulroney, in 1992, to ask an experienced minister, Robert de Cotret, to review the cabinet structure. He was supported in this task by staff from the Privy Council Office and advised by a committee that included Osbaldeston.

The timing of the report produced by this review was such that Mulroney delayed action to allow his successor to perform the surgery that virtually everyone, the public included, considered necessary. His successor, Kim Campbell, limited the Cabinet to 25 members and cut the number of cabinet committees from 11 to five. The number of departments was reduced from 32 to 23. With an election pending, she declined to appoint any junior ministers although it was announced that in the future, parliamentary secretaries, who had not previously been considered members of the government, would "play a stronger and more visible role in support of Ministers, both in the House of Commons and in dealing with issues and clients in their Ministers' portfolios."[7]

In opposition, the Liberals denounced the decision to restructure government departments before a review of the roles of the federal government, but did not object to a smaller Cabinet. Indeed, the Liberal transition team had done considerable work on machinery of government issues and was well aware of the arguments in favour of significant change. Once elected, the Chrétien government made only one major change to the Campbell design, namely the elimination of a portfolio and department of Public Security. At the same time, Chrétien appointed eight junior ministers, now titled "secretaries of state," but did not include them in the Cabinet. For the first time then, the Canadian Cabinet was distinguished from the full ministry. The Chrétien government also decided that there would be no formal "inner-executive" committee, as had existed from 1968 to 1993 in one form or other (Priorities and Planning, Inner Cabinet or Operations); the full Cabinet would be the "senior forum for collective decision-making."[8] In addition, the number of cabinet committees was reduced to four.

In accepting the idea of a streamlined executive structure, ministers and officials sought to have fewer ministers representing what were identified in negative terms as "special interests." Having fewer ministers would also tilt the balance between spenders and guardians in favour of the latter. The consolidation of portfolios and departments, combined with the subordination of junior ministers to portfolio ministers, was further seen as a way to promote a more integrated approach to the critical task of reviewing the program commitments of the federal government. Finally, much of what previously had to entail interministerial, and therefore often Cabinet or cabinet committee, decisions could now be devolved to individual portfolios. The advantages of this were clearly seen in the major policy and program reviews during 1994 and 1995, given that individual portfolio ministers possessed greater scope to assume responsibilities than would have been the case prior to the restructuring.

Along with the consolidation of authority that resulted from the 1993 restructuring, a new Expenditure Management System (EMS), introduced in 1995, acknowledges the need to concentrate expenditure decision-making authority in the hands of the Prime Minister and the Minister of Finance. The "integration" of the "budget planning process" is the key feature of this new system. The fiscal budget assumes first priority, while expenditure decision making becomes essentially "reallocations" within the limits set by the Prime Minister and Minister of Finance, who are to "make the final decisions" on "fiscal targets, new spending initiatives and reductions."[9] A new Coordinating Group of Ministers is responsible for the program review process that has become integral to the budget process.

Comparative Experiences

In Great Britain, Margaret Thatcher did not set out to redesign the formal organizational structures of cabinet government when she became Prime Minister in 1979. However, she did use her prime ministerial powers to the fullest to alter the dynamics of power within the machinery of government. This meant enhanced prime ministerial intervention across a wide range of policy areas related to her major priorities. Thatcher's intentions were clear in all this: she had an agenda and she was going to manage it her way. Her strategy was to reduce the influence of those ministers whom she considered either her internal opposition or not sufficiently supportive of her agenda. Above all, she sought to restrict the degree to which the government would be forced to compromise on her fundamental political agenda because of competing interests and views in the Cabinet and ministry. Her efforts to control the agenda were thus equally focused on the members of her own government and the career public service, notwithstanding the fact that her public rhetoric was most often directed at the permanent bureaucracy.

Thatcher's approach was facilitated by two features of cabinet government in Britain that, while not unique to this Westminster system, were clearly more pronounced than in Australia, Canada or New Zealand. The first was the extent to which secrecy applied to the structures and operations of Cabinet and its committees. Brian Hogwood and Thomas Mackie refer to this as "decision sifting in a secret garden."[10] The secrecy that pervades the British system has clearly augmented the powers of prime ministers. The second and perhaps more important feature was the extent to which the collective dimensions of the British Cabinet had not become excessively institutionalized over time.

In such a context, a British prime minister can be as dominant as he or she wants. Thatcher was able to avoid a good deal of compromise on what she wished to do, precisely because she could not only by-pass collegial decision making but, in some cases, keep her initiatives a well-guarded secret until she was ready to spring decisions on her colleagues. As Peter Hennessey put it: "[S]he was not a Cabinet-committee person. She would do business with her fellow ministers free of the curse of committees."[11] The use of committees for decision-making purposes declined significantly as a consequence.[12] However, to the extent that she needed allies among ministers, she was able to structure decision making on an *ad hoc* basis to suit her purposes. This was perhaps best illustrated in her use of an expenditure decision-making committee, entitled the "star chamber," comprising trusted ministerial colleagues that excluded the major spending ministers.[13]

As well as managing Cabinet in this way, Thatcher also provided critical support to those key cabinet ministers and departments with corporate policy responsibilities. Most important, the Chancellor of the Exchequer and the Treasury were able to signal her support for expenditure restraint in their dealings with other ministers and their departmental officials. Her approach, while it did not always ensure that she got her way, enabled her to function, as George Jones put it, "as [the] guardian of collective government."[14] A strong prime minister, in other words, need not necessarily imply an erosion of cabinet government in the pursuit of the government's political agenda.

In contrast, Thatcher's successor, John Major, by no means as strong a Prime Minister, has been both inclined and required to re-emphasize the collective dimension of cabinet government. In the realm of the expenditure decision-making process, for instance, this took the form of a new cabinet committee headed by the Chancellor to make the major expenditure decisions of the government on a more collective basis, even if restricted to those ministers serving on this senior committee.

In New Zealand, for a somewhat different set of reasons, the Labour government that came to power in 1984 with David Lange as Prime Minister did not have to change the basic design of Cabinet. The size of the New Zealand Cabinet, at 20 or so ministers, with an additional handful of junior ministers not in Cabinet, meant that the formal architecture was conducive to strategic leadership, even though the total number of departments meant that several ministers had to hold more than one portfolio.

The New Zealand cabinet design was not altered following the election of the Lange government, notwithstanding what emerged as a radical reform agenda. The major change in response to a critical economic situation was the restructuring of the commercial undertakings of the New Zealand state that had been deeply embedded in the departmental structures of government. This was realized through the "corporatization" of state-owned enterprises; they became corporations operating at arm's length from ministers, under the direction of a board of directors, but within a tightly defined commercial and accountability regime. In many cases, these corporations were subsequently privatized. Following these initiatives, a second round of changes involved a major restructuring of the traditional departmental system of public management in order that ministers could better direct the desired outcomes of public policy and hold their departments and agencies to account for the management and delivery of the outputs purchased by ministers.

The political leadership that drove these changes and also effected a major assault on public spending, especially in eliminating a wide range of industrial subsidies, came from a small group of key ministers, backed by an equally small number of key officials primarily from the Treasury department, who forced their radical agenda through Cabinet. As in Britain, this concentration of power did not require major changes in the machinery of cabinet government; it merely required a demonstration of political will by the Prime Minister and his most influential colleagues.[15]

The New Zealand National party, elected in 1990 when the Labour government's leadership self-destructed over the continuing need for radical change, had expressed concerns about the effects of the Labour reforms on the collective management of government by Cabinet. This concern was echoed in a review commissioned by the new government,[16] but the principal features of Labour's reforms were judged sound and retained. It was thought that the collective dimensions of cabinet government could be strengthened by improving the new system of contractual relations between ministers and the chief executives of departments put in place by Labour. This was particularly true with regard to the information base for cabinet decisions on the government's expenditure budget and the enhancement of the role of central policy agencies as well as collective public service advice to cabinet committees.

In Australia, in the immediate aftermath of the 1983 election of the Hawke government, the principal objective was to secure political control over what was perceived to be the major problem facing the incoming government, namely the budgetary deficit and its cumulative effects on the government's debt situation. The new government pursued a wide range of economic policy measures to deregulate the Australian economy and to promote industrial restructuring. In addition, an Expenditure Review Committee chaired by the Prime Minister took direct aim at the government's deficit. Hawke and his Treasurer, Paul Keating, constituted the heart of the "razor gang" of "economic rationalists" who regarded the elimination of the deficit as central to the government's reform agenda. With great enthusiasm and significant personal involvement by the Prime Minister, they attacked this issue in ways that ensured political control over the expenditure decision-making process and, in so doing, secured the commitment of those ministers who were less enthusiastic about downsizing the state.

In 1987, immediately after Labor was re-elected, Hawke instituted a new design for the Australian Cabinet. Although the government retained a two-tier ministry with senior ministers in the Cabinet and junior ministers outside it, the Cabinet, with 16 portfolios, was structured so that all departments were represented in Cabinet by a portfolio minister. Previously, departments headed by junior ministers were not represented in Cabinet. Under the new design, junior ministers were assigned to a portfolio and thus were subordinate in status to their portfolio minister. The number of departments dropped from 28 to 18 (two of which were headed by junior ministers but reported through a portfolio minister).

Several reasons were advanced for this reorganization of Cabinet, but clearly the most critical were enhanced ministerial control, a more strategic focus on public policy and increased budgetary discipline. In each of these respects, the Cabinet was to be better positioned to manage the state apparatus. Ministerial control was to be enhanced by a clearer hierarchical arrangement within the smaller number of portfolios. Junior ministers and parliamentary secretaries were to relieve portfolio ministers of the more mundane political and administrative matters that previously had required ministerial attention but could not be delegated to political assistants or public servants. Ministerial decision making was to be better coordinated by the consolidation of decision points in the system; and Cabinet was to have a greater capacity to coordinate major policy initiatives by removing "the dross which once overloaded the Cabinet agenda."[17] Coherence was to be enhanced by eliminating the policy and program duplication and overlap resulting from the organization of government into 28 departments. Finally, budgetary discipline was to be strengthened by better use of the system of portfolio budgeting (introduced in 1984) that could result from the reduced number of ministerial portfolios.

Although there were significant transitional costs to productive management associated with this major reorganization, especially as it required the consolidation of departments, the changes have been judged successful on the basis of the above criteria.[18] Not only have the number of organizational changes within the government subsequent to this reorganization declined significantly, but the basic design has been maintained. The principal reasons for this are threefold.

First, like the British and New Zealand Cabinets, the Australian Cabinet was now a manageable size for executive decision-making purposes. While there is no magic number here, a Cabinet much larger than two dozen is rarely able to contain factionalism in an effective manner, either in full Cabinet or in cabinet committees. Second, and again like the British and New Zealand Cabinets, the Australian ministry now possesses an explicitly hierarchical structure, with junior ministers subordinate to portfolio ministers. Third, ministers now have a greater capacity to manage their portfolios without interference from other ministers. With a limited number of departments, the number of interministerial and interdepartmental committees required for coordinating the state apparatus is reduced.

Comparative Perspectives

The major lesson to be drawn from the comparative experience over the last decade is that the political leadership must structure the policy and expenditure decision-making processes in ways that facilitate tight control over strategic decisions. In particular, this means an effective centralization of global budget decision making that sets firm limits on the total size of the expenditure budget and shapes the major contours of the total budget in the direction of the government's priorities. Concentration of authority has been pursued in the designs of each of the four systems, with the Australian Expenditure Review Committee (now the Expenditure and Revenue Committee), New Zealand's Expenditure Control Committee, the British expenditure committee that formalized Thatcher's "star chamber," and the revamped Expenditure Management System in Canada.[19]

Of course, the structures of an expenditure budget system do not necessarily produce the required political will to exercise discipline and effect restraint. This is the major reason why legislated controls over spending have become a central feature of some reform programs, as prescribed by public choice theorists. Such initiatives arise from the fundamental limitation inherent in even well-designed budgetary systems, namely that they do not in themselves ensure the required political discipline. Restructuring the central capacity of the executive is obviously not a panacea; there continue to be ministers who see their political fortunes tied closely to "delivering the goods" to their regional or sectoral constituencies. Indeed, the New Zealand Fiscal Responsibility Act was placed on the statute books in anticipation of the possible consequences of the next election with its prospects of a coalition government resulting from the new proportional representation electoral system approved by a referendum in 1993.

A streamlined system for central policy and expenditure decision making requires that a greater measure of authority be devolved downward to ministers and their departments. In its basic design, the Canadian Policy and Expenditure Management System (PEMS) was at the forefront in recognizing this paradox. It provided for a centrally determined budgetary allocation of "resource envelopes" to policy committees, and a decentralized allocation of resources by these cabinet committees to the programs of individual ministers. Within these limits, cabinet committees were to allocate, and reallocate, resources to meet government policy priorities.

However, there were two fundamental flaws in the design of PEMS. The existence of a central policy reserve allowed ministers a second chance at obtaining new resources when they failed to make their case in policy committees. The use of cabinet committees to determine the reallocation of resources offered up by individual ministers was devoid of practical incentives to restrain spending since ministers could not be certain that they would obtain new resources by way of reallocations. The obvious resolution to these flaws are centrally determined allocations to ministerial portfolios. This approach need not rule out any role for policy committees, but it does require that final authority reside with either the Prime Minister and Finance or Treasury minister, or a cabinet committee wherein the guardians of the public purse are well positioned to extract the necessary collective discipline. With tight limits, some responsibility for reallocating resources within portfolios can then be assigned to individual ministers and departments, particularly where the portfolio structures themselves are designed to encompass a related set of policy programs. In these cases, especially where a coherent policy strategy exists, some trade-offs can be made in reallocating resources among programs without constant reference to Cabinet or cabinet committees.

Simply giving ministers broader responsibilities does not in itself secure effective policy making. The appropriate design of portfolios is crucial, notably incorporating the right mix of related policy and program instruments. This can never be done in ways that produce watertight compartments, but the policy interdependencies among programs can be contained better with some designs than others. In the Canadian case, this objective has always been confounded by the role assigned to regional ministers: the advocacy of different sets of regional interests overlays ministerial responsibilities for public policies and programs meant to serve public interests defined in non-territorial terms.[20] The essentially nonpartisan commitment to this federal imperative of governance, at least on the part of the Conservatives and Liberals, was clearly demonstrated in the streamlining of portfolios in 1993. Neither Campbell nor Chrétien was willing to abolish the regional portfolios and agencies put in place by the Mulroney government.[21]

Devolving Authority

The consolidation and concentration of authority that have characterized the efforts of governments to be able to assert their authority in policy and expenditure decision making have been accompanied by efforts to devolve authority and decentralize decision making in the management of government operations. Strengthening line authority in order to enhance productive management has been at the forefront of the new public management for at least two reasons. First, public managers themselves identify the external constraints emanating from central corporate management agencies and the internal constraints imposed by functional staff authorities within departments as major impediments to the economical and efficient use of their financial and human resources. Second, reformers at the centre of government insist that line managers must assume greater responsibility for resource use if public management is to be improved. These two principal tenets of the new public management are no longer publicly challenged or debated. The conjunction of the twofold demand to let managers manage and to make managers manage, however, has resulted in different responses in the four systems.

Removing Constraints to Productive Management
In the Canadian context, demands for a devolution of management authority came initially from within the public service itself in recognition of the

numerous perverse, even if unintended, effects on productive management emanating from the highly centralized management systems put in place over the last two decades. This view was well represented in the Auditor General's 1983 report. One of its chapters, entitled "Constraints to Productive Management in the Public Service," looked at the effects of control from the centre. As this report noted, "the extent and intensity of the frustration we encountered [in the conduct of this study] was striking."[22] The response within government was a Productivity Improvement program, an initiative that sought to reduce the burden of centralized corporate controls while putting in place "a policy framework" that would "tailor [the central management] regulatory regimes to reflect the circumstances of different departments."[23]

Support for this program and associated initiatives from the three central agencies responsible for management in government (the Treasury Board Secretariat, the Office of Comptroller General and the Public Service Commission) dissipated when the Conservatives assumed office in 1984.[24] However, in its electoral campaign, the Conservative party had promised not only to tackle the size and scope of government expenditures, but also had accepted the need for changing the administrative regime in order to promote productive management. The party's campaign platform encompassed a set of general proposals outlined briefly in a document entitled "Towards Productive Management – The P.C. Approach." It drew extensively on the Auditor General's 1983 chapter.

The Ministerial Task Force on Program Review, launched immediately after the Conservatives' election to office in 1984, was thus not only "in response to the government's concern about waste, duplication and red tape," but also promised "to overhaul government programs so that they would be 'simpler, more understandable and more accessible to their clientele' and that decision making should be 'decentralized as far as possible to those in direct contact with client groups'."[25] The program review did not result in the elimination of many programs – in part because of the unwillingness of ministers to do so or even to reduce program expenditures as such. However, it did foster a continual effort to reduce the overhead costs of government. Reductions thus focused on operating budgets and the size of the public service. Given this approach, the need to alter the centralized management regime and reduce its regulatory burden on operating departments was also accepted. In place of the former government's Productivity Improvement program, the Conservative government in 1986 implemented its own program, labelled Increased Ministerial Authority and Accountability (IMAA).

The IMAA program, at one point in the planning stages entitled Increased Ministerial *and Departmental* Authority and Accountability (reflecting the fact that this was very much a public service initiative), was based in some large measure on work done by the Treasury Board Secretariat as part of the previous government's Productivity Improvement program. IMAA's focus was directed primarily at enhancing the management authority of deputy ministers, giving them greater leeway to make decisions on the deployment of departmental resources without reference to the Treasury Board and reducing their reporting requirements to the Board. This increase in powers was in exchange for a more effective accountability regime. To accomplish these objectives, agreements between the Board and departments were negotiated on a voluntary basis. The logic of IMAA assumed that this instrument of devolution should not be imposed from the centre.

The success of IMAA in devolving authority in order to promote greater productivity was limited at best. Only 10 Treasury Board-department agreements were concluded over the following four years, at which time the initiative was overtaken by other developments. The Canadian experience with the IMAA program revealed the extent to which the Conservative government's approach to devolution was devoid of political leadership or strategic direction. The federal bureaucracy was essentially left on its own to improve public management and to cope with an increasing malaise in the public service. This situation was the consequence of bureaucracy bashing by the Conservative political leadership and its political staff; frustration with the perpetuation of centralized administrative systems; the continuation of wage restraints introduced before the Conservatives gained office; the impact of budget and staff cuts on morale and on the capacity to maintain expected levels of public service; and a profound lack of confidence in the abilities of public service leadership to manage personnel, especially those in the executive cadre.

To its credit, the leadership of the public service under the direction of the Clerk of the Privy Council, Paul Tellier, not only commissioned an attitudinal survey of public service managers but was willing to publish its findings.[26] All these factors eventually led the senior public leadership to seek approval for launching a major internal assessment and renewal of the public service and public management. Mulroney agreed, and in 1989 this began under the banner of an initiative entitled Public Service 2000.

The government was willing to approve this initiative in part because of the urging of the Public Policy Forum, a newly formed joint private sector-public sector venture in the cause of good government. At the same time, ministers continued to have little interest in reforming the system of public management. The government was willing to proceed with some statutory changes to public service personnel legislation and with some alterations to central agency policies that enhanced departmental management authority, for example, over the disposal of Crown assets. For the most part, however, the Public Service 2000 program was contingent on senior managers adopting a wide range of practices to effect a "culture change" in public management. The explicit assumption of senior officials was that attitudinal change would be a sufficient determinant of behavioural change. In this respect, the program of renewal, while not inspired by the central tenets of the "total quality management" movement[27] and other management movements then fashionable, was subsequently cast in a way that linked its proposals to these private sector schemes. Publicly, renewal was justified by its claim that the driving force was improved service to the public.

Left essentially on its own to give effect to Public Service 2000, the senior bureaucracy nevertheless had to cope with a continuing set of political demands for restraint in operating budgets (including public service pay) and further public service staff reductions (resulting both from contracting out and organizational mergers and closures). Both of these factors undermined efforts to demonstrate the need for, or virtues of, public service renewal in the lower ranks of the management cadre – let alone among public servants on the front lines. The fact that the renewal effort was not politically driven also meant that there were few sanctions that could be imposed on those senior managers who failed to conform to the spirit of Public Service 2000. All of this was compounded by the uncertainty about government-imposed restraint measures, as the federal government lurched from one round to another without a serious plan for addressing its fiscal situation.

The PS 2000 process was consciously led by senior officials, a situation viewed in public service union quarters as an indication that the exercise was primarily geared to giving managers greater control over the management of staff. In some large measure, this view was correct. The point of the exercise was to enable managers, first and foremost, to gain enhanced authority to manage a system that had become excessively rigid and inflexible. This was most clearly demonstrated in what managers perceived to be necessary changes in public personnel management. They saw these changes as a way of eliminating the restrictions of the personnel system; union leaders saw these proposed changes as the way of eliminating the rights of public servants.

Although the renewal program had a top-down management focus, it lacked sufficient coherence to guide reform measures. In accepting just about every tenet of management reform advanced by the several, and often competing, schools of management thought in vogue at the time, it failed to articulate or advance what Ian Clark, at the time of his departure as Secretary to the Treasury Board, called "a realistic management posture."[28] Neither was it connected to any major plan for alternative organizational designs that might serve as the basis for altering behaviour either at the centre or within ministerial departments. Lacking a mandate from the government for significant restructuring and, in any event, having lost faith in organizational engineering given the record of the previous two decades, the senior public service resorted largely to exhortation.

Across a broad front, nonetheless, some progress was made in devolving authority, although a good deal of what was done was only loosely connected to Public Service 2000 as such. The burden of central agency regulations and rules was reduced in several areas of financial, personnel and common services policy. Changes were made to both Treasury Board policies and legislative requirements, most notably those of the Financial Administration Act, to eliminate, reduce or streamline various controls and standards in financial administration. In many instances, general policies replaced regulations; in others, guidelines replaced policies.

Although there have been fewer changes in the area of human resources or personnel management to devolve authority to line managers, some flexibilities have been granted, in part as a consequence of the 1992 Public Service Reform Act. Among other things, these encompass a greater capacity for deputy ministers to redeploy, demote and release staff and to appoint certain categories of managers to levels rather than to specific positions. While significant staffing authority was delegated to line managers by the Public Service Commission in the 1970s and 1980s, there has been an inability to find solutions to further devolution on which senior officials agree and public service unions find acceptable, despite the extensive and high-level efforts of the PS 2000 task forces and associated union consultations. Finally, by including optionality in its common services policy, the Board gave line managers the opportunity to secure a much greater range of goods and services from the private sector, choices based on their own assessment of benefits and costs to their departments.

Equally significant was the Treasury Board's emulation of the Australian "running costs" model with the adoption, first on a pilot basis and later across the board, of a policy of single operating budgets for government departments. By enabling a department to manage its budget for salaries, wages, administrative and overhead costs, and minor capital expenses as a single expenditure category, this approach provides the flexibility for movement between the various items of expenditure. In adopting this scheme, the Treasury Board ended a longstanding element of control over management flexibility, namely control over the staff complement, or number of "person-years," assigned to a department by the Board in the annual expenditure budget process. This scheme, as in Australia, also contains provision to carry forward a percentage of this budget (now set at five percent) from one fiscal year to the next.

The Treasury Board Secretariat was also anxious to promote experimentation with organizational designs. Thus was created the special operating agency (SOA) model, a modest emulation of executive agencies in Britain. It was hoped that this provision of an even further degree of managerial flexibility would enable these new organizations to improve productivity and services. Six years after the first five such agencies were created, however, only an additional 12 such agencies have been established, employing a total of 7,000 staff. Moreover, these new agencies remain subordinate to their parent departments: the heads of these agencies, for instance, report to the deputy minister of the portfolio in which they are located rather than directly to the minister, as in the British model.

The rhetoric of Public Service 2000, especially its emphasis on "empowering" public servants generally – that is, not just senior managers – was cast at a high level. But in addition to a widespread view that senior managers failed to "walk the talk," there was no coherent plan for devolving authority. As a consequence, devolution took place in a context where uncertainty was ever present. In some cases, devolution from central agencies to departments resulted in senior departmental managers substituting centralized departmental corporate controls over the management of departmental operations. Given the preoccupation with central agency-deputy minister relations in many of the changes emanating from Public Service 2000 initiatives, the limited effects of devolution down the line were perhaps not surprising. For many deputy ministers, the challenge of managing in the turbulent political, policy and budgetary environment of the late 1980s and early 1990s, combined with an absence of demand from ministers for public management reform, was sufficient justification for keeping authority at the centre.

Finally, by the early 1990s it was hardly a state secret, at least in the senior echelons of the public service, that some form of substantial restructuring and downsizing was on the horizon. Gordon Osbaldeston's personal campaign for a restructuring of the machinery of government as outlined in his study, *Organizing to Govern,* as well as the de Cotret evaluation of the cabinet system, were evidence that change was forthcoming.[29] In addition, as noted, the question of the size of the Cabinet and the number of departments was raised as a political issue by those advancing streamlined government; and a number of provincial governments had already reduced the size of their Cabinets. All this meant that just about everything associated with Public Service 2000 could be regarded as preliminary to the main event.

The main event was the 1993 restructuring, initiated by Prime Minister Campbell and accepted by the Liberals after their 1993 electoral victory. This consolidation of portfolios and departments shifted the focus of organizational change from devolution to organizational mergers for many departments and to the downsizing of the corporate overhead in all departments. Nevertheless, the consolidated portfolio and departmental structures, especially when combined with the Liberal government's new Expenditure Management System, may well provide an organizational and decision-making framework within which increased deregulation of central agency controls and enhanced delegation of authority are more probable.

Comparative Experiences

In Britain, increased devolution of authority was viewed as an essential element of public management reform. This message was a central theme of the many efforts of Thatcher's personal efficiency adviser, Derek Rayner. Under his direction a program of scrutinies aimed at securing efficiencies in the management of government operations was initiated. In addition to the concrete suggestions for efficiencies resulting from scrutinies undertaken by departmental officials with the support of his unit in the Prime Minister's Office, Rayner pressed for the adoption of new management practices and sought to instill a new management culture in the public service. In combination with a separate innovation in the Department of the Environment spearheaded by its managerialist minister, Michael Heseltine, who was uniquely interested in managing his department in the mode of "minister-as-manager," these calls for reform resulted in the Financial Management Initiative (FMI).

Launched in 1982, the FMI sought to introduce a new management regime and was heralded at the time as a significant departure from traditional practice.[30] Decision making was to be decentralized to departments; central corporate controls were to be reduced; departmental objectives were to be clarified; outputs and performance were to be measured; the effectiveness of programs was to be monitored; responsibility centres were to be held accountable for controlling costs; and, most important, information systems supporting ministerial and senior departmental management were to be put in place. Cost-consciousness was to be promoted in ways that until now had not penetrated the management of departments.

Significant changes did occur following the implementation of the FMI. Improvements were made to budgetary and financial management information and to control systems at various levels in departmental hierarchies, especially as these related to operating budgets – "running costs," as the British (and Australians) label them. As Andrew Gray and Bill Jenkins note: "As a programme of financial management, FMI has introduced and institutionalized a change of emphasis in civil service management: primary responsibilities no longer lie exclusively with the management of policy but include the management of resources."[31] Little attention was given to human resource management, however, except insofar as "running costs" came to include personnel costs, although here the priority was the downsizing of the civil service to effect economies. Improvements were also made in measuring performance, but managers down the line were given little new authority to improve performance beyond cost-cutting measures.

The limitations of the FMI as a regime for devolved authority were soon acknowledged by the Efficiency Unit. In its 1988 report, *Improving Management in Government: The Next Steps*,[32] the Unit concluded that ministers could not be expected to be managers; that effective management could not be realized if the entire governmental apparatus was centrally managed as a single corporate entity; and that the management tasks of government could not be performed well if they were not distinguished from the policy tasks of governance.

The implications were clear. Ministers and their departmental policy advisers should confine themselves to establishing the strategic purposes and directions of the operational units of government and allocating budgetary resources to them; central management agencies should confine themselves to assisting ministers in ensuring that proper and appropriate control, monitoring and evaluation systems are in place for each unit; new organizational structures called "executive agencies" should be established within departments to carry out the operational tasks of government, namely the implementation of policies and the delivery of services; and within this framework, those responsible for operational management should be given the flexibility to manage and conduct their operations to secure the maximum degree of economy, efficiency and effectiveness. At the same time, they would be subject to a rigorous performance measurement and accountability regime.

The adoption of this new executive agency structure met some resistance within government, especially from the Treasury, but Thatcher, once convinced, was adamant that the restructuring proceed. The appeal of this approach was essentially threefold. The overload on ministers was not about to go away simply by virtue of the government's effort to roll back the state. Changes in expenditure budgeting and financial management had assisted ministers, collectively and individually, to get a better handle on public management at a macro level. But, at the micro level of departmental administration, the complexities of public management continued to overwhelm even the most managerially minded ministers. Devolution was seen as not simply desirable but essential.

At the same time, whether because of British tradition or due to circumstances inherent in the task of assisting ministers in their roles (the Efficiency Unit, following the Fulton Committee Report, implied the former), the senior departmental public service had neither the operational experience nor the managerial disposition to provide the executive leadership required of the organizations that implemented policies and delivered services. This meant that those who headed such organizations had to have a new relationship not only with their ministers but also with their senior departmental officials and, by extension, with central corporate management agencies. Their "subordinate" status within the bureaucratic hierarchy had to be redefined to give them the necessary scope to behave as "executives." A separation of policy and operational responsibilities was necessary if operational responsibility was to be given to those who could provide the required leadership.

Finally, the experience of the FMI, with its concentration on a purely financial management approach to public management reform, had demonstrated that increased cost-consciousness and better control over spending, however important to taxpayers, did not constitute, in and of themselves, a sufficient condition for improving services to the public. What the British refer to as the "executive" operations of government, that is, the delivery of public services, had to be managed according to a new ethic that focused on improving services in ways that better met customer or client expectations. Devolution was seen as a prerequisite to changing the attitudes of public servants, particularly managers who had to ensure that their organizations served citizens first and foremost. Managers were to manage "down" their organizations to serve citizens;

they were not to manage "up" the hierarchy to serve ministers, let alone the senior bureaucracy.

The acceptance by government of this restructuring (called the Next Steps program) has had a profound effect on the organization and management of the British government and its public service. Almost two-thirds of British public servants are now working in executive agencies,[33] encompassing organizations that are both tiny and mammoth and both operationally innocuous and politically charged. Agencies are still being created, and a large number of departmental units encompassing a further 17 percent of the civil service are under active consideration for agency status.

Executive agencies are headed by chief executives who report directly to departmental ministers. The regime prescribes a formal agreement between the chief executive and the responsible minister that specifies the services an agency is to deliver, its performance targets, the management authority of its chief executive and the agency's reporting requirements. Agreements are tailored to the particular circumstances of each agency. The devolution of authority from ministers, departments and central management agencies, accordingly, is not uniform across all agencies.

The experience of executive agencies to date has demonstrated that deregulation of central corporate and departmental controls and decentralization of management authority through devolution can improve management in the delivery of public services. At the same time, significant devolution has not been easily accomplished, in some large part because the Treasury department, in contrast to its counterparts in Australia and New Zealand especially, was not the driving force behind the Next Steps program. As was the case with the FMI, executive agencies were the creation of the Efficiency Unit operating at the time out of the Prime Minister's Office.

What is perhaps most important from the perspective of the new public management is that there is widespread support for the basic principle of devolution on which executive agencies were established. The most recent evaluation, and perhaps the most independent to date, indicated that general agreement exists to the effect that the system ought not to revert to past practices.[34] In addition, a recent report from the House of Commons Treasury and Civil Service Committee has endorsed the executive agency regime. The Major government has committed itself to further devolution, in particular by delegating responsibility for pay and grading of staff below the senior levels.[35]

In New Zealand, the Lange government embarked on an equally extensive restructuring to devolve authority in the management of government.

The New Zealand system was clearly in need of major reform. As previously noted, numerous government departments had a bewildering array of commercial and public service activities. Great scope existed for restructuring these commercial activities as state-owned corporations and for introducing a wide range of measures to effect the commercialization of these enterprises. Although some aspects of these reforms merely brought New Zealand into line with other systems, in other respects commercialization introduced a significant measure of economic deregulation and privatization. At the same time, New Zealand had lagged behind other governments in diminishing excessive central controls. In particular, its two central management control agencies, the Treasury department and the State Services Commission, together managed what was undoubtedly the most intrusive management regime of the four Westminster systems.

What distinguished the New Zealand adoption of the new public management was the clarity and comprehensiveness with which the principal agents of change approached reform. Although reform proceeded in several stages, the briefing that the incoming Labour government received from the Treasury in 1984 was a devastating critique of the effects of the existing system. Political commitment to change was immediately forthcoming, and a process of devolution, encompassing both a deregulation of central corporate control and a decentralization of authority to managers, was initiated.

Following the "corporatization" of commercial enterprises, in itself a program of devolution, the government overhauled the structure of public management through legislative changes. These changes were fashioned after the legislative and organizational model established for the public management of the new state-owned enterprises. The most important dimensions of devolution as applied to the core public sector resulted from a massive restructuring of ministerial departments. The premise for this restructuring was the need to separate organizational responsibilities for determining the outcomes that ministers want to pursue as a matter of government policy and for the management of the outputs that ministers fund to realize these outcomes. This separation of responsibilities was adopted as a general principle because those departments or agencies that supply or provide outputs on behalf of ministers should not also monopolize advice to ministers on the outputs they should "purchase" from their suppliers.

There are three critical dimensions to this new set of organizational arrangements. First, ministers must be specific about what operational departments and agencies are to deliver. Second, what operational departments deliver is the subject of a formal agreement between ministers and the chief executives of operational departments – an agreement that is to spell out the services, costs, management practices and performance targets and measures for assessing performance. Third, chief executives are given authority over the resources to be deployed in the management and delivery of their services. This model was given legislative status by the State Sector Act of 1988 and the Public Finance Act of 1989. The contractual approach to ministerial-chief executive relations thereby produced the most extensive delegation of management authority in any of the four Westminster systems.

The chief executives of departments, employed by the State Services Commission on term contracts, are now the employers of their staff and have full authority over their operational budgets, including decisions on the procurement of the goods and services. At the same time, they must provide the specified outputs for which they contract with ministers, and their management of resources is closely monitored by the Treasury, to which they must report with some frequency. This regime is by no means a loosely managed affair. Indeed, chief executives must not only meet their performance targets within budget, but they are also responsible to ministers for the good management of their departments.

However, in contrast to the previously centralized and highly controlled regime, chief executives are given both the authority and the incentives to promote good management. For instance, the public sector is now subject to the same labour laws as the private sector, thereby eliminating many of the regulatory restrictions on personnel administration. Chief executives may also hire staff on contract and are responsible for the conduct of industrial relations with their employees. In these and other ways, individual chief executives rather than the central management agencies are accountable for the achievement of best practices in their organizations and are clearly more exposed on this score than under the old regime.

Various government reviews of the changes to the New Zealand system, as well as statements by ministers and officials themselves, are invariably favourable. There have been no major challenges to the basic ideas that underpin the new model although concern has been expressed that the model has yet to be fully implemented. The Controller and Auditor General stated in 1994: "I do not regard the process of financial management reform as complete."[36] There is also continuing concern that devolution of authority to line managers must not undermine the collective responsibilities or corporate interests of the government by virtue of the increased specialization of operations inherent in the model. The adoption of the concept of a "senior executive service" to foster a unifying force within the public service is widely acknowledged to have achieved much less than expected. In response, increased attention has been given to ways to secure adherence to fundamental public service ethics, to reduce the risks to ministers and to improve the specification of departmental performance in relation to ministerial objectives.[37]

The New Zealand approach differs from the executive agency model in Britain primarily in the degree to which central agency controls have been deregulated and authority devolved to chief executives. In each case, however, ministers are still responsible for both policy and operations and receive advice from public servants on each dimension of public management. Both models presume that ministers, assisted by their policy advisers, can be reasonably specific about what services they want as outputs, the resources needed to provide these services at the desired level of quantity and quality, and the measures needed to determine the performance of operational agencies and their management. It follows, therefore, that ministerial intervention in the management and delivery of public services is meant to be restricted by these framework agreements, just as it is in the operational management of nondepartmental agencies such as state-owned enterprises or other organizations established with an arm's-length relationship to ministers.

However, ministers must not be deprived of the advice of line managers either on the policy outcomes that they should pursue or on the outputs for which they should contract in pursuit of these outcomes. As one chief executive, R.G. Laking, put it: "as in any other 'service' relationship, the supplier helps the consumer decide what is required"; and, "there is something intrinsic to the output contract which makes it impossible to exclude the supplier from the formation of value."[38] As Laking views the model: "Ministers can and probably should take advice from someone other than the supplier, but they will inevitably be influenced by their own departments' views on what needs doing. It makes no sense to try to exclude operating agencies from policy debates, particularly when they enter the implementation stage."[39]

In Australia, the Financial Management Improvement Program (FMIP) built on ideas about decentralizing financial management that had gained currency in other systems, most particularly the FMI in Britain. As the Australian government's 1992 evaluation study expressed it, for some reforms such as the new budgetary and financial management systems, devolution was "a necessary condition."[40] As subsequently developed, the most important measures included a "running costs" regime, similar in principle but more extended in scope to what had been introduced previously in Britain and later in Canada (using the term "single operating budgets"); a system to decrease annually these running costs (entitled an "efficiency dividend"); and the flexibility to "carry forward" a percentage of these costs beyond a single fiscal year. These changes were coupled with considerable devolution in personnel administration which transformed the Public Service Board, renamed the Public Service Commission, from a central management agency to an advisory and audit agency.

The Australian approach, to date at least, has differed from the British and New Zealand models in rejecting the idea of separating responsibilities for policy and operations. Instead, the Australians have sought to achieve devolution through an integrated system of program management and budgeting. This has meant that ministerial departments and not just ministers retain responsibilities for both policy and operations. The overriding objective here has been to ensure that public servants are not only responsible for the delivery and management of services as outputs but also to "feel responsible for the results [that is, the actual outcomes] of the programs they are administering,"[41] even though they are "held accountable only for those things over which they have some control."[42]

The Australian approach to expenditure management, as noted, entailed tight central control over expenditure decision making through the Expenditure Review Committee of Cabinet. Improved management of public spending was augmented by a new system of "rolling three-year forward estimates of budget outlays," which was considered the "linchpin" of the control framework.[43] This system was meant to counter the traditional practice of "creeping incrementalism in government outlays."[44] However, the new program management and budgeting system was intended not only to contain costs in the pursuit of greater economy or efficiency, but also to link greater economy and efficiency concerns to an explicit focus on results – the impact of programs on intended outcomes. In this way, the Australians saw themselves engaged in a reform process that would heighten attention to the "cost effectiveness" of their programs and their management.[45]

The emphasis given to results has reinforced the emphasis on devolution as a managerial means to greater productivity. In some important respects, the Australian system is now more rigorous than it was under the traditional regime in pushing corporate responsibilities for improved public management. Line managers, for instance, must return an efficiency dividend from their running costs to the Treasury; commercialization has changed the ways by which various goods and services are provided and purchased by government agencies; program evaluations have demanded a greater focus on actual outcomes of programs; and various changes in industrial relations and human resource management have required line managers to assume greater responsibility for what had been largely the concerns of central agencies.

The record of the Australian reforms respecting these changes demonstrates that clarity, consistency and stability are important ingredients of success. In these three respects, reformers are given high marks both by their peers[46] and by scholars.[47] This being said, there are concerns that devolution down the line in some government departments has not gone far enough, although the record here among departments is clearly mixed. Nor is there general agreement that further delegations are required for improved public management.[48]

Comparative Perspectives

The Canadian effort to effect devolution in public management stands in sharp contrast to developments in Britain, Australia and New Zealand. In each of these last three cases, changes have been politically driven; devolution has been seen by the political leadership, if not all ministers, as a necessary condition to greater productivity. In the Canadian case, however, there has been little in the way of ministerial, let alone prime ministerial, interest in management reforms to promote greater productivity beyond expenditure reductions to the overhead costs of government. For the Mulroney government, fiscal restraint measures including reductions in public service personnel were viewed as a sufficient ministerial response to the "productivity" question. In the case of the Liberal government, the emphasis switched to program review. Efforts to devolve authority under each of these regimes have had to be pursued as part of the public service's own initiatives for reform.

Devolution, of course, is but a means to an end. The purpose is to promote greater productivity in the use of resources, while maintaining or improving the quality of public services. The key to success here is the extent to which policy and operational responsibilities can be separated without diminishing the responsiveness of operations to policy objectives. This can be accomplished only insofar as policy objectives, including corporate administrative policies, are clearly specified, make sense in relation to the actual missions of operational departments and agencies, and are sensitive to the particular managerial and operational circumstances of the tasks performed by departments and agencies.

The comparative experience indicates that much more can be done to meet these requirements than has traditionally been assumed by practitioners and theorists alike. For example, the New Zealand effort to distinguish between responsibilities for outcomes and outputs and the British effort to distinguish between policy and operations constitute a fundamental recognition of what is central to the reconciliation of the twin pillars of the Westminster tradition, namely the conjunction of responsible government and good government. To achieve this, ministers must be as clear as possible about what outcomes and policies they wish to see effected and what outputs and services they are willing to fund. At the same time, they must devolve authority and responsibility to their chief executives for the management of departmental or agency operations.

The attempt to apply these distinctions is not entirely novel in public administration. It draws on the traditional separation of policy and operational responsibilities that is inherent in the approach to the independent staffing of the public services and associated aspects of personnel administration insofar as they are managed independent of ministerial authority. It also acknowledges that, as in the Canadian case, authority for certain aspects of financial administration and control has been delegated directly to deputy ministers and not to ministers. More generally, it builds on the more extensive experience of separating policy and operational responsibilities by the statutory creation of corporations or agencies that function at arm's length from ministers.

What is new, however, is the effort to devolve responsibility for the management of operations across the full spectrum of management functions for those operations subject to direct ministerial authority and responsibility. While managers of these operations may be expected to provide advice to ministers on policy and to assess constantly the level of effectiveness in realizing the desired outcomes, and while policies may be adjusted by ministers in the implementation process, the management of the resources to produce outputs and provide services is deemed to be a responsibility of managers and not ministers.

It follows that if this distinction is to be rigorously applied in the management of government, an organizational separation between those responsible for policy and those responsible for operations is necessary.

Contrary to the way in which it is often portrayed outside New Zealand or Britain (as illustrated in the 1992 Australian government review of its own reforms that includes comments on foreign experiences[49]) neither the New Zealand nor the British model relinquishes ministerial responsibility for decisions on policy and its implementation. Moreover, in each case, ministers are served by public servants with respect to these two responsibilities. The confusion arises from the failure to recognize that these governments have sought to distinguish between responsibility for policy and for the management of operations. Two types of organizations serve ministers, namely policy departments/ministries, and operational departments/agencies respectively. Ministers are not left to their own devices to decide on policies; nor do they relinquish responsibility for what outputs should be funded or operations undertaken.

The British approach is perhaps better developed because each departmental minister has what is essentially a policy department and one or more executive agencies to give advice on his or her full range of responsibilities. However, executive agencies are primarily responsible for managing the operations that provide public services. In principle, the same model applies in New Zealand, but its application across government is uneven. In some cases, ministers are not well served because the desired separation of policy and operational responsibilities among the departments or agencies within their portfolios, or with which they contract for services, has not yet been fully realized.

Although the application of this distinction varies across the two governments, and even across portfolios within each government, its crucial advantage for good government is its requirement that ministers contract with chief executives for the delivery of specified outputs or services. This makes it possible to devolve responsibilities for the management of the resources to be deployed in the delivery of these outputs or services.

The rigorous application of the model in New Zealand has meant a significant degree of devolved authority, encompassing various aspects of financial management, control and accounting; staffing, industrial relations and human resource management; and a wide range of administrative and support services and facilities. This devolved authority is governed by framework legislation, corporate administrative policies and, equally important, ministers' annual contracts with their chief executives. Given this approach, central corporate management controls, especially over personnel administration, have been significantly diminished, as best illustrated by the termination of the extensive powers of the State Services

Commission. This was accompanied by a major deregulation of financial management controls and the virtual elimination of common service agencies and their standardized policies.

In each of these respects, devolved authority has meant a more rigorous responsibility and accountability regime for chief executives. They remain responsible and accountable to ministers, however. Devolved authority has not altered the basic premises of responsible government, but the accountability of chief executives has become more transparent. Nor has devolved authority eliminated the requirement of chief executives to adhere to corporate management policies and principles of good management. Devolution has not done away with corporate management policies; rather, it has shifted the responsibility from control agencies to chief executives.

The British executive agency model is similar in principle, even though executive agencies are formally housed within ministerial departments and do not have separate legislative status. In addition, three features of the British approach have distinguished it from the New Zealand experience. First, both central agencies and parent departments exercise much greater control over the management of executive agencies.[50] This is the case both formally, in that the scope of devolution to the chief executives of executive agencies is less, and practically, in that central agencies and parent departments have sought to intervene in the management of executive agencies to a greater degree. Second, certain corporate policies of the British government have been viewed as contradicting the principles of a regime of devolved authority. The market-testing policy, for instance, was regarded in this way. It diverted executive agency resources to centrally imposed exercises unrelated to their primary missions and tasks, but also denoted a lack of confidence in the willingness of executive agencies to take the necessary steps to be productive and to demonstrate the same. As a result, this policy has been altered to give managers greater authority to decide on how efficiencies should be achieved in their own organizations.[51]

Finally, neither central agencies nor parent departments in Britain have shown much interest in reducing their staff complements in light of the responsibilities assigned to executive agency managers. Not surprisingly, chief executives of executive agencies spend a great deal of time attempting to fend off interventions in what they view as their responsibilities. Equally important, debate over the question of public accountability continues to persist, a point that is considered in chapter 8.

The Australian government did not develop its reforms on the basis of a distinction between policy and operational responsibilities, at least not as these applied to the core public service. On the contrary, as Malcolm Holmes notes, "bringing [policy and delivery] together has been one of the central planks of FMIP and Program Management and Budgeting." The purpose in doing so, he argued, was twofold: first, to have the "needs" of clients better advanced in the policy process by those who have the most direct contact with clients, namely service providers; and second, to promote on the part of those who deliver services a greater focus on "achieving outcomes cost-effectively." This approach, he argues, is superior to that adopted in either New Zealand or Britain where, in his view, the overriding concern has been primarily cost efficiencies and, somewhat later, service improvements.[52]

Although they maintained the integrated departmental approach, the Australians sought to devolve greater managerial authority. Insofar as this entails a deregulation of central agency management controls, a good deal has been accomplished. Insofar as this entails delegation within departments, relatively less has been accomplished. This ought not to be surprising. Senior departmental officials, starting with departmental secretaries, remain responsible for the management of operations and are likely to want to retain management control even if they are willing to decentralize management functions to lower levels in the departmental hierarchy. In these cases, as an Australian review notes, decentralization of functions occurs, but devolution of authority does not.[53] If a department has a stable policy environment, its departmental secretary is more likely to delegate authority for the management of operations. However, in less stable policy environments, the tendency will be to keep tighter control on the assumption that the management of operations must be constantly subject to changing policies. Moreover, the more complex the operations of a department, the more likely that this will result in a less stable policy environment.

On this score, the structural differences between the Australian and Canadian approach and that of New Zealand and Britain are significant. In the latter two systems there has been greater devolution by virtue of the much greater number of operational units (departments and agencies) to which authority has been devolved. In contrast, devolution in Australia and Canada has entailed assigning greater authority to integrated ministerial departments. This is true even though Canada has introduced special operating agencies, and Australia, on an even more selective basis, has established similar kinds of sub-departmental agencies, particularly the several business units of the Department of Administrative Services that provide a range of common services on a commercial basis to other line departments.

As with other aspects of attempted public service reform, the Canadian approach to special operating agencies has been judged harshly by both those in and outside the system.[54] A number of reasons for this have been advanced, including a lack of ministerial interest; the absence of a clear, coherent and accepted strategy for linking this initiative to a broader scheme of reform; the failure to provide a catalytic change agent at the centre to drive this reform; and an inability at the centre to provide the necessary technical support for those departments where special operating agencies were established. But two factors are perhaps the most critical here.

First, the design of these agencies places their heads in a subordinate position to departmental deputy ministers (or, in some cases, to assistant deputy ministers). These heads do not report directly to ministers, as is the case with both the chief executives of executive agencies in Britain and the chief executives of departments in New Zealand. While neither the British nor the New Zealand government has resolved all the issues entailed by these new arrangements, the Canadian experience has been subject to even greater convolution and confusion, leading one agency official to describe the SOA initiative as "Screwed Once Again."[55]

In some cases, the personal relationship between a deputy and an agency head can make an effective accommodation possible, as long as the two persons in question remain in their respective positions. But this idiosyncratic circumstance hardly constitutes a viable organizational design solution across the entire system, especially given the high turnover in both positions that characterizes federal staffing practices. As long as departmental deputy ministers retain their current authority and thus responsibility, they are likely to intervene in agency management whatever formal agreements they devise for this relationship. For all of the reasons that limit the devolution of authority in departments themselves, as both the Canadian and Australian experiences demonstrate, special operating agencies will be subject to departmental controls whenever deputy ministers feel they are warranted.

The second critical factor is the continuing resistance to the very idea of separating policy and operational responsibilities. Although this idea lies behind the adoption of the SOA initiative, the scope for real change has been restricted by a widespread unwillingness to accept that this idea has much application beyond a very narrow range of operations. This is perhaps seen most clearly in the report and recommendations of the stocktaking study commissioned by the Auditor General and the Secretary of the Treasury Board in 1993, which reported in May 1994.[56] While the steering group for this study concluded that "for certain government activities,

SOAs should be able to provide better service at lower cost," it stated that this form of government organization "should be continued" only if certain conditions are met. These conditions included widespread acceptance of the very idea of SOAs – from ministers to deputy ministers, from public service unions to private sector competitors and from the general public to parliamentarians. They also included an organizational design that encompassed criteria for using the SOA model in particular cases; a framework for public reporting; clear guidelines for commercial competition with the private sector; and a performance measurement regime relating to goals and priorities, responsibilities and results. More important, the steering group suggested that SOAs "would seem best suited [for government activities]...whose objectives and outputs can be reasonably measured...do not require significant ongoing ministerial involvement and, although this is quite subjective...operate in a relatively stable policy framework." It would also help if these activities were "revenue dependent...self-financing on the basis of their outputs."[57]

This approach to SOAs illustrates the extent to which Canadian thinking about devolution departs from the British and New Zealand reforms. There is no general acceptance of the idea that government should seek to separate policy and operational responsibilities. Rather, the converse is accepted: those who want an organization to become an SOA must demonstrate that it meets each and every condition for the separation of operational responsibilities from the conventional ministerial department. As the report put it: "The SOA is not, in the view of the Steering Group, suited for situations where: the public expects, or the minister wishes, significant ongoing ministerial involvement in operational decisions and the use of management discretion; [or] the primary activity is developing government policy."[58] The assumption here is that the SOA model has a very limited application to some common service agencies; agencies *en route* to privatization; and those activities so devoid of policy significance or contestation that no one would notice what organizational form they took.

In some limited ways, the SOA design enables greater devolution than the traditional departmental design. For the most part, however, it is a recipe for frustration and confusion beyond anything that executive agencies in Britain have experienced in seeking greater organizational autonomy from their parent departments while remaining directly responsible to their ministers. This was most clearly demonstrated in the unsuccessful attempt to apply the SOA model on an extensive scale in the design of the new Department of Public Works and Government Services (the result of the merger of two departments) following the 1993 restructuring.[59]

The result was a major disappointment to those Treasury Board officials who wished to see the SOA given greater prominence in departmental designs. Although these two formerly separate departments and the two units that joined them from other departments already encompassed four SOAs, and one unit in the process of becoming an SOA, the failure to achieve a new organization along the lines desired by the Treasury Board Secretariat was due, perhaps more than anything else, to a lack of agreement or common understanding of how SOAs should fit within a departmental structure headed by a deputy minister. The major concern here focused on the fact that deputy ministers, and not the chief executives of SOAs, are responsible to their ministers for the management of all parts of a minister's department including its SOAs. This concern, combined with confusion over the model itself, has diminished support for SOAs in both ministerial and senior public service quarters.

Conclusion

In several important respects, the Canadian federal system is at a crossroads. The basic designs of Cabinet and ministerial portfolios, as well as the Expenditure Management System, have improved the organizational capacity of the government to manage its strategic objectives including budgetary restraint. Continuing steps have also been taken to devolve management authority from central agencies to departments. Yet as the 1995 report of the Head of the Public Service makes clear, more thought needs to be given to enhancing the capacity to deal with the imperatives of horizontal policy issues on the one hand and to promoting good management in the delivery of public services on the other.[60]

The principal lesson to be drawn from comparative experiences, especially those of Britain and New Zealand, is that it is possible to advance the cause of good government through devolution as long as a fundamental distinction is drawn between organizational designs for policy and operational responsibilities respectively. There are longstanding models of this approach in several continental European political systems, including federal systems such as Germany where the separation of policy and operational responsibilities is found at both the federal and state levels of government. However, it is not necessary to go abroad to find applications of this distinction. As the Canadian experience with Crown corporations demonstrates, significant devolution of management responsibilities is possible when policy and operational responsibilities are kept separate. But as demonstrated in the case of Canadian Crown corporations, the advantages of devolution can be negated if these nondepartmental organizations are not subject to reasonably precise mandates, not given clear and consistent policy directions and not subject to an effective accountability regime.

This is not to suggest that important relationships and connections between policy and operations do not exist. Indeed, policy should drive operations in the sense that it should determine what public services a government provides, how these are designed as a means of realizing desired outcomes and what level of resources a government can afford to allocate to each of its services. Moreover, policy decision making continues through the implementation process to accommodate required adjustments and unforeseen circumstances. But in the management of operations for the delivery of public services, economy, efficiency and effectiveness can be best achieved where those responsible have maximum authority over the deployment of resources and are held accountable for the exercise of their authority.

Determining the best structures to achieve these purposes is not a simple task. Because public administration is such a complicated and complex business, governments need the best possible capacity to undertake or obtain sound policy analysis. Political will is no substitute for the application of knowledge and objective advice in governance. Moreover, it is critical that those who manage operations also advise on policy, even where governmental designs consciously seek to separate policy and operational responsibilities. This is essential to avoid capture by those with an interest in operations and to enhance management performance.

In the best of circumstances, the men and women of government business make their contribution to good government by rendering policy advice and managing government operations. Recent developments, particularly the new cabinet decision-making structure and process, suggest that the Canadian government is cautiously moving in this direction. It promises to consider additional "options" for devolution,[61] including further deregulation of central agency controls and decentralization by expanding the scope of delegated management authority.

To the extent that the Canadian government maintains the traditional form of ministerial department, it is unlikely to achieve major changes in behaviour. Central agencies and deputy ministers in line departments will be hesitant to devolve authority, or to refrain from interfering even when they do, unless and until their failure to delegate authority is perceived by ministers as constituting an obstacle to good government, and one that creates political risks for ministers. If good government requires the best possible policy advice to cope with the imperatives of achieving desired outcomes and addressing horizontal policy issues *and* best practices in the management of operations to cope with the imperatives of limited resources and quality service, the crucial question is whether this can be better achieved by separating policy ministries from operational agencies.

The lessons from the Canadian experience as well as from the other three Westminster systems are that these two crucial requirements are unlikely to be met within the traditional structures of ministerial departments. As a general rule, deputy ministers no longer have the time to give adequate attention to both their policy and management responsibilities. In addition, those who now get to the top tend to have neither the required managerial experience or expertise nor the inclination to manage in ways that advance best practices in their organizations. This should not be surprising. Given their responsibilities for advising ministers, deputies will and should give primacy to assisting ministers in establishing policy directions, clarifying policy objectives and designing programs that effectively secure the best possible outcomes.

In much the same way that ministers, during the last century in Britain and then later in the three other Westminster systems, had to accept that they could not personally manage their departments but would have to rely on the services of professional "men of business," a single deputy minister cannot manage both the policy and operational dimensions of a department. The time has come to acknowledge that, at least as a general rule, it is no longer possible for an individual deputy minister to accomplish these dual imperatives, especially in departments with the increased scope of responsibilities resulting from the 1993 consolidation.

There are a variety of nondepartmental organizational forms that can be used to address this matter, including Crown corporations, regulatory boards and even special operating agencies. However, attention should also be given to the British and New Zealand models. Applied to the particular circumstances of the Canadian government, the separation of policy and operational responsibilities could help solve the inherently difficult task of addressing what James Desveaux calls "the strategy-structure problem in public bureaucracy." As he notes: "Bureaucrats are expected to deliver technically feasible solutions to problems within a political framework. This suggests that policy outcomes depend not only on linkages between agencies and elective political institutions but also on the shape of bureaucratic structures themselves."[62] The British and New

Zealand models provide a considerable range of organizational options to address this problem. They do so by preserving a strong role for ministerial departments in assisting ministers to perform their essential functions, particularly those that cut across portfolios horizontally. At the same time, they provide an institutional framework within which authority for managing operations can be devolved to a larger number of operational units yet remain subject to tight policy expectations and rigorous accountability.

Adopting the basic principle of such models across the Canadian government would not require the wholesale dismantling of ministerial departments, let alone ministerial portfolios, as currently constituted. However, policy and operational structures could be better aligned, especially in those departments where operational units have been bent to fit within a departmental framework simply so they remain part of an integrated line of hierarchical authority under a single deputy minister and an associated set of corporate management controls. Ministers, in short, would not need to lose the advantages brought about by portfolio consolidation; they would still maintain the same array of policy instruments within their mandates. But greater attention to the technical dimensions of operations could be achieved by adopting different structures, such as are represented by executive agencies with direct relationships to ministers. The paradox here is that a greater degree of organizational differentiation for operating units can promote both greater devolution for managerial effectiveness and greater ministerial control over the strategic direction of state agencies than is possible with highly integrated ministerial departments.

Notes

1. Peter Aucoin, "The Mulroney Government, 1984-1988: Priorities, Positional Policy and Power," in Andrew Gollner and Daniel Salée (eds.), *Canada Under Mulroney: An End-of-Term Report* (Montreal: Vehicule Press, 1988), pp. 335-56; Colin Campbell, "Mulroney's Broker Politics: The Ultimate in Politicized Incompetence," in Gollner and Salée (eds.), *Canada Under Mulroney,* pp. 309-34.

2. Thomas Axworthy, "Of secretaries to princes," *Canadian Public Administration,* Vol. 31, no. 2 (Summer 1988), pp. 247-64.

3. Herman Bakvis and David Mac Donald, "The Canadian Cabinet: organization, decision-rules, and policy impact," in Michael M. Atkinson (ed.), *Governing Canada: Institutions and Public Policy* (Toronto: Harcourt Brace Jovanovich Canada Inc., 1993), pp. 57-59.

4. A.W. Johnson, "Reflections on administrative reform in the government of Canada 1962-1991," Discussion Paper, Ottawa, Office of the Auditor General of Canada, 1992, p. 34.

5. Réjean Landry, "Administrative reform and political control in Canada," *International Political Science Review,* Vol. 14, no. 4 (1993), p. 341.

6. Bakvis and Mac Donald, "The Canadian Cabinet," pp. 58-59.

7. Canada, Office of the Prime Minister, "Release," June 25, 1993, p. 3.

8. Canada, Office of the Prime Minister, "Release," November 4, 1993, p. 2.

9. Canada, Government of Canada, *The Expenditure Management System of the Government of Canada* (Ottawa: Minister of Supply and Services, 1995), p. 9.

10. Brian W. Hogwood and Thomas T. Mackie, "The United Kingdom: decision sifting in a secret garden," in Thomas T. Mackie and Brian W. Hogwood (eds.), *Unlocking the Cabinet: Cabinet Structures in Comparative Perspective* (London: Sage, 1985).

11. Peter Hennessey, *Cabinet* (Oxford: Basil Blackwell, 1986), p. 100.

12. Hennessey, *Cabinet,* p. 101; G.W. Jones, "Presidentialization in a parliamentary system,"

in Colin Campbell and Margaret Jane Wyszomirski (eds.), *Executive Leadership in Anglo-American Systems* (Pittsburgh: University of Pittsburgh Press, 1991), pp. 111-37.

13. Hogwood and Mackie, "The United Kingdom: decision sifting in a secret garden," p. 45.

14. Jones, "Presidentialization in a parliamentary system," p. 128.

15. Canada, Office of the Auditor General, *Toward Better Governance: Public Service Reform in New Zealand (1984-94) and its Relevance to Canada* (Ottawa: Minister of Supply and Services, 1995), p. 79.

16. New Zealand, State Services Commission Steering Group, *Review of State Sector Reforms* (Wellington: State Services Commission, November 29, 1991).

17. Michael Keating, "Mega-departments: the theory and objectives," in Patrick Weller, John Forster and Glyn Davis (eds.), *Reforming the Public Service: Lessons From Recent Experience* (South Melbourne: Macmillan Education Australia Ltd., 1993), p. 10.

18. Emma Craswell and Glyn Davis, "Does the Amalgamation of Government Agencies Produce Better Policy Co-ordination?", in Weller, Forster and Davis (eds.), *Reforming the Public Service,* pp. 180-207.

19. Colin Campbell and John Halligan, *Political Leadership in an Age of Constraint: Bureaucratic Politics Under Hawke and Keating* (St. Leonards, Australia: Allen and Unwin, 1992); June Pallot, "Financial Management Reforms," in Jonathan Boston, John Martin, June Pallot and Pat Walsh (eds.), *Reshaping the State: New Zealand's Bureaucratic Revolution* (Auckland: Oxford University Press, 1991), pp. 166-97; Colin Thain and Maurice Wright, "Planning and Controlling Public Expenditure in the UK, Part 1: The Treasury's Public Expenditure Survey," *Public Administration,* Vol. 70 (Spring 1992), pp. 3-24; Colin Thain and Maurice Wright, "Planning and Controlling Public Expenditure in the UK, Part 2: The Effects and Effectiveness of the Survey," *Public Administration,* Vol. 70 (Summer 1992), pp. 193-224; *The Expenditure Management System of the Government of Canada.*

20. Peter Aucoin and Herman Bakvis, "Regional responsiveness and government organization: the case of regional economic development policy in Canada," in Peter Aucoin (ed.), *Regional Responsiveness in the National Administrative State* (Toronto: University of Toronto Press, 1985), pp. 51-118.

21. Peter Aucoin, "Cabinet government in Canada: corporate management of a confederal executive," in Campbell and Wyszomirski (eds.), *Executive Leadership in Anglo-American Systems*, pp. 144-45.

22. Canada, Auditor General of Canada, *Report to the House of Commons for the Fiscal Year ended March 31, 1983* (Ottawa: Minister of Supply and Services, 1983), p. 60.

23. Ian Clark, "Restraint, renewal, and the Treasury Board Secretariat," *Canadian Public Administration*, Vol. 37, no. 2 (Summer 1994), pp. 214-15.

24. Clark, "Restraint, renewal, and the Treasury Board Secretariat," p. 215.

25. Quoted in Peter Aucoin and Herman Bakvis, *The Centralization-Decentralization Conundrum: Organization and Management in the Canadian Government* (Halifax: Institute for Research on Public Policy, 1988), p. 1.

26. David Zussman and Jak Jabes, *The Vertical Solitude: Managing in the Public Sector* (Halifax: Institute for Research on Public Policy, 1989).

27. Francine Séguin, "Service to the public: a major strategic change," *Canadian Public Administration*, Vol. 34, no. 3 (Autumn 1991), pp. 465-73.

28. Clark, "Restraint, renewal, and the Treasury Board Secretariat," pp. 230-39.

29. Donald J. Savoie, "Restructuring the government of Canada: leading from the centre" (Ottawa: Canadian Centre for Management Development, forthcoming).

30. Les Metcalfe and Sue Richards, *Improving Public Management* (London: Sage, 1987), pp. 177-210.

31. Andrew Gray and Bill Jenkins with Andrew Flynn and Brian Rutherford, "The management of change in Whitehall: the experience of the FMI," *Public Administration*, Vol. 69 (Spring 1991), p. 56.

32. United Kingdom, Efficiency Unit, *Improving Management in Government: The Next Steps* (London: HMSO, 1988).

33. United Kingdom, Cabinet Office, Next Steps Team, *Briefing Note*, September 1, 1995, p. 4. As Brian Hogwood notes, the British case is more complex than a "simple core [department]/agency characterization" would suggest. See Brian W. Hogwood, "Whitehall families: core departments and agency forms in Britain," *International Review of Administrative Sciences*, Vol. 61, no. 4 (December 1995), p. 511.

34. Sylvie Trosa, *Next Steps: Moving On*, prepared for the Office of Public Service and Science (United Kingdom), February 1994, p. 4.

35. United Kingdom, Prime Minister, Chancellor of the Exchequer and Chancellor of the Duchy of Lancaster, *The Civil Service: Taking Forward Continuity and Change* (London: HMSO, January 1995), p. 13.

36. Quoted in Canada, Office of the Auditor General, *Toward Better Governance*, p. 56.

37. New Zealand, State Services Commission, *New Zealand – Public Sector Reform* (Wellington: State Services Commission, 1993), pp. 26-28.

38. R.G. Laking, "The New Zealand Management Reforms," *Australian Journal of Public Administration*, Vol. 53, no. 3 (1994), p. 317.

39. Laking, "The New Zealand Management Reforms," p. 317.

40. Australia, Task Force on Management Improvement, *The Australian Public Service Reformed: An Evaluation of a Decade of Management Reform* (Canberra: Australian Government Publishing Service, December 1992), p. 67.

41. *The Australian Public Service Reformed*, p. 252.

42. Malcolm Holmes, "Corporate management – a view from the centre," in G. Davis, P. Weller and C. Lewis (eds.), *Corporate Management in Australian Government* (South Melbourne: Macmillan, 1989), p. 34, quoted in *The Australian Public Service Reformed*, p. 252.

43. *The Australian Public Service Reformed*, p. 225.

44. Michael Keating and Malcolm Holmes, "Australia's Budgetary and Financial Management Reforms," *Governance*, Vol. 3, no. 2 (April 1990), p. 171.

45. *The Australian Public Service Reformed,* p. 252.

46. *The Australian Public Service Reformed.*

47. Campbell and Halligan, *Political Leadership in an Age of Constraint.*

48. *The Australian Public Service Reformed,* p. 118.

49. *The Australian Public Service Reformed,* pp. 523-24.

50. See Patricia Greer, *Transforming Central Government: The Next Steps Initiative* (Buckingham: Open University Press, 1994), p. 115.

51. *The Civil Service: Taking Forward Continuity and Change,* p. 9.

52. Holmes, "Corporate Management," pp. 32, 34, quoted in *The Australian Public Service Reformed,* p. 252.

53. *The Australian Public Service Reformed,* pp. 89-90.

54. Donald J. Savoie, *Thatcher, Reagan, Mulroney: In Search of a New Bureaucracy* (Toronto: University of Toronto Press, 1994), pp. 239-41; Canada, Steering Group on Special Operating Agencies, *Special Operating Agencies: Taking Stock, Final Report,* May 1994. For a more positive analysis, using the same data basis as the second study, see J. David Wright and Graeme Waymark, *Special Operating Agencies: Overview of the Special Operating Agency Initiative* (Ottawa: Canada Centre for Management Development/ Minister of Supply and Services, 1995).

55. Savoie, *Thatcher, Reagan, Mulroney,* p. 241.

56. *Special Operating Agencies: Taking Stock.*

57. *Special Operating Agencies: Taking Stock,* Summary of Conclusions.

58. *Special Operating Agencies: Taking Stock,* p. 52.

59. Alasdair Roberts, "Building a Common Services Department: The Establishment of Public Works and Government Services Canada" (Ottawa: Canadian Centre for Management Development, forthcoming).

60. Canada, Clerk of the Privy Council and Secretary to the Cabinet, *Third Annual Report to the Prime Minister on the Public Service of Canada* (Ottawa: Minister of Supply and Services, 1995), pp. 38-46.

61. *The Expenditure Management System of the Government of Canada,* p. 6.

62. James A. Desveaux, "Anticipating Uncertainty: The Structure-Strategy Problem in Public Bureaucracy," *Governance,* Vol. 7, no. 1 (1994), p. 32.

SIX

Moving Beyond Bureaucracy

The new public management suggests that organizational designs to devolve authority and responsibility in the operational departments and agencies of government are required to improve public management. But, while these designs may be necessary, simply changing the focal point of decision making is not sufficient. It is essential to do more than remove the structural impediments to good management. Good management must "move beyond bureaucracy." In this sense, bureaucracy is regarded as a particular approach to management that fosters attitudes and practices that impede good management. It does so because it fails to appreciate that "management" is more than the implementation of rules and the administration of systems. If public management is to overcome the limitations of bureaucracy and focus on increased economy, efficiency and effectiveness in the conduct of government business, it must be transformed in significant ways. Attention must be given to those management practices that are essential to the development and maintenance of what Otto Brodtrick calls "well-performing organizations."[1]

The Bureaucratic Ideal

In his classic account of the "bureaucratic ideal," Max Weber characterized bureaucracy as the most rational form of management because it applies general rules to particular cases. Weber defined bureaucracy in the following manner:

> The reduction of modern office management to rules is deeply embedded in its very nature. The theory of modern public administration, for instance, assumes that the authority to order certain matters by decree – which has been legally granted to public authorities – does not entitle the bureau to regulate the matter by commands given for each case, but only to regulate the matter abstractly.[2]

Regulating "the matter abstractly" requires "general rules, which are more or less stable, more or less exhaustive, and which can be learned."[3]

Given the importance of rules, it is not surprising that Weber's bureaucratic ideal emphasizes the written "files" of an organization. These are the depository of its rules and, equally important, the record of its decisions, on which knowledge is developed through experience and precedent. For this store of applied knowledge to be used in its operations, an organization must secure staff with the appropriate technical competence not only to learn the knowledge of the organization but also to apply it to particular cases.

It does not follow from this that discretion is never exercised. Discretion cannot always be avoided in the application of general rules to particular cases even when the rules are provided in extensive detail. Moreover, discretion is required at all levels in the organization. But regardless at what level within the hierarchy it is exercised, discretion is meant to be informed by applied knowledge. This knowledge consists of the learned experience of the organization. At one level, it constitutes a form of "jurisprudence"; at a second, it takes the form of "standard operating procedures"; and at a third, it entails the "rules of thumb" embedded in an organization's values and culture.[4]

This does not necessarily mean that an organization's jurisprudence, standard operating procedures and rules of thumb will always have been formally instituted by superior officers. In many instances, new practices or strategies for dealing with new problems emerge from the lowest echelons in a bureaucracy. In these instances, they are tolerated by superiors until they are challenged. When challenged, they are either rejected or found useful and then officially endorsed.[5]

Rules as Public Policy

While all bureaucratic organizations, public and private, share these characteristics, the general rules that public servants apply to particular cases constitute public policy. In Westminster constitutional systems, public policies are governed first and foremost by laws passed by Parliament. The implementation of laws in a constitutional regime requires that the administration of public affairs not only conform to the letter of the law but also adhere to its policy objectives, that is, the spirit of the law. The fact that the executive is part of the legislature under the Westminster system and has assumed important legislative functions, both in proposing new laws (or amendments to existing laws) and in exercising delegated legislative powers, does not detract from this requirement. In principle, what Cabinet and ministers do in exercising executive authority must be sanctioned by law. The implementation of public policy, in short, is the implementation of law, whether the business of government is the provision of public goods and services or the making and enforcing of regulations.

The significance of rules in public management, as in private management, is based in part on the assumption that they constitute the applied knowledge of the organization. Their purpose is to achieve results, on the one hand, and to minimize the need for discretion to avoid error, on the other. But in government, as compared to business, they also serve another fundamental objective. They ensure that citizens are not subject to arbitrary rule by those who exercise the coercive powers of the state. The rights of citizens to public goods and services, as well as to freedom from unjustified government interference, are protected by law: citizens must be accorded their due but no more than that to which they are entitled. The principles of natural justice require that all citizens be treated alike under the law, yet equity among unequals is itself to be determined by reference to these principles and not by administrative fiat. Moreover, where the law is inadequate for securing its objectives, or where it introduces unintended inequities in the distribution of goods or services or unjustified restrictions on freedoms, recourse should take the form of amendments to the law or policy. These shortcomings or deficiencies are not meant to be rectified by public servants in the process of its administration.

Given the very nature of its business, public management relies heavily on rules: the public interest is to be secured in the distribution of goods, the provision of services and the regulation of socio-economic behaviour by adherence to the law on the part of those responsible for its implementation. The pursuit of the public interest also extends to the administrative systems and processes used in the implementation of the law. Although there are differences among the four Westminster systems in how public policies infuse administrative activities, each has adopted policies relating to staffing and management of its public service, the procurement of the goods and services used by government and the disbursement of funds from the public purse. These policies impose general rules on the internal conduct of government business. In other words, administrators must conform to public policy not only in delivering goods or services or in enforcing regulations but also in managing the internal operations of government.

In these respects, government may be considered "rule-bound". Yet governance requires more than a simple application of rules. The work of government must also be managed, in at least three ways. First, new or revised rules are required to respond to changing circumstances. Second, decisions must be made concerning the resources to be deployed in the implementation of laws, particularly when, as is invariably the case, the demand for resources exceeds the supply. Third, the organizations and personnel who implement the law must be directed in ways that secure performance; government operations cannot be put on automatic pilot.

Managing Public Policy

The management of policy in the Westminster system of government requires that new or amended rules to give effect to public policy respond to the political priorities of ministers and Cabinet. There may be public input in this process, especially when the policy constituencies most affected are well organized. In these cases, ministers and officials may determine public policies primarily in response to clearly articulated and forcefully presented demands. More often than not, however, policies are designed on the basis of tradeoffs between competing demands. Given the extensive role of the modern state in providing public goods and services and regulating citizens, the management of policy absorbs a great deal of governments' time as they cope with changes in circumstances and priorities.

Managing policy requires that officials focus, first and foremost, on the requirements of ministers. These requirements invariably centre on the need to formulate or revise general rules, even when the demands are for changes to highly specific aspects of government operations. The focus of such management is therefore "up" the organization to those with authority to set general rules. Moreover, as one moves up the organization, the range of factors to be considered in addressing the public interest in policy becomes broader.

In any complex organization, policy design factors invariably extend beyond the particular concerns of the departments or divisions whose operations are being considered. Changes in policy may improve public management in terms of greater effectiveness, economy and efficiency in government operations. The bottom line, however, is whether they resolve policy conflicts and thus reconcile competing public demands. Such over-riding objectives may make operational criteria, as they apply to particular government undertakings, secondary considerations.

Managing Public Administration

The management of administrative processes and resources within government constitutes a second function of public management. This is the consequence of the degree to which public policy, including administrative law, has been applied to the administrative dimensions of management in government. Personnel administration, for instance, became subject to public policies when the merit principle in appointments and promotions was instituted. Since then, numerous other aspects of personnel administration, especially policies respecting employment equity, have been governed by legislation or executive directives. In a similar manner, the procurement of the goods and services required in government operations came to be governed by public policies to restrict political patronage, to enhance fair and equitable treatment of those who compete for government contracts and to promote the public interest in the development of particular national or regional enterprises. Likewise, the administration of financial resources, including those used to pay the salaries and benefits of the public service, became subject to policies to protect the integrity of the public purse.

In the four Westminster systems there has been a general development of functional specialization in the several administrative dimensions of public management. In all cases, corporate management has been heavily controlled by central administrative agencies responsible for personnel, financial and common services administration. As well, functional specialization has meant increased separation of these administrative responsibilities from line management, whether at the centre of departments, in their various operational divisions or in the field.

This means that those who manage government operations, especially down the line and in the field, are subject not only to rules established by line managers up the hierarchy, but also to rules established by those who have functional authority over the various administrative dimensions of management. Given that functional authorities for personnel, financial and other corporate services administration have developed at the centre of government, at the centre of departments and even at the centre of departmental divisions, operational managers are subject to multiple authorities in the determination and interpretation of administrative rules.

Managing Operations

The third function of public management is the operational dimension. This entails the actual implementation of public policies through the delivery of goods and services and the enforcement of regulations. It is here that the highly technical competence of the bureaucracy is applied. Those who manage these operations must manage "down" the organization. They must ensure that public policy, including public policy applied to the administrative dimensions of management, is implemented in the concrete actions of those performing the tasks of the state. This means applying general rules to particular cases in the delivery of public services and the enforcement of regulations.

Managing operations is subject to the greatest degree of bureaucratization because this task involves the most specificity in jurisprudence, standard operating procedures and organizations' rules of thumb. This specificity, as previously noted, is based on the need to protect the organization against technical and administrative errors in the implementation of policy and to protect citizens from arbitrary decisions.

The bureaucratic ideal also emphasizes rules as the means to ensure the integrity of public policy implementation. These rules assist public servants insofar as they protect them from citizens – as individuals or groups – who seek to subvert public policy by pressuring or inducing public servants in ways that undermine the law or, at least, do not conform to the spirit of the law and its ethical application. Bureaucracy is thus meant to counter corruption from those who try to penetrate the state from the outside, using illegitimate, if not illegal, means.

The Critique of Bureaucracy

With the rise of the new public management, the practice of bureaucratic management has been heavily criticized in recent years. The criticisms have several different foci. Some relate to the bureaucratic mindset, some to perceived pathologies that are said to be inherent in the bureaucratic model and some to particular forms or practices of bureaucratic management in government.

Criticism of the presumed bureaucratic mindset is legendary; indeed, in the four Westminster systems it has become part of the political culture. Bureaucracy, in this view, refers to an officialdom in which bureaucrats avoid doing anything not prescribed by the rules of their organization. This mindless following of the rules, it is concluded, creates an organizational ethos that fosters a proliferation of rules to cope with all uncertainties arising in the implementation of laws. Bureaucrats, accordingly, need not think; their work is "routinized" in every detail.

It is further assumed that, when situations arise where decisions are required outside the framework of rules, the inevitable response is to stall and to pass the buck to superiors. Since there is often more than one superior to be consulted, delays follow as superiors procrastinate on finding the most appropriate rule to apply. Bureaucracy is thus not responsive to citizens because matters cannot always be accommodated within its established rules. As well, authority to resolve issues facing individual citizens is fragmented across more than one department or agency or even within the divisions of a single department or agency.

Bureaucratic Pathologies

Bureaucracies are criticized as essentially passive institutions. At best, they promote compliance with rules. They do not foster initiatives that address concerns that fall outside the framework of rules or, as is often the case, fall within the crevices of these rules. The purposes of the law are either ignored or become secondary to the rules used to implement the law. The "goals" of the organization are "displaced" by the "means" deployed to achieve them.[6] Bureaucracies are thereby subject to organizational pathologies that detract from the realization of their primary missions.

In large and complex bureaucracies, there is also what Michel Crozier describes as the "vicious circle" in the "phenomenon" that is bureaucracy. If bureaucrats are subjected to a perceived excess in rules, they react in one of two ways. They "retreat" from the organization by doing only what is prescribed, contributing nothing to the organization except the routine; they do not "go the extra mile." They do only as much as is formally required of them and as little of that as they can get away with without risking their positions. They take little or no pride in their work or in the performance of the organization. Alternatively, they "rebel" against the organization, on their own initiative or, more commonly, under peer pressure. They slow down its work by doing only the minimum or by bargaining with their superiors for even further elaborations of rules to protect their work, and thus their positions, within the organization.[7]

Within government, it is argued, the bureaucratic mindset and its inherent pathologies are reflected in particular practices that have perverse consequences for good management. Traditional financial administration systems, for instance, are regarded as deficient because they focus almost exclusively on maintaining the integrity of public spending in accordance with parliamentary appropriations. Within the bounds of approved spending, therefore, what is appropriated will be spent. The most extreme illustration of this is found in the presumed unnecessary spending that occurs at the end of every fiscal year to avoid having unspent monies in an organization's budget.[8] Unspent monies would indicate that an organization had a budget exceeding its requirements. The incentive, accordingly, is to spend to the limit of the organization's appropriations, because unspent appropriations do not remain with the organization but revert to the Treasury and may result in an organization's budget being cut by that amount for the following fiscal year.

The assumed consequence of this approach to financial administration is that managers and their staff pay little attention to economies or efficiencies that might lead to savings for the public purse. Financial information and accounting systems are considered deficient and discourage managers from being cost conscious. They take their revenues as a given resource to be expended on specific items and spend only as prescribed and permitted. Except to ensure that expenditure rules are applied and that costs are contained within budget, they do not manage their costs. They are careful spenders but not for reasons of economy and efficiency. Under these circumstances, financial administration becomes a separate and specialized function of the organization and not necessarily a significant one in the management hierarchy. Its fundamental purpose is to ensure that those who spend comply with the rules and stay within their budget. Concerns for "value for money" are secondary at best.

From this general approach to financial administration, it follows that rules governing various administrative practices – from travel regulations to policies concerning the procurement of goods and services used by operating units – are also designed with less than adequate attention to economy or efficiency. The objective is to avoid discretion that might lead to error or malfeasance. Standardization of financial administrative practices is thus the norm regardless of the economies or efficiencies managers might achieve by exercising discretion suited to the particular circumstances and requirements of their individual organizations. They have little incentive to go beyond the norm: the time and effort required to obtain permission on a case by case basis is not worth it. In any event, their particular organization would not benefit. To the extent that economy and efficiency result from standardized practices, for instance in the use of common service agencies for the procurement of goods and services across government, they do so in relation to government as a whole. Conversely, to the degree that they do not produce such results, line managers may not even notice if the costs are not assigned to them but absorbed by the government as a whole.

Public service personnel administration is perceived to suffer from similar deficiencies. It is argued that managers pay insufficient attention to managing staff as an essential element to the performance of the organization. Rather, personnel administration becomes an exercise in which the rights and obligations of public servants, codified in law and/or policy, are applied to relations between superiors and subordinates across the organization. The emphasis is on rigid and detailed job descriptions to minimize uncertainty in responsibilities. Task specialization is thus a central feature of bureaucracy.

Beyond the command and control model usually associated with bureaucracy, this emphasis on task specialization diminishes the value attached to managing people in ways that advance the goals of an organization. The operative assumption is that the management of staff consists primarily in the administration of personnel systems. The personnel function is thus assigned to functional specialists. Managers can then proceed on the assumption that their staff are qualified for their specialized positions, know their assignments and merely need to be supervised to ensure their work is done as prescribed.

The work of managers beyond the implementation of financial and personnel administrative rules is therefore twofold. First, they must process decisions that require approval beyond the defined powers of their subordinates whenever the latter are confronted by new circumstances or changing priorities. Second, to minimize the number of such decisions, they must seek to devise new rules. In managing down the organization, accordingly, managers do not engage their subordinates as their staff, because they are not the employers of their staff. The government is. The public service as a corporate institution may have significant authority over staffing and personnel policies, and individual managers may have some influence over the promotion of their subordinates, but there are precious few rewards or sanctions at the disposal of the individual manager to affect the performance of her or his subordinates, especially in times of restraint.

Impoverished Management

The cumulative effects of these bureaucratic practices, it is argued, have resulted in an impoverished state of management in government. It is preoccupied with managing *up* the organization because of the importance attached to formulating new policies in response to changing circumstances and the changing priorities of ministers; and it is preoccupied with managing *across* the organization because of the importance attached to standardized administrative policies and practices as well as to the inter-departmental aspects of policy development. At the same time, it is fragmented, because these preoccupations create three streams of management: policy, administrative and operational.

Each of the four Westminster systems has evolved differently in these regards. As a result, the critique of bureaucracy in each case takes a somewhat different tack. Of the four systems, the British tradition has given highest priority to policy management as defined above. This was expressed most clearly in the efforts of British reformers in the mid-19th century to distinguish between "intellectual" and "mechanical" tasks in the public service. The former were deemed to require those able to discern the public interest in advising ministers on public policy. They would constitute the superior class of public servants, directing those who performed "mechanical" tasks of policy implementation.

The most trenchant criticism of the British bureaucracy, not surprisingly, has been directed at the myth of the superiority of the "gifted amateur" – the British tradition that has given primacy to the recruitment of those who are liberally educated and are offered opportunities to learn across government departments in both central and line departments through a succession of appointments and promoted on the basis of their demonstrated capacity to master the high arts of policy management. It has been argued, most forcefully by the Fulton Committee, that this tradition has diminished the importance of management. The "generalist" class was not expected to master the skills necessary to manage resources or operations; these functions could be left to subordinates, more specialized and technically trained.

From the outset, the systems of recruitment, grading and promotion in the other three Westminster systems differed from the British. Most important, their less rigid personnel structures allowed public servants to move up the hierarchy as they mastered progressively the operational, administrative and policy dimensions of public management. However, a convergence in practice has occurred over time: the senior public service in each of the three systems has become dominated by "policy managers." The tradition of working one's way up the ladder of an operational department gave way to the practice of according priority to those whose careers focused on the policy dimensions of government.

The expansion of policy work in government that accompanied the increasingly interventionist state meant that policy management inevitably became a distinct function. As these public services expanded to provide more government undertakings, the administrative dimensions of management also evolved into more distinct specialities. The consequence has been a growing number of senior public servants without significant operational experience. Their promotions have depended primarily on their capacity to serve their public service superiors and ministers in designing policy or administrative systems.

Specialists in personnel, financial and common services administration have not achieved the same status accorded to policy specialists. They have not had, therefore, the same degree of access to the most senior positions in the public service. This has been compensated for in part by the professionalization of many of these specialities and by the consequent near-monopoly that specialists have secured across government in staffing these functions, both within departments and in central administrative agencies. The principal exception here has been the functional speciality of budgeting, which constitutes a major dimension of public policy, especially when resources are tight, and restraint and cut-backs are the order of the day.

Under these circumstances, bureaucratic elites possess neither the technical expertise nor the practical experience necessary to provide the leadership required to develop and maintain the desired attributes of well-performing organizations. In the Canadian context, for example, Barbara Wake Carroll has argued that the lack of technical education and operational experience has adversely affected the capacity of senior mandarins to be innovative:

Paralysis in the face of changes in the environment and an inability to develop new or innovative solutions to problems are symptomatic of organizations in which the managers are out of touch with both their environment and their technology, or 'what it is the organization does'...Thus one of the causes of nonadaptiveness and the inability of public bureaucracies to resolve policy problems may be that the technical aspects of the organization have come to be underrepresented within its senior management.[9]

David Zussman and Jak Jabes make the same point: "[T]here has been the tendency to reward those individuals who were particularly adept at understanding the decision-making system, at the expense of the content experts and the managers."[10] Their conclusion, based on surveys of managers in the Canadian public service, was that "it appears that there has been too little attention paid to managerial skills."[11]

It is no surprise that bureaucratic elites without sufficient "managerial skills" would rely on administrative systems and rule-bound program delivery. They depend for good management on the functional specialists in personnel, financial and common services administration who apply their systems to the supervision of those lower down the ranks. Good program delivery in this context means the design of delivery systems that minimize discretion and thereby avoid error.

Moving Beyond Bureaucracy

Prescriptions for management reform to move "beyond bureaucracy" have emanated from experiential learning in both the private and public sectors (particularly the former but increasingly the latter) as well as from the new public management. Various theoretical formulations have been constructed on the basis of successful case histories from which are deduced "best practices." These theorists also seek to provide more broadly based empirical explanations for the deficiencies of bureaucracy and to justify prescriptions that take public management "beyond bureaucracy".

The reform movement in public administration can be seen as an effort to contrast the merits of a managerial approach against the traditional emphasis given to administration. As I have noted elsewhere:

Managerialism, in contrast to the traditional bureaucratic ideal of 'administration', has developed in the public sector for the same reasons it has emerged in the private sector, namely an increased concern with 'results', 'performance' and 'outcomes'. Hence higher priority is given to the 'management' of people, resources and programmes compared to the 'administration' of activities, procedures and regulations.[12]

Managerialism has much in common with traditional management theory as applied to the tasks of complex organizations.[13] But few advocates of contemporary managerialism suggest that public management reform should emulate traditional management theorists of the "scientific management" school in seeking to develop the "one best way" to manage. Serious efforts at promoting management reform favour a more consciously eclectic approach. Les Metcalfe and Sue Richards, for instance, state that: "The flexibility required to cope with uncertainty and facilitate innovation involves a further cultural shift to stimulate the development of competencies in managing by design, over and above competencies in managing by direction."[14] Scientific management, in short, is regarded as too mechanistic to cope with the rapidly changing environment of governments as political institutions, or the ever-changing technologies they must use to be productive.

Well-Performing Organizations
There are, nonetheless, several attributes that are claimed to be present in well-performing organizations. In his study of a set of Canadian government organizations, Otto Brodtrick identified 12 principal attributes as significant determinants in securing performance. He grouped these into four categories, as follows:

(1) *emphasis on people*: whereby staff are empowered with authority and responsibility and autonomy; the values of the organization are based on the belief that performance is a product of people; success is made part of the culture;

(2) *participatory leadership*: whereby leaders articulate purpose and goals and foster commitment; leaders guide by being creative rather than coercive; leaders strive to reach ideals, they inspire and foster communication;

(3) *innovative work styles*: whereby staff learn from their experiences; they thrive on identifying and solving problems; they collaborate in order to control themselves rather than being controlled from the outside; and

(4) *strong client orientation*: whereby goals are congruent between political leaders, central agencies and departments; staff derive satisfaction from serving the client; staff are able to talk in concrete terms about the missions and values of their organization.[15]

Brodtrick claimed that "the most significant finding" of this study was that "people need to have a certain mindset" to "develop and maintain" these attributes within an organization. "This mindset," he suggested, "seems to be a function of strongly-held beliefs, of values such as dedication and the innate need to improve the organization in which they work." This could be contrasted with the "bureaucratic mindset [which] tends to see problems essentially as problems of compliance [with prescribed rules and procedures]."[16]

These attributes are commonly identified by reformers in all four Westminster systems as necessary to improve public management. In every respect, these attributes imply that managers need to move beyond bureaucracy; as John Noble points out, "[a]ll the way through [Brodtrick's] report, for 'bureaucratic' you can read 'bad'."[17] At the same time, most reformers recognize that well-performing organizations still require formal organizational designs, administrative systems and even rules.

In one sense, this recognition constitutes an acknowledgement that, while bureaucracy is necessary for a minimal level of good management in government, performance beyond this requires something more. In several of its manifestations, managerialism can be regarded as the contemporary version of the "human relations" movement which, in its hey-day, sought to humanize the traditional scientific management approach. The four emphases of well-performing organizations are thus hardly novel to normative management theory. Nevertheless, they are necessary ingredients of improved public management if public service organizations are to tap their most essential resource, namely the people who work in them.

These emphases also acknowledge that good management in government requires constant attention to identify, counter or overcome the pathologies claimed as being inherent in bureaucracy. In this view, bureaucracy in government, like government itself, is necessary but need not be evil. Vigilance is required to ensure that inane red tape and perverse rules are eliminated as often and with as much dispatch as possible. Accordingly, constant "de-bureaucratization" ought to be a primary task of good management. Another is concerted action to ensure that there is an emphasis on people and participatory leadership. Only on this basis will organizations foster the attributes of well-performing organizations.

Post-Bureaucratic Paradigm

The theoretical critiques of bureaucracy of the last two decades take aim at bureaucracy on two fronts. They criticize public service bureaucracies for not being responsive to those they are meant to serve, namely citizens, and for their failure to deliver quality public services. Rule-bound bureaucracy means that bureaucrats, as agents of the state, relate to citizens as subjects, rather than as clients or customers. Rule-bound bureaucracy also means that bureaucrats, again as agents of the state, manage government operations as the administration of laws rather than as services to effect desired outcomes.

Implicit in these two fundamental criticisms of the bureaucratic paradigm is a crucial assumption about where the bureaucracy fits into state-citizen relations. For the bureaucracy to be responsive to citizens and to be able to provide quality public services, it must be given significant discretion in its relations with citizens and thereby considerable autonomy from the political apparatus of the state, that is, government and Parliament.

The logic behind the need to move beyond bureaucracy to what Michael Barzelay calls the "post-bureaucratic paradigm"[18] rests on a twofold premise. First, the traditional practice of representative government combined with professional public service has failed to secure what he calls "results citizens value."[19] It has failed, so his argument goes, precisely because this practice has assumed that elected representatives, advised by professional public servants, can discern what is in the public interest with respect to what governments should or should not do. In one sense, there is little that is novel in this critique. In another sense, it advances the "post-modernist" assault on the idea that professional experts know best what is in the interest of the publics they are meant to serve.[20]

The second part of this premise is more subtle. It conceives of public management as a process of state-citizen relations in which dialogue and deliberations between citizens and the agents of the state, especially public servants, constitute both a necessary and a sufficient response to the perennial questions of governance. This process is necessary because citizens have lost faith in the institutions of representative government as electoral democracy as well as in the capacities of professional experts to meet their needs. This much is shared by those on both the right and left of the ideological spectrum.

Such a process is deemed sufficient because it advances, if only implicitly, a theory of public management that is essentially stripped of any sense of governance as a function of power, conflict and competing interests. In place of these inherently political phenomena, the foci of the new public management requires a response, as Anna Yeatman approvingly notes, to:

three related contemporary dynamics: 1. increased social and cultural complexity; 2. increased uncertainty...a requirement that we develop the capacity to adapt to ongoing change of kinds which we cannot predict or plan for; [and] 3. increased democratic expectations of government and all kinds of service where individuals and/or their particular communities of interest ask that they get to participate in the design and delivery of the service.[21]

Here too, the right and left share common cause, although they part company on the role of the state in the public management of socio-economic affairs.

As the focal points for the post-bureaucratic paradigm, complexity, uncertainty and client service require that public servants treat citizens as customers of some public services, as co-producers of other public services and as voluntary compliants of those public services that are regulatory in form. Complexity, uncertainty and customer service also require a public service culture in which personal responsibility and accountability for quality service, empowerment for problem solving and norms of mutual trust and accommodation dominate. Accordingly, Barzelay claims that concepts such as public interest, efficiency, control, functions, authority, structure, costs, organizing, directing and coordinating must be "purged" from the mindset of public managers.[22]

The post-bureaucratic paradigm envisages public management as a kind of governance that is devoid of power, conflict and competing interests because it assumes that dialogue and deliberations between citizens and public servants can achieve consensus about "results citizens value." Adversarial politics and partisan politicians are entirely absent from this account except as remnants of the old bureaucracy which, indeed, is passing away as the dominant paradigm, even if vestiges remain necessary for those citizens and public servants unwilling to make the transition to the new order.

Moreover, "[t]he central feature of the post-bureaucratic model of public management," states Yeatman, "is its challenge to the separation of policy *conception* and its implementation which is built into the bureaucratic model...This means of course that those who are involved with ideas of public management must also be engaged with their implementation."[23] Policy conception and its implementation are the domain of public servants acting in concert with citizens in an environment characterized by great uncertainty, complexity and democratization. In this context, politicians, whether in the executive or legislature, are presumably those who do no more than approve policies as they are "conceived" by others. Policy conception and implementation are thereby integrated rather than separated because managers are free to manage, in partnership with citizens. Letting the managers manage requires a sharp demarcation between partisan politics and public management in order that the former not pollute the latter. This requires that the business of government be conducted according to a set of values that stands in fundamental contrast to the values that operate in the partisan political realm.

Changing the Rules of the Game

A second approach to moving beyond bureaucracy argues that the political apparatus of the state must require the public service to improve its responsiveness and performance: the prescription is "to make managers manage." If managers are made to manage by the political apparatus, then responsiveness and performance must be tackled in ways that alter the "rules of the game" governing the collective and individual behaviours of those engaged in public management. These rules constitute the values, norms and incentives operative in the management of public services.

Advocates of this approach to reform acknowledge the central importance of rules and therefore recognize that constant attention to their effects is necessary if organizational leaders are to promote responsiveness and results. This approach departs from Barzelay's post-bureaucratic paradigm in its explicit focus on power, conflict and competing interests. It seeks ways to restructure power, resolve conflict and reconcile competing interests by changing the rules. This approach derives from public choice and agency theory. It is perhaps best viewed as institutionalist in character because it assumes that behaviour is a consequence of the rules that define relations among individuals in an organizational setting and between them and their customers or clients.

To improve public management with respect to responsiveness and results, a reconsideration of those rules that deflect the attention of public managers both from the publics they are meant to serve and from the evaluation of the effectiveness of their services in realizing desired outcomes is necessary. Foremost among the rules that must be reconsidered are those that contain incentives, positive and negative, to manage up rather than down the organization and to manage inputs rather than outputs.

Public managers in the bureaucracies of Westminster systems, it is argued, have incentives to manage up the organization not only because they are subordinates to their political masters, but also because their ministers are publicly accountable for the actions of their public servants. How well public managers and their staff support their ministers in the performance of their political duties determines to a large extent how ministers and their advisers assess, and thus reward or sanction, their public service personnel both directly and indirectly. Although complex and subtle in actual practice, the priority given to error-free administration traditionally has resulted in rules that constrain public servants from managing down their organizations in ways that promote responsiveness and results.

Improving public management by eliminating the rules that prevent public servants from managing down the organization requires getting rid of the rules that impede the devolution of authority, responsibility and accountability down the line. The assumption here is that devolution will make public servants more responsive to citizens' needs and require them to assume greater responsibility and accountability for what they do with their increased authority. This does not necessarily assume that public servants must become accountable to Parliament rather than to their ministers. But it does assume that managers will have the incentive to support, encourage and coach their staff to be responsive to citizens.

If organizations are to be managed according to these principles, then managers must be given clear objectives and missions so their tasks can be defined in ways that relate to these goals. At the same time, these managers must have sufficient authority to manage the resources they use in the conduct of their operations. This requires that managers, as agents, have explicit contracts or performance agreements with their ministers, or superiors, as their principals. Only on these two bases can the risks of devolved authority be managed and managers be held accountable for the delivery of specified outputs or desired outcomes.

This approach to public management assumes that attention will be given to achieving the attributes of well-performing organizations. However, Yeatman claims, "we see a thorough reinstatement of the policy-administration dualism."[24] There must be an assertive cast of principals – that is, ministers – who, assisted by their policy advisers and corporate management support staff, set clear objectives, define concrete organizational missions, establish rigorous performance targets and measures and incorporate these in explicit principal-agent contracts or agreements. Agents are then given increased authority to deliver their outputs or programs and to manage their resources.

The Politics of Moving Beyond Bureaucracy

These two approaches to improving public management assume that the ideal attributes of well-performing organizations must actually be valued in government. Traditionally, these attributes have not been valued precisely because they are perceived to contribute little to the resolution of issues that affect the electoral fortunes of the party in power. If public managers perceive that their political masters hold the view that "there are no votes in good management," the bureaucratic model will be regarded as sufficient to minimize error, to control malfeasance and to secure compliance with policy infused rules. This is all that governments expect of public management as "management." Politicians may periodically rail against bureaucracy, but when in power they appreciate its virtues. "Moving beyond bureaucracy," for them, simply means effective assistance from the senior public service in managing their political agenda.

Some political leaders and governments have begun to make public management reform central to their political agenda. The combination of expenditure restraint, global competitiveness and citizen demands for quality service has placed management performance front and centre on the political agenda. In these cases, securing and maintaining electoral support depend not only on good policy designs but also on successful policy implementation. The results of successful implementation are measured according to how the undertakings of government meet the tests of increased economy, efficiency and effectiveness.

From this perspective, the shortcomings of public service managers are not seen as the results of a lack of technical expertise, limited operational experience or even impoverished managerial skills. Rather, they are seen as due to the lack of a political demand for public services to adopt a different model of public management. In effect, management in the public service is bureaucratic only to the extent that governments insist that it be so.

Accordingly, the fragmentation of public service management into policy, administrative and operational streams is, in some large measure, the consequence of governments demanding that senior public servants pay close attention to ministerial requirements for policy advice and policy management, on the one hand, and ministerial insistence on the establishment of rigid administrative systems to govern the deployment of financial and personnel resources, and associated administrative practices, on the other. The policy requirements have encouraged the development of a public service elite comprising those who are skilled in the policy advisory and policy process services required by ministers. One does not develop these skills by spending time in operational units where services are delivered or regulations enforced, or even by staying in one place for very long. One must prove oneself as a "generalist," however much this means having limited "content" expertise or "managerial skills."[25]

Ministers' insistence on rigid administrative systems has resulted in the development of specialized management functions in the public service that further fragment public management. As a result, line managers at all levels in the hierarchy defer to these specialists in their respective spheres. They do so because they cannot possibly stay abreast of the myriad of detailed regulations governing the administrative dimensions of public management. For managers up the line, this fact of life is not a major concern; in any event, they are too busy attending to the policy requirements of ministers. For those down the line directly responsible for managing the operating core, these regulations do constitute constraints to productivity. The fact that well-performing organizations can be found in government is evidence that these constraints can be overcome.

The separation of the three management streams outlined above has a further effect. It diminishes morale in the public service, especially when government operates under expenditure restraint. Equally important, conditions of work will deteriorate since demands for services are unlikely to diminish. Opportunities for advancement will be restricted, and morale will suffer further because the leadership of the public service will be both ill equipped and not disposed to manage people well. Indeed, it is likely to become more ineffective in the management of people under conditions of restraint. The "vertical solitude" described by David Zussman and Jak Jabes[26] – the lower one goes in the management hierarchy, the less one finds positive attitudes about management practices in the public service – may not be a consequence of restraint. However, it is more than likely exacerbated by restraint when the senior public service is unable, or not required, to provide leadership in practising and demonstrating effective people management or, more generally, in exhibiting the characteristics of managers in well-performing organizations.

Governments intent on reforming public management to foster performance face a serious dilemma. They cannot simply transform their senior public servants into managers whose primary attention is directed down their organizations. Serving ministers, individually and collectively, must also be a priority of the senior public service. This means paying attention to the policy responsibilities and priorities of ministers and the government.

It also means ensuring that systems are in place to assure ministers that the administrative policies of the government are enforced. Only then can the senior public servants who directly serve ministers attend to ensuring that those who must manage down the organization do so in ways that promote the ideals of well-performing organizations.

However, in many traditionally designed ministerial departments in the four Westminster systems, the most senior officials have precious little time for such managerial tasks. And the dilemma is not resolved by the presence of several levels of management. The full implementation of best managerial practices requires a degree of formal, or at least *de facto*, devolution that is found in few ministerial departments. Even where such devolution is attempted, these practices are not always adhered to with sufficient consistency to maintain the attributes of well-performing organizations. Ministers and senior officials frequently come and go, and the most mundane of administrative or operational matters can become politicized or subject to constantly changing policy directives.

Reforming public management to move beyond bureaucracy, in order to promote greater responsiveness and performance as prescribed by the post-bureaucratic paradigm, is limited by its seriously flawed conception of policy and operational responsibilities. Although this paradigm is helpful in thinking about the limitations of the formal organizational designs and management control systems in coping with complexity, uncertainty and customer service, it too easily glosses over the constraints imposed on managers in any organizational setting, particularly in the public sector. Just as previous models of cooperative, consultative and participatory management, which collectively constituted the human relations paradigm, advanced our knowledge of the dynamics of organizational behaviour but did not eliminate adherence to the bureaucratic paradigm, so the post-bureaucratic paradigm provides an incomplete empirical account of reality. It thus has limited application as a normative prescription for management reform. It assumes a form of integration of "policy conception and implementation," as Yeatman puts it, that places those responsible for policy, namely ministers, on the sidelines, while public servants in partnership with their customers get on with the tasks of designing and delivering public services.[27]

The post-bureaucratic conception of public management is essentially a reformulation of the traditional argument for a separation of politics and administration rather than a separation of policy and operational responsibilities. It may cast the dichotomy in new terms, particularly as it seeks to join empowered public servants to empowered customers. But, by ignoring the need to resolve conflict and address competing interests in public policy, it is a recipe for reform that has little application in the Westminster system of governance.

The prescriptions that flow from the paradigms of public choice and agency theories are grounded more firmly in the realities of public management as governance. Because the constraints imposed on public managers derive primarily from public policy, they cannot be wished away, however much public managers seek to foster cooperation, consultation and collaboration. Contrary to Yeatman's claim, this institutionalist approach to reform does not in fact promote a separation of "policy and administration." Rather, it distinguishes between the roles (and thus authority, responsibility and accountability) of ministers and their public servants respectively: ministers are principals while public servants are their agents. Ministers make public policy, including decisions necessary to give effect to policy objectives in the actual implementation process. In these tasks, ministers are advised and assisted by public servants. In all these respects, there is an integration of policy and implementation within a framework of public management as governance.

At the same time, this institutionalist approach does seek to separate the management of policy and operational responsibilities, even to the point where, in some cases, the latter are contracted out to the private sector. In every case, however, the operative assumption is that responsiveness and performance are enhanced by the use of explicit contracts between principals and agents (whether these agents be public service managers, quasi-autonomous boards or private-sector contractors). The "business of government" can thus be subject to considerable devolution in its operational dimensions. In order to achieve results and not be undermined by bureaucratic pathologies, the rules that govern the management of operations and thereby structure incentives (rewards and sanctions) must be altered.

Moreover, this institutionalist approach does not rule out adherence to the norms of an empowered public service or the pursuit of values that encourage public servants to function in a consultative or partnership relationship with citizens. Nonetheless, it does prescribe a management regime that is still tightly controlled. The focus of these controls shifts from the use of inputs to accountability for the delivery of outputs. Those who fail to see the distinction between this approach and that advocated by adherents of the post-bureaucratic paradigm are likely to think of the former as "bureaucracy" under another guise. To the extent that real devolution does not accompany a more tightly controlled regime focused on outputs, they are not far off the mark. In such cases, public managers are subject to even greater controls, with correspondingly perverse effects for responsiveness and performance.

Conclusion

Reforms to make managers manage within the Westminster system can be successful only if ministers are willing to establish management regimes that alter the rules of bureaucracy to give managers greater authority, responsibility and accountability. Public management can move beyond bureaucracy but cannot eliminate it. Bureaucracy is inherent in public management as governance, precisely because its most fundamental "rules" constitute public policy. But within this understanding of bureaucracy as essential to constitutional government, ministers can establish a management regime that better achieves both responsiveness and performance. The key to improved public management lies in the recognition that some rules contain rewards and sanctions that actually undermine good management. Changing these rules need not result in ministers being exposed to increased risk of bad management with its attendant political consequences.

Removing certain rules, however, may well expose the deficiencies of some ministerial policies and decisions. And greater transparency in government is not necessarily something that ministers subscribe to with enthusiasm. Yet a greater devolution of managerial authority, coupled with the requirement that ministers provide clear(er) objectives, goals and targets for those responsible for government operations, has the potential to increase public knowledge of the effectiveness and costs of programs, as well as the limitations government faces in meeting competing demands.

Finally, the institutionalist approach to public management is crucially dependent on the capacities of government to formulate public policies that can subject the management of operations to a reasonably rigorous regime of performance measurement, service standards, output audits and program evaluation. These are essential to effective regimes of both ministerial and public service accountability. It is here that the new public management meets its greatest challenge.

Notes

1. Otto Brodtrick, "A Second Look at the Well-Performing Organization," in James C. McDavid and Brian Marson (eds.), *The Well-Performing Government Organization* (Toronto: Institute of Public Administration of Canada, 1991), pp. 16-22; Canada, Auditor General of Canada, *Report to the House of Commons for the Fiscal Year ended March 31, 1988* (Ottawa: Minister of Supply and Services, 1988), chap. 4.

2. Max Weber, "Bureaucracy," in H.H. Gerth and C. Wright Mills (eds.), *From Max Weber: Essays in Sociology,* translated (New York: Oxford University Press, 1946), p. 198.

3. Weber, "Bureaucracy," p. 198.

4. James Q. Wilson, *Bureaucracy: What Government Agencies Do and Why They Do It* (New York: Basic Books, 1989), pp. 90-110; Kenneth Kernaghan, "The emerging public service culture: values, ethics, and reforms," *Canadian Public Administration,* Vol. 37, no. 4 (Winter 1994), pp. 614-30.

5. Henry Mintzberg and Jan Jorgensen, "Emergent strategy for public policy," *Canadian Public Administration,* Vol. 30, no. 2 (Summer 1987), pp. 214-29.

6. Robert K. Merton, "Bureaucratic structure of personality," *Social Forces,* Vol. 18 (May 1940), pp. 560-68.

7. Michel Crozier, *The Bureaucratic Phenomenon* (Chicago: University of Chicago Press, 1964), pp. 187-208.

8. Australia, Task Force on Management Improvement, *The Australian Public Service Reformed: An Evaluation of a Decade of Management Reform* (Canberra: Australian Government Publishing Service, December 1992), pp. 239-41.

9. Barbara Wake Carroll, "Politics and Administration: A Trichotomy?", *Governance,* Vol. 3, no. 4 (October 1990), p. 361.

10. David Zussman and Jak Jabes, *The Vertical Solitude: Managing in the Public Sector* (Halifax: Institute for Research on Public Policy, 1989) p. 203.

11. Zussman and Jabes, *The Vertical Solitude,* p. 203.

12. Peter Aucoin, "Contraction, Managerialism and Decentralization in Canadian Government," *Governance,* Vol. 1, no. 2 (April 1988), p. 152.

13. Christopher Pollitt, *Managerialism and the Public Services: The Anglo-American Experience* (Oxford: Basil Blackwell, 1990), pp. 1-27.

14. Les Metcalfe and Sue Richards, *Improving Public Management* (London: Sage, 1987), p. 225.

15. Auditor General of Canada, *Report to the House of Commons for the Fiscal Year ended March 31, 1988,* paras. 4.71-4.88.

16. Auditor General of Canada, *Report to the House of Commons for the Fiscal Year ended March 31, 1988,* paras. 4.91, 4.90, 4.91, 4.46.

17. John Noble, "Reflections on the Not-so-Well-Performing Organizations," in McDavid and Marson (eds.), *The Well-Performing Government Organization,* p. 37.

18. Michael Barzelay, *Breaking Through Bureaucracy: A New Vision for Managing in Government* (Berkeley: University of California Press, 1992), pp. 115-33.

19. Barzelay, *Breaking Through Bureaucracy,* p. 117-19.

20. Hilary Wainwright, "A New Kind of Knowledge for a New Kind of State," in Gregory Albo, David Langille and Leo Panitch (eds.), *A Different Kind of State? Popular Power and Democratic Administration* (Toronto: Oxford University Press, 1993), pp. 112-21.

21. Anna Yeatman, "The Reform of Public Management: An Overview," *Australian Journal of Public Administration,* Vol. 53, no. 3 (September 1994), p. 289.

22. Barzelay, *Breaking Through Bureaucracy,* pp. 115-33.

23. Yeatman, "The Reform of Public Management," p. 290; emphasis added.

24. Yeatman, "The Reform of Public Management," p. 293.

25. Zussman and Jabes, *The Vertical Solitude,* p. 203.

26. Zussman and Jabes, *The Vertical Solitude.*

27. Yeatman, "The Reform of Public Management," p. 290.

SEVEN

Enhancing Performance

Enhancing performance in governance to move public management beyond bureaucracy and promote greater economy, efficiency and effectiveness is the bottom line of public management reform. Advocates of reform recognize that changes to the structures of governance and public management, while a necessary condition for enhanced performance, are not sufficient on their own. Additional measures are required.

At the level of strategic policy and expenditure decision making, and beyond the need for political discipline, improved performance can only be achieved through measures such as business plans, performance targets and service standards. Above all, there must be greater clarity in the objectives ministers wish to achieve with their policy initiatives.[1] Strategic policy is better secured when policy objectives are clear. But, equally important, public management is less likely to succumb to bureaucratic pathologies when policy objectives are given concrete operational meaning through defined plans, targets and performance measures. Finally, when policy objectives are clear, organizational learning is more likely to occur as a result of evaluations of policy and program initiatives.

At the level of the provision of public services and the enforcement of regulations, enhanced performance requires that services and regulations be administered in ways that secure quality service to the public or, as Michael Barzelay puts it, "results citizens value." This requires, at a minimum, a greater degree of consultation with citizens, increased access to information for the public and increased flexibility in responding to the particular needs and circumstances of certain citizens in the application of general rules. Achieving these results implies, in turn, explicit service standards that meet the requirements of quality service as understood by citizens and clients, at the same time adhering to traditional public service values and ethics, including probity, fairness, impartiality and equal treatment under the law. If quality service initiatives lead to alternative forms of service delivery and regulatory enforcement, and thus encompass partnerships between the public service and the private sector and voluntary organizations (and/or two or more orders of government), it is imperative that traditional values and principles be maintained, lest private interests undermine, compromise or put at risk the public interest in quality public service.

In pursuing results citizens value, greater authority must inevitably flow to the front lines. Greater clarity in missions, tasks and standards is essential in order that this delegated authority be guided by policy. General rules will not be absent, but when recourse to superiors for interpretation and guidance is not a ready option, best practices in the form of continuous learning must emerge from the front lines, or they will not be developed at all.

In this chapter, the approaches taken by each of the four Westminster systems are considered in relation to what is required to enhance performance. The differences in approach among the systems are a useful basis for an evaluation of how public management reforms contribute to enhanced performance in governance.

Clarifying Objectives

Chief among the concerns of public management reformers in each of the Westminster systems has been the need to establish greater clarity in public policy objectives as a precondition of improved public management. While this is hardly a new theme in public administration, it has constituted a major preoccupation of reformers either as a starting point, as in Australia and New Zealand, or as a priority that emerged from initial attempts at reform, as in Great Britain and Canada. This focus is not surprising. If bureaucrats are not to rule by discretion, objectives must be stated clearly in the law or in government policy.

While bureaucrats may play a central role in advising ministers on public policy, the laws and policies they implement in delivering public services and enforcing regulations should be governed by the decisions of the democratic political process. Clarifying policy objectives, accordingly, is crucial to improved public management if government departments and agencies are to achieve their missions within the context of the rule of law.

The concept of clarity in objectives is easily dismissed as unrealistic by both political and administrative theorists and practitioners. Realists quickly point to the multiplicity of objectives in any given area of policy, the inevitable compromises when efforts are made to accommodate competing interests in public policy and the uncertainties that characterize most, if not all, areas of government intervention in the socio-economic order. These realities are cause to maintain executive and administrative authority at the highest levels; in Westminster systems, this means as close as possible to the source of constitutional authority, namely individual ministers and Cabinet.

At the same time, realists also acknowledge that neither individual ministers nor Cabinets have the time to manage, directly and personally, the implementation of law and policy in all its dimensions. Efforts to turn ministers into managers are noteworthy for their limited success, if not outright failure, as amply demonstrated in the attempt to apply the minister-as-manager concept in Great Britain under the Financial Management Initiative (FMI). If ministers cannot manage in this sense, even with the advantages of the new information technologies, but nevertheless want the implementation of law and policy to be responsive to their objectives, the only recourse is to clarify these objectives to govern implementation.

The Canadian Experience

In the Canadian government, efforts to clarify objectives have a long-standing, if uneven, history. From the introduction of the Planning, Programming and Budgeting System in the late 1960s to the 1995 Expenditure Management System, it has been assumed that clearly stated objectives are crucial to improved public management. The language has changed over time, but the fundamental idea has remained constant: ministers, individually and collectively, must translate their strategic goals and priorities into policies and programs that can be understood by those responsible for their implementation. Although the real world of governance has played havoc with efforts to clarify objectives in these respects, reformers have persisted.

Clarifying policy objectives was implicit in the establishment by the Mulroney government, immediately after assuming office in 1984, of the Task Force on Program Review. The legacy of the programs of the long-tenured Liberal government was to be subject to the test of whether the programs continued to serve public policy objectives. According to Erik Nielsen, the Deputy Prime Minister who chaired the Task Force, "the government's intention [was] to create a new array of programs with definite objectives, with clearly defined tasks and with purposes related to the public interest."[2] The results, in terms of clarifying the policy objectives of government as they applied to the vast complex of government programs, were scant to say the least, even as recorded by those who participated.[3]

For a new government, and especially one that did not come to power with a clearly enunciated platform beyond a general inclination to follow the lead of British and American neo-conservative governments, the lack of results was no surprise. Given this general policy orientation, and in part supported by the work of the Task Force, some regulatory reforms improved policy objectives in the regulatory decision-making process. Reforms did clarify policy objectives in relation to Crown corporations in cases where they were not privatized.

Beyond these changes, there were precious few successes in the clarification of policy objectives. In some large measure, this was due to the size and representative character of the Cabinet as well as the brokerage politics style of the Mulroney government. This was reinforced by what the government saw as a pressing national need, namely the priority of "reconciliation" – not only between Quebec and the rest of the country but also between the federal and provincial governments, and between the public and private sectors. The overriding policy objective was simply to hold the line on government spending. The strategic policy here did not mean a return to the issue of program spending, given the failure of the Nielsen Task Force exercise but rather led to initiatives to reduce operating budgets and the size of the public service.[4]

At the same time, the 1986 Increased Ministerial Authority and Accountability (IMAA) initiative did pay at least lip-service to the idea of clarifying "strategic objectives and desired results, to enhancing accountability based on results achieved, and to increasing the utilization of results and program effectiveness information in Treasury Board decisions."[5] The actual focus, however, was on strategic objectives and results primarily in relation to the management of those departmental resources not subject to legislated or discretionary program spending requirements. This was complemented by a Treasury Board Secretariat initiative – the Shared Management Agenda program – whereby the Secretary to the Treasury Board and each deputy minister agreed annually on the key strategic priorities for each deputy.

The most recent manifestations of the pursuit of clarity in objectives were twofold. First was the consolidation of cabinet portfolios and departments; second was the design of the Expenditure Management System (EMS). The EMS gives central place to "strategic planning" generally and to the role of "departmental business plans," in particular. Departmental business plans are expected to outline:

- major challenges, directions and objectives for the planning period – that is, the Estimates year plus two future years as a minimum – within the context of government priorities and the department's current and prospective position;
- strategies, actions, associated costs and the flexibilities required to deal with major changes;
- associated goals, targets and performance measures to assess program results and management strategies during the planning period; and
- performance information focused on service lines affected by significant change.[6]

Departmental business plans, however, are "formal submissions from departmental ministers to the Treasury Board,"[7] and do not require the approval of the Board, except where increased flexibilities are sought. They provide information to the Board to ensure that this central authority understands the working plans of a department. Accordingly, they are considered confidential to government and "will not be available for public release."[8] How this lack of transparency is to advance the cause of greater clarity in objectives is not at all certain.

The experience of special operating agencies (SOAs) is instructive given that the idea of "business plans" was first introduced with the adoption of the SOA model. According to the most recent assessment, a major shortcoming in the implementation of the idea of business plans by SOAs has been the establishment of "performance objectives and priorities."[9] In the words of the internal government review of SOAs, the difficulty lies "in the political system in which the SOA is embedded. For the SOA head, alone, to declare that any objective is not of the highest priority is to invite pressure from the stakeholders for whom the objective is the only priority."[10] As a consequence, this review notes, objectives "tend to focus on financial objectives."[11] Given that ministerial departments are equally "embedded" in "the political system," if departments are to be explicit and specific about priorities, then additional elements are required.

The EMS contains four related elements to serve this purpose. First, departments are required to prepare for public release "outlooks on program priorities and expenditures" which "outline the key strategies that departments will pursue to adapt to the fiscal and policy environment."[12] Second, these documents are subject to review and report by House of Commons standing committees. Third, these committees also examine the reports on performance to be contained within the annual Estimates documents as well as published departmental program evaluations. Fourth, departments are required to publish "service standards," to "tell program clients what kind of service they can expect to receive,"[13] as well as information concerning the department's performance in relation to these standards.

If performance reporting is to be improved over past practices, objectives will have to be more clearly established by ministers and their departments, and reflected in departmental performance targets and measures. This will require major departures from recent Canadian practice, in particular to enhance reporting on program performance in relation to policy objectives.

While the genesis of what came to be called "program evaluation" lies in the adoption in the late 1960s of the Planning, Programming and Budgeting System (PPBS), the crucial phase in assessing program performance did not begin until the latter part of the 1970s. This was when the Auditor General began to take dead aim at what he declared to be major shortcomings in the government's approach to financial planning, management and control. Besides establishing the Royal Commission on Financial Management and Accountability, which endorsed the claims and recommendations of the Auditor General, the government committed itself to the program evaluation function. Somewhat later it also agreed to adopt new measures for reporting on departmental performance in the annual Estimates process.

The subsequent experience in performance reporting and program evaluation, by every account including those contained in the 1992 and 1993 reports of the Auditor General, has fallen well short of the mark.[14] Al Johnson attributes the shortcomings in program evaluation (or what he prefers to call "effectiveness evaluation") to the unrealistic assumption about the "compatibility" of this function with "the parliamentary system."[15] Ministers will not normally be enthusiastic about committing "political hara-kiri" if the publication of program evaluations amounts to a public exposure of "all the warts of [their] public policy."[16] Despite this cautionary exhortation by an experienced mandarin, the Chrétien government has recommitted the Government of Canada to the function of program evaluation, including the publication of evaluations and their review by Commons standing committees, and to improving performance reporting in the Estimates process.

There are at least three reasons for this measure of acceptance of program evaluation and performance reporting in the Chrétien government's agenda for reform. The first relates to the widespread public view that value for money is not achieved in government spending. The above measures are one response to this. In different ways, each has the potential to demonstrate value for money if departments can prove that programs are in fact achieving policy objectives and are administered in cost-effective ways. In this sense, these measures have the capacity to help restore confidence in government, in itself a major objective of the Chrétien government. This may be overly optimistic, of course, but these measures, if sufficiently transparent and credible, are among the instruments available to government to restore confidence in public institutions and processes in an objective, that is, nonpartisan, manner. In the partisan arena of Parliament, the best defence may well be a good offence.

The second reason for the Chrétien government's espousal of program evaluation and performance reporting is their potential contribution to ministerial decision making under the new EMS. This system is predicated on the assumption that "program reviews," not only to effect reductions in total public spending but also to reallocate resources between programs, must be an ongoing dimension of government renewal, at least for the foreseeable future. In the 1994-95 program review process, for instance, a form of program evaluation was very much in evidence, even if it drew largely on the collective experiences of officials rather than on systematic formal program evaluations.

These evaluations, by several accounts, were central to the cabinet planning and budget processes. They may well have constituted a "watershed" with respect to "the prospect of some more rational approaches to the functioning of government in the future."[17] At the least, they demonstrated that ministers and departments need all the evidence they can muster to fend off those whose oxen will be gored by expenditure cuts and to defend those who continue to be indulged. In this context, ministers, collectively if not individually, are more likely to welcome evidence that some programs are unsuccessful or too costly. This, too, of course, is an optimistic reading of the potential contribution of program evaluation, but, in the conundrum of redefining the role of the state, ministers may well take whatever they can get.

The third reason for promoting these measures relates to their potential to improve public service performance. Ministers and their advisers can use the evidence from these measures to hold departmental officials to account. Such an incentive can spur public servants to pay greater attention to the realization of policy objectives, to do so in cost-effective ways and to seek out alternative approaches to realize ministerial policy objectives better.

Clarifying policy objectives to enhance performance requires significant input from public service managers if these objectives are to provide meaningful direction to policy implementation, result in missions and tasks that can actually be accomplished and constitute a framework for performance measurement. Precious little will be achieved, however, if ministers do not meet their responsibilities in these regards. Assigning the task to deputy ministers and departmental officials invariably causes inaction in some departments and obfuscation in others, as departments seek to protect their ministers from commitments that are too explicit for political consumption. The first result constitutes the bureaucratic pathology of goal displacement. The second, while it at least acknowledges the supremacy of ministers, does little to enhance performance. Officials down the line and in the field are too often left to discern for themselves how to interpret what policy objectives actually mean.

Comparative Experience
In Australia, improving clarity of objectives was a first order of public management reform. Its Financial Management Improvement Program (FMIP) rested on the assumption that much greater attention had to be given to the identification of government objectives and priorities and their translation into specific program structures and resource allocations, as well as the creation of measures to assess performance. The crucial components of reform, in addition to changes embodied in the FMIP itself, were the subsequent creation of a new program management and budgeting system, and the consolidation of ministerial portfolios.

Unlike the IMAA in Canada, however, Australia's FMIP was a government-wide corporate initiative encompassing all departments and agencies. Beyond it, the Australian reforms have emphasized changes to improve the capacities of government in three critical areas. First, there was the explicit forging of a closer link between strategic and expenditure decision making to strengthen the role of ministers in collectively establishing strategic priorities. Second, the management capacity of individual ministers and departments was enhanced to foster closer connections between portfolio objectives and programs, including the requirement that departments engage in corporate planning. Third, program evaluations were introduced to assist ministers and departments in determining whether their programs were in fact achieving their strategic objectives.

This trinity of reforms has improved public management in Australia. While successive efforts have been required to realize more fully the objectives of the reform program and especially to move beyond enhanced efficiency to enhanced effectiveness as assessed in program evaluations, there has been a considerable degree of consistency. Equally important, especially given the major focus of Australian reforms on "managing for results," officials report that progress has been made in using program evaluations in strategic and expenditure decision making.[18]

Relative to Canada, the Australian experience is noteworthy in at least three respects. Securing greater clarity in objectives was expedited early in the mid-1980s by the Expenditure Review Committee's efforts to set priorities. The government then moved quickly to consolidate ministerial portfolios, thus facilitating corporate planning and management. Finally, a concerted effort was made to use program evaluations as a basis for improved decision making. The actual evolution of these reforms was not part of a grand design, however. In retrospect, it may appear so, although the machinery of government changes were disruptive and the program evaluation function was slow to materialize in practice.

In certain respects, the Australian government was merely catching up to Canada, especially with its implementation of a program planning and expenditure management system. Nevertheless, two elements of the Australian experience led to real progress. Its program management and budgeting system was put in place in close conjunction with a streamlining of government departments and their operations. And the system dovetailed with a policy of restraint in spending, the introduction of financial management reforms and a major commitment to results in terms of policy outcomes. Compared to earlier Canadian efforts, greater clarity and coherence in policy objectives were more easily obtained. According to the Australian review of its reform program, the clarification of policy objectives has made them more meaningful to managers at the centre and down the line. At the same time, it is clear that the system in place is only one determinant of success; equally important have been the ability and willingness of a key set of ministers and senior officials to manage the system according to its logic.[19]

The British experience parallels developments in Canada and Australia in some respects but departs from them in others. The British Financial Management Initiative (FMI), for instance, differed from the Canadian IMAA initiative but was similar to the Australian FMIP in that it was a centrally imposed government-wide program. As with both, however, it too promised to provide ministers and central agencies with a greater capacity to hold departmental officials to account for their performance in exchange for greater departmental flexibility in the use of resources, especially financial resources. It gave an increased emphasis to the development of performance indicators as the mechanism for holding departmental managers to account. While some progress occurred under this regime, it was not long before the limited impact in improving departmental management generally was acknowledged. As noted, the move from the ministerial form of departmental organization to the executive agency model was initiated by Prime Minister Thatcher's own advisers in the Efficiency Unit. They saw the need for having public service delivery managed through a contractual relationship between individual ministers and the chief executives of the agencies within a minister's portfolio.

In adopting this approach, the government, in effect, admitted that Thatcher's initial expectation that ministers would clarify their objectives and then get on with managing their departments had not been met. The adoption of a contractual mode required ministers to establish their objectives in published policy and resource framework documents, bind their executive agencies to explicit performance targets and measure their performance against negotiated performance indicators. In this respect, the executive agency model went beyond the FMI approach in that it sought to secure for executive agencies a greater measure of managerial authority than the Treasury had been willing to confer on departments under the FMI.

While the chief executives of executive agencies have a role in negotiating their framework documents with ministers and their departmental officials, the intent of this separation of policy and operational responsibilities was a major departure from British practice. It is predicated on the assumption that ministers and their departments can be explicit in setting performance targets that both reflect policy objectives and establish credible performance measures in relation to these objectives.

In practice, the British model has focused on enhancing performance in the efficient delivery of public services, which is not surprising since the push for these reforms emanated from the Efficiency Unit. Although this was complemented by the widespread application of service standards, as required by the Major government in its Citizen's Charter initiative, efficiency in the use of resources, especially the operating budgets of agencies (their "running costs"), has been the overriding concern. This focus was reinforced by the adoption of a "market testing" scheme. Under this second Major initiative, agencies have been required annually to subject significant portions of their operations to competitive bids from the private sector to determine if the private sector could deliver public services more efficiently.

This "Competing for Quality" initiative, as it was called, took the contractual approach to public service delivery one step beyond contracting for services *to* or *within* government by encompassing contracts with the private sector to provide public services directly *to* citizens. Under this scheme, large portions of departmental and agency operations have been regularly tested against market competition. In 1994, the government indicated its willingness to alter this policy. In its place, executive agencies are now required to develop efficiency plans that indicate in what ways, including but not restricted to market testing, agencies will achieve efficiencies in their running costs.[20]

Clarifying policy objectives in this context has been driven largely, if not exclusively, by questions of economy in government. Competition between the public and private sectors, and in certain areas of public service, such as health and education, between public service providers themselves, has been viewed as the principal lever to enhanced performance, defined primarily in terms of economy and efficiency, with quality service added later as a criterion.[21] As a consequence, precious little attention has been given to program evaluation as a mechanism to assess the effectiveness of public services.[22] Policy analysis, accordingly, is focused on three questions. First, should the government be involved in an activity at all? The emphasis here is on eliminating "unnecessary tasks" in order to use resources where they are most "needed" or to reduce the "cost to the taxpayer."[23] Program or effectiveness evaluation is not ruled out but little, if any, priority is attached to this dimension of policy analysis.

If the answer to this first question is positive, the second is: could government tasks be performed more economically by the private sector? Third, if the conclusion to the second is negative, how should the delivery of services within the state apparatus be structured to achieve the greatest degree of efficiency? Paralleling this restricted approach to policy analysis and reinforcing its economy in government orientation are the ongoing efficiency scrutinies meant to tease out even further economies in the management and delivery of services. Proposals to expand the use of executive agency management advisory boards – which could include representatives from the private sector – to help ministers and departments manage their contractual relationships with executive agency heads, point in the same direction, although they also reflect an increasing concern for service quality.

Without program evaluations to assess whether services achieve ministerial policy objectives beyond meeting performance targets, the only criteria used are those of economy and efficiency. Under the circumstances, some worry that the British approach has not adequately addressed the classic dilemma in public management of doing the wrong things well. Sufficient attention has not been given to clarifying policy objectives in relation to the horizontal interdependencies of the various departmental policies and agency services as they affect the outcomes in particular areas of government activity. The increased specialization in the delivery of services brought about by the executive agency structure, which inevitably has led to further fragmentation of government, demands more horizontal coordination to integrate policies necessary to produce desired outcomes.

"Getting policy right" requires attention to the effectiveness of programs if policy analysis, including the assessment of policy options, is to have a solid grounding in empirical evidence and actual experience. Without this, the most likely effect is to focus almost exclusively on questions of economy; better policy may well become tantamount to cheaper public services. Moreover, while performance targets and measures may contribute to greater clarity in operational outputs, they are not a satisfactory substitute for program evaluation in relation to their effectiveness in realizing outcomes.

In New Zealand, the development of its model of public management was preceded by an effort to enhance ministerial direction over departmental management in ways that mirrored the IMAA in Canada, the FMI in Britain and the FMIP in Australia. In moving to a contractual model of ministerial-departmental relationships, the ideas underpinning the New Zealand separation of policy and operational responsibilities were even more explicit than those that underlie the British executive agency structure.

Using the distinction between outcomes and outputs has been perceived as critical in two respects. First, it has been assumed that ministers can expect improved public management only if there is a "greater clarity of objectives." This was defined as "the key principle which must underlie any reform if management is to be improved."[24] To achieve a greater clarity of objectives requires that the outputs of government be distinguished from the outcomes desired by government, because the former are but the means to the latter.

Greater clarity of objectives in governance is not easily obtained simply by distinguishing between outcomes and outputs. The causal connections between desired outcomes and delivered outputs are difficult to establish because the actual outputs are not the only factors that determine whether the desired outcomes are realized. In recognition of this, the New Zealand model established contractual relationships not only for those who deliver outputs, as in Britain, but also for those public servants who advise ministers on policy, that is, another kind of output.[25] Moreover, these relationships are more transparent in several respects, including the manner by which the distinction between outcomes and outputs is built into both budgetary appropriations and accountability regimes.

The most significant developments here are twofold. On the one hand, the distinction has enabled ministers to see more clearly just what they are "purchasing" in the form of outputs.[26] On the other hand, there is greater specificity in what those responsible for outputs are to deliver and the measures by which their performance is to be judged. All of this is relative, of course. Many outcomes are still presented like wish lists with little connection between what is desired and what is pursued. And performance contracts for outputs have not eliminated all uncertainties, such as what is to be done or who is to do it.

As noted, the incoming National government in 1990, following its review of this approach, endorsed its basic principles. It did express concerns that the new model, with its multiplicity of new departments and agencies, had fragmented the New Zealand governmental apparatus in ways that led to what the National Prime Minister Bolger labelled "little islands" of public service.[27] His principal concern was that this new model did not secure the "degree of integration, collaboration and co-operation between ministries and departments [necessary] to achieve the best results."[28] Although the "collective interests" of the government had also been a concern for the previous Labour government, the National government has taken steps to reassert the corporate responsibilities of departmental chief executives, including provisions to this effect in their contracts with ministers. At the same time, some officials have worried that policy evaluation has not adequately addressed the contribution of outputs, however well managed and delivered, to outcomes.[29]

Comparative Perspectives

The collective experiences of these four systems in seeking to improve the clarity of policy objectives to enhance public service performance all point in the same general direction. In each case, greater transparency has been sought on two fronts: what ministers want accomplished and what public service managers are to deliver; and how effectiveness, efficiency and economy are to be assessed. In Canada and Australia, the focus has been on improving ministerial and departmental "plans" to achieve these two requirements. In Britain and New Zealand, "contracts" between ministers and public service organizations are used.

The principal merit of the former, it is argued by its advocates, is that the plans ensure that the objectives of government remain front and centre, and are not subsumed by the activities used to pursue them; the "what" of government is clearly distinguished from the "how." To secure enhanced performance, however, this approach demands that priority be given to the effectiveness of plans in realizing intended results. The connections between policy objectives and program designs require the rigorous use of program, or effectiveness, evaluations. Australia has gone further than Canada in this regard, at least in using evaluations in strategic decision making, even though Canada adopted a formal system of program evaluation earlier. The new expenditure decision-making system adopted by the Chrétien government is meant to get Canada back on track.

The principal merit of the contractual approach to relationships between ministers and their public service agencies or departments, as argued by its advocates, is that the separation of responsibilities for outcomes and outputs is a more realistic route to enhanced performance because it specifies more precisely what public service agencies must accomplish. The assumption here is that a reliance on planning and evaluation, as the principal means to enhance performance, stretches the capacities of the state beyond what can be reasonably expected given the limits of public management as applied social science or social engineering. A more pragmatic, if more limited, approach is to be as specific as possible about what those responsible for operations are to deliver as outputs, and then to establish rigorous measures of performance and performance monitoring mechanisms.[30] In this regard, the New Zealand system, compared to the British approach, is clearly more advanced, both in terms of coverage and transparency. These two approaches need not be mutually exclusive, however. Indeed, both the Australian and Canadian approaches contain elements of the contractual model, particularly in the emphasis given to

196

performance reporting by departments in relation to the delivery of programs as outputs.

Greater transparency and objectivity require clear policy objectives and information on performance. Efforts to secure both have met with political and bureaucratic resistance because of the constraints on executive and administrative discretion that these requirements entail. Notwithstanding its early adoption of planning and evaluation systems, Canada's experience in focusing on performance measurement has lagged behind that of the other three systems. Indeed, it may well be that the willingness of the Canadian public service to concentrate on performance measurement has been adversely affected by the perceived failures of past efforts in this area. What Donald Savoie refers to as the "disbelief culture" of the Canadian public service,[31] spawned by the many previous unsuccessful efforts at reform, was close to the surface in the 1990 Public Service 2000 White Paper in its commentary on performance measurement as it applies to accountability. It argued that "[m]echanical accountability based on simplistic, quantified objectives is not what is needed."[32]

In a similar vein, the former Secretary to the Treasury Board, the agency responsible for performance measurement in government, noted with approval those scholars who have drawn attention to "the difficulty of measuring the variables that are most important for public sector management" and have warned "of the perverse results that can occur when private-sector models of performance measurement are adopted [in government]."[33] It is little wonder that the public service has been so unenthusiastic about the adoption of performance measures. Although the government remains committed to the idea of performance management, it was conspicuous by its absence in the 1995 report by the Clerk of the Privy Council on public management changes.[34]

Focusing on Clients

Throughout the Westminster systems, several initiatives have been undertaken by departments and agencies in response to citizens' demands for better public services (and within government, by common service agencies in response to their client departments and agencies wanting better internal government services).[35] Many have been government-wide initiatives driven from the centre, as governments generally seek to cope with restraint while maintaining quality service. Citizens' expectations for quality public services have not been diminished by the need for cutbacks, particularly insofar as they are conditioned by quality service initiatives in the private sector. Governments must also take advantage of new opportunities to communicate with citizens, especially as provided by new information technologies.

In these respects, governments are reacting to stimuli and opportunities in their environments. In addition, however, public servants are responding to their own sense of what needs to be done to improve services to the public. Professionalism and a commitment to quality public services are also crucial determinants of change as evidenced by the extent to which changes have taken place independent of government-wide initiatives.

The Canadian Experience

To improve public services, Canadian departments and agencies have sought to enhance citizen and user access to information and services through integrated government information centres and coordinated delivery systems; to make services and regulations more user-friendly through streamlined administrative processes and methods of voluntary compliance; to consult with users through advisory panels, surveys and focus groups; and to establish partnerships with users and others through joint delivery systems or joint financing of public projects.[36]

These kinds of initiatives illustrate what can be done within government even under the existing management regime. Enhancing access to information and services by way of the Canada Business Service Centres and other ways to provide "clusters" of services recognizes that the dispersal and duplication of contact points with citizens and client groups may constitute an obstacle to quality services. Interdepartmental cooperation in service delivery on the front lines is an obvious corrective.

Making services and regulations more user-friendly by way of a consolidation of business registration numbers, fewer forms, forms written in plain language or more flexible office hours, for instance, is an indication that governments can provide better service, including better regulatory enforcement. Such changes are significant to users and in many instances do not require a massive overhaul in management systems. Consulting more widely with citizens, and using new techniques to this end, constitute a recognition that services can be improved if those who are at the receiving end are more effectively engaged in the design of programs and their delivery or enforcement systems. Although there is little that is novel in this, the effort being made implies a greater collaboration with citizens than has been the practice in many areas of public administration.[37]

At least two factors are crucial to the success of improved public services in the above respects. One is the need to foster a culture that gives high priority to a focus on clients; the other is the need to establish criteria for assessing performance in responding to clients' expressed demands. The record of achievements within the federal public service suggests that leadership can be found in several departments and agencies, and that this leadership has contributed to the adoption – formally or informally – of total quality management principles. In some cases, this has led to innovations that have improved service quality; in other cases, quality service has emerged once certain constraints are removed.

As a generalization, the absence of established criteria for assessing performance and demonstrating improvements in service quality has diminished the recognition of achievements where they have occurred. All too often, successes have had to be demonstrated in forums unconnected to the regular processes of governance and public management. It is ironic that the best evidence of successes has been supplied by scholars or private organizations, such as the awards competitions of the Institute of Public Administration of Canada, rather than formally structured processes of the institutions of government and Parliament. Central agencies, such as the Treasury Board, and departments have increased efforts to recognize those who have made significant contributions. With few exceptions, however, this recognition is internal to the public service. In a more public manner, the Auditor General has in recent years assisted in recognizing progress, but the absence of established criteria for service quality has limited the capacity of even this agency to attest to performance. In addition, of course, neither the media nor Parliament pays much attention to positive audit commentaries by the Auditor General.

Although Public Service 2000 focused largely on internal administrative matters, its Task Force on Service to the Public brought forward recommendations to enhance public service, including proposals to institute public departmental service standards.[38] These proposals were incorporated in the government's 1990 White Paper on Public Service 2000, which included the following commitment:

> Deputy Ministers will establish clear standards of service and will be accountable both for the reasonableness of those standards and for the quality of the service provided to the public. They will ensure that information about client satisfaction and suggestions for improving service are regularly sought both from clients and employees. Simple procedures for responding to complaints will be established.[39]

By late 1994, however, the former secretary to the Treasury Board could write that: "The Treasury Board has *requested* that departments develop service standards...and a committee of assistant deputy ministers meets regularly to exchange ideas about implementing service standards."[40] He also noted that the new Liberal government had committed itself to providing a "declaration on service quality" in 1994 and to having service standards "in all departments" by 1995.[41] Progress in implementing this dimension of Public Service 2000, in short, has been slow.

This slow pace in establishing service standards has done a grave disservice to the Canadian public service in particular and to the Canadian federal government in general. Those who provide public services have a diminished capacity to demonstrate performance against standards. Without established standards, two things tend to happen.

First, the performance of federal departments and agencies is measured against whatever criteria partisan opponents and critics wish to use. These invariably ignore any consideration of the actual requirements and constraints under which departments and agencies must operate. And public service leaders can hardly defend their performance against either unrealistic or changing criteria.

Second, in the absence of established service standards, assessments too often become *ad hoc*, invariably relating to specific instances of shortcomings. In these circumstances, the general impression of the overall performance of an organization can easily become skewed by highly publicized revelations of particular shortcomings. The score card is distorted by the absence of measures that would place such shortcomings in perspective.

The principal consequence of this state of affairs is that public confidence in government is not as advanced as it might be. It matters little in this context that departments and agencies may be accorded high levels of citizen or client approval for particular public services and service delivery on the basis of user surveys or other methods to measure user response. Such evidence of good performance and quality service is shunted to the political sidelines, even if it is not perceived as self-serving or self-promoting on the part of government departments and agencies.

The Achilles heel of performance measurement in the Canadian experience lies less in the arts and sciences of measurement, as challenging as these are in their application to public services, than in the tendency to try to measure performance on outputs and outcomes at the same time. The move that began with the Public Service 2000 initiative to introduce service standards linked with performance measurement constitutes a significant change in this regard. Although service standards were seen as a way to separate these two foci, the continual decline of resources for services, coupled with the consequent problems of tracking service costs and performance in a rapidly changing context, led many managers to question the wisdom of setting standards at all. This has been compounded by the turmoil associated with the 1993 restructuring, followed closely by the major program reviews that began in earnest in 1994. In this milieu, staff enthusiasm for further reform exercises has been severely tested.

Indeed, the first phases of the restructuring were predicated on the assumption that they would not adversely affect the business of government in delivering services and enforcing regulations. It was to be in the final phase of the process that ministers and departments were to tackle the major question of affordability in public services. Departments, with considerable pride, point to the lack of serious criticisms and complaints from citizens and clients as evidence that performance on the front lines was maintained throughout the restructuring.[42] In several respects, quality service initiatives implemented before the restructuring, including measures to engage citizens and clients, may well have been of assistance here.

The program review exercises have caused greater stress on the system. Some citizens and clients have found that certain changes are not to their liking, if only because they must adapt to changes in, or loss of, services. Improved public services will no doubt result in some cases as departments and agencies do business differently. Using "alternative program delivery," as the Treasury Board has called it, is recognized as a response to declining resources. The bottom line to doing business differently is that it must not cost more. Indeed, affordability, in this context, is invariably taken to mean alternatives that cost less.

Achieving affordable government business in the Canadian context encompasses the full range of options now common across the Westminster systems. These include interdepartmental cooperation at the point of service delivery; partnership arrangements with other levels of government and non-profit organizations; joint ventures with the private sector; commercializing services; using regulatory instruments in place of direct services; using tax measures in place of spending programs; contracting out the delivery of services; and increased emphasis on voluntary compliance mechanisms in the areas of regulation and tax administration. None of these alternatives is new: they constitute the range of the policy instruments that have always been at the disposal of governments, and for each instrument there are precedents to be followed. What has changed, however, is the willingness of government to consider the greater use of certain instruments over a broader range of public services and fields of regulatory activities.

Clearly, greater emphasis is now given to a client focus in the design and delivery of public services and regulatory activities. Senior line department officials, from deputies on down, are responding to pressures from citizens generally and from specific clienteles. These pressures are reinforced by demands for "empowerment" from staff at the delivery end. While the degree of responsiveness varies among departments, even departments and agencies that have prided themselves on their relations with citizens and client groups are making efforts to be, or at least to be seen to be, more client focused.

Across the federal government generally, this increased client focus is having an effect. The Treasury Board Secretariat declared in 1995 that it "will make affordable 'client-focused quality service delivery' its top priority."[43] One consequence of this is that senior managers, especially those who have had little or no experience with field operations, have become more aware of how receptive public servants are, especially in the field, to the ideal of a client-centred focus. It is here that one finds managers and staff who are willing to acknowledge that they take risks, bend the rules and push the boundaries of their discretion.[44] Indeed, in a recent study of front-line managers in federal and provincial public services, Barbara Wake Carroll and David Siegel found that these officials see themselves, but not those at head office, as conforming to the principal elements of the post-bureaucratic paradigm in this crucial respect, even if they are not completely conversant with the theory or its literature.[45]

Managing down the organization is thus becoming a more salient feature of federal public administration. In the process, ironically, there are now increased concerns at the centre, in central agencies especially but also in the headquarters of some departments, that this not result in increased fragmentation (or "stove-pipes" or "silos," as the current jargon expresses it) in the delivery of services. There is no substitute for well-designed undertakings with a clear client focus that addresses the full range of requirements of their clients. This is easier said than done, and there is no single remedy. However, quality service is best promoted when it is recognized that organizational specialization can take several forms, including both vertical and horizontal designs. Nonetheless, the construction of services that citizens want must be expressed in concrete operational tasks for public servants,[46] even if this means tasks performed in an interorganizational context.

Comparative Experience

If well-performing government organizations are characterized by reasonably clear and discrete missions, it follows that the British and New Zealand models should be more likely to meet the tests of improved public services than those found in Canada or Australia. This is true even leaving aside the differences in direct service responsibilities that arise from the fact that the first two are unitary states and the second two are federal systems. Both Britain and New Zealand have established a greater focus on service by virtue of their organizational distinction between policy and operational responsibilities. This has resulted in an emphasis on performance or output targets and measures, especially for quality service to the public, including factors of accessibility, timeliness, accuracy and courtesy.[47]

The British focus on service quality has gone beyond the use of performance targets and measures to encompass the Citizen's Charter. This initiative was adopted with the explicit intention of focusing on, and empowering, citizens as customers of public services. It includes not only explicit standards that relate to the levels and quality of service, but also matters of choice, at least in certain services, as well as complaint and redress mechanisms. Citizens, as taxpayers, loom large in this scheme, the assumption being that individual citizens should receive value for their tax payments. It is also explicitly assumed that, in those instances where quality service is not provided, the service should be a candidate for a change in management, contracting out or privatization.

Numerous commentators have been quick to note that the charters of the numerous service organizations that are required to develop them do not confer new rights on citizens.[48] For some, this is a fundamental flaw, even though it is not at all clear that a statutory basis for these charters would actually improve public services, except for the few who could afford to be, or threaten to be, litigious. In a political system that lacks a strong constitutional tradition of individual rights, however, the appeal of greater statutory recognition of individual rights has an obvious appeal. For some others, the adoption of the Citizen's Charter scheme constitutes little more than lip-service to the rhetoric of "citizens as customers," but in a context where public service "customers" cannot be, and therefore have not been made, "sovereign." The official view is that the Charter is a reinforcement for the idea of quality service that began with the institution of performance targets and measures, as first adopted under the Financial Management Initiative and then strengthened by the establishment of executive agencies.

The scepticism and cynicism that have engulfed the British Conservative government's approach to improving public services by focusing on clients are due in some large measure to the hostility toward the public service that has characterized the Conservative regime. The serious management shortcomings of the upper echelons of the public service, as amply documented in the post-war years, combined with the inevitable deficiencies to which a badly managed public service must succumb, have fuelled this hostility. These factors also gave this animosity a degree of public credibility that went well beyond the jocular view of the public service reflected in "Yes, Minister." Hence, the government's ever-increasing subjection of public services to competition from the private sector and, where this has not been possible or politically feasible, to increased regulation and/or central government intervention.

The Citizen's Charter initiative reflects this hostile view insofar as it seeks to set citizens against public service agencies. Citizen empowerment, in this view, is hardly to promote a sense of collaboration or partnership between public servants and citizens as clients, or even customers. The fact that the Conservative government has introduced no major constitutional or institutional reforms that might empower citizens in relation to their political masters is perhaps further evidence of the Conservatives' hostile stance against the public service. The "state" has been equated with the British public service and not the government. If all these measures to subjugate the public service do not contradict the principles underpinning the idea of executive agencies, as many claim, they at least exhibit a form of schizophrenia on the part of government toward the public service. Those who advocate strengthening the charters by giving them a statutory foundation exhibit this same tendency.

Notwithstanding this morale-crushing environment, the British public service, especially in line operations, has demonstrated in many cases, even before the Citizen's Charter initiative, that it is able and willing to enhance the client focus in the design and delivery of services.[49] Much of what has been accomplished is the result of managers and staff using the increased flexibilities and scope for initiative brought about by public management reform, including efficiency scrutinies, the Financial Management Initiative, executive agencies and even the Citizen's Charter itself. Even provisions for contracting out, at least when deployed as a management tool by executive agencies, have assisted here. A "managerial revolution"[50] has been effected and in several instances has improved morale,[51] and these components of reform are probably immune to a change in government.

What is much less likely to survive a change in government is the ideological commitment to the Conservatives' contracting out. As noted, the Major government has changed its policy on market testing in some ways, but it still stands committed to the idea of contracting out as a principal way of achieving efficiencies. The empirical evidence from several jurisdictions makes clear that there are limits to the efficiencies achieved by contracting out and that there are costs to be borne in certain circumstances.[52] Contracting out public services is a reform option, but the international experience indicates that its usefulness in achieving better performance – that is, cheaper and better service – depends on the context.[53] Some contextual factors can be identified by objective criteria as identified in theoretical models. But other factors are specific to the particular context which means that, for instance, the outcome of competitions between public service providers and private sector providers to secure government contracts cannot be predicted. The fact that the latter do not always win, even when the playing field is level, is evidence that the provision of public services by public service agencies can be cost-effective.

When the playing field is level, a critical factor in determining the performance of public service agencies is the extent to which public servants (managers and staff) are committed to serving clients. This commitment must offset, even exceed, the advantages of those economic incentives, rewards and sanctions assumed to be the greatest assets of private sector organizations, even when profits are built into private sector costs. The flexibilities afforded executive agencies have better positioned British public service agencies to compete with the private sector for government business, but there are still restraints not found in the private sector.

The elitism of the British public service goes a long way to account for the relative absence of a strong client focus in the upper echelons of the service. The Conservatives' hostile view of the public service, including both its mandarins and its front-line workers, has also done little to advance a commitment to public service. However, aside from the market testing scheme, the reforms to the British public service have laid a foundation for increased economy and efficiency in the managerial dimensions of public administration and for better service to citizens.

Organizational cultures take time to transform themselves. Some have not transformed fast enough and have fallen victim to privatization or contracting out. Others have survived, but have had a hard time responding to the mixed signals emanating from the centre of government, and their performance reflects this state of affairs. Still others have risen to the occasion and have demonstrated a capacity to accommodate the demands of restraint while improving services. In these cases, scattered as they are across various agencies, the combination of a commitment to serving clients and a high level of morale has been sufficiently strong to counter the hostility toward the public service.

In New Zealand, the legislative and organizational focus of management reforms has led to changes that have had a dramatic effect on economy and efficiency. There has also been an increased focus on the users of public services, in part because of the user charges that have been applied to several services and in part because many of the performance targets of departments and agencies are clearly related to service quality, at least in their transactional dimensions.

For the most part, reformers in New Zealand simply assumed that better and more transparent management systems would inevitably lead to improved management and therefore to improved public service. Greater "client responsiveness" was among the Labour party's objectives when it assumed office in 1984,[54] yet the principal means to achieve this was deemed to be increased responsiveness to ministers. This meant that public servants and interest groups had diminished influence on the design of public services. Ministers, as agents of the public, determined the public interest to be secured in the provision of various public services and then gave these meaning through the performance targets to be achieved in the outputs purchased from their departments and agencies.

As the new public management regime in New Zealand took effect, managers in line operations began to realize that securing performance meant at least two things. First, they had to adopt new management styles to achieve their performance targets. Devolved authority required managers to change how they managed their staff. With chief executives now "employers" with the authority to determine wages and conditions of service of their staff, a clear responsibility is in place to promote quality service among staff. Second, departments and agencies have an incentive to "improve responsiveness to customers" to "add value to their outputs."[55]

Despite a greater recognition of the need to improve "responsiveness to customers," the New Zealand experience has been slow to develop the full range of measures to promote customer responsiveness as found elsewhere, especially in Britain. The new management system was predicated on the perceived need to enhance economy and efficiency in the public sector generally. Achieving this meant a major "reshaping" of the New Zealand state,[56] including the elimination or substantial reduction of services to many "customers." Although this reshaping assumed that service quality could be improved for those services that remained in the public realm, it also assumed that political leaders would no longer bow to the pleadings of "special interests" or seek "consensus" among them. Given the priority attached to decisive political decision making, the idea of improved public services did not encompass the notion of a bureaucracy interacting with an empowered citizenry. Those who drove reform in government and in the central public service agencies were confident that sufficient public approval for the reshaping of the state would be forthcoming. For some time, at least, this confidence appeared to have been well founded.

In Australia, as in New Zealand, the reform agenda focused on improving the responsiveness of the public service to ministers. Here, however, the fundamental rationale was not so much the reshaping of the state, although there was some of this, as it was improving the performance of the state. This meant reforms that would be characterized as "managing for results."[57] Within the context of reforms to improve performance, "an increased focus on clients" was said to be the "most commonly identified positive outcome" by public service staff with respect to the effects of reforms on their work.[58] This has meant a "very substantial change in culture" on the part the Australian public service.[59]

Given the focus of Australian reforms on results, a major emphasis has been to enhance the capacity to evaluate programs and to use these evaluations in budgeting and strategic policy making. This emphasis need not conflict with a focus on quality service; indeed it should support it. However, in practice, the links between evaluations focused on outcomes and assessments of quality service, especially related to service transactions, have yet to be pursued with the required vigour. At least three reasons account for this.

First, the Australian reforms have not paid sufficient attention to service standards although some agencies have taken initiatives in this area.[60] The result is that inadequate attention has been given to ensuring that "clients" have a good "understanding of what can be provided" and that client "feedback" is secured.[61] Second, the emphasis on restraint has compounded the problem since agencies have fewer resources with which to provide the accessible and timely services demanded by citizens. Third, the limits on devolution, resulting in part from the continued emphasis on the integration of policy and operations in ministerial departments and thus the maintenance of several levels in departmental hierarchies, has meant that front-line managers and staff have not only less authority but also less incentive to be client focused. As in Canada, the question of improved quality service by way of a sharper distinction between policy and operational responsibilities may well be necessary, both to flatten hierarchies as they affect service delivery organizations and to introduce a greater incentive for superiors to manage down the organization. This would result in making devolution, in pursuit of quality service, a more realistic and feasible possibility.

The Australian reforms have paid somewhat less attention to issues of quality service precisely because the primary focus, beyond the "economic rationalism" that has pervaded public policy reforms, has been the outcomes of public services. More recently, the focus has shifted to other aspects of performance assessment, especially "benchmarking" against best practices in other organizations,[62] that speak more directly to quality service. Up to this point, however, Australian reformers have resisted what they perceive as the excessively narrow focus of service quality and customer responsiveness, as contained within the British approach, despite their appeal to some state governments in Australia. As in Canada, this view is partly because the federal government is less involved in direct service provision.[63]

Comparative Perspectives

The major lesson emerging from the comparative experiences of these four systems in trying to enhance a client focus in the design and delivery of their services is that the distinctive character of public services confounds simplistic notions of responsiveness to clients. Although some services have identifiable clients who do not constitute the entire citizenry, in every case the policy justification for services is that they serve the public interest of the body politic. While the precise public interest to be served by certain services may be subject to intense controversy, or lack of clarity, those who manage and deliver these services cannot in principle treat their clients as "customers," even in cases where partial, or even full, user charging applies. To do so is to assume that such "customers" are "sovereign" and to imply that there is no public interest to be served beyond the interests of those who are perceived to be the direct beneficiaries of particular services. To acknowledge, explicitly or implicitly, that there is no broader public interest to be served is to undermine whatever justification had been advanced for the service in the first place. The fact that there is a growing body of literature on public management that advances the notion of public service recipients as "customers" is beside the point. While these prescriptions may be well intentioned, they are misplaced in relation to the tasks of public management and the policy purposes of public services.[64]

Managing and delivering services to be more responsive to clients need not necessarily lead to a perversion of the public interest that particular services are meant to secure. But more effective public management is needed if those on the front lines are to secure the public interest in the design and delivery of services. The need for such improvements varies among departments and agencies, in part as a function of their professional character, in part as a function of their size, and in part as a result of the leadership styles dominant in their organizations. The more an organization is staffed with professionals in a particular field, the more it is likely to possess cultural norms that provide guidance on how to reconcile the general public interest and specific client needs or wants in particular cases. The smaller an organization, the more likely it will have channels of communication that allow front-line staff to obtain advice from supervisors on the interpretation of general rules in specific circumstances. The more organizational leaders pay attention to the operational requirements of front-line staff, the more likely that training and coaching will facilitate adherence to public policy purposes.

The importance of public management improvements in each of these regards has become increasingly critical for two related reasons. First, front-line staff are exposed to citizens with increased expectations of service. These increased expectations derive not only from a greater consciousness of rights generally but also, especially in Canada, from a heightened awareness of issues of service quality resulting from dramatic changes in service quality in the private sector in response to greater competition for customers, including those sectors long protected from competition by government regulation. Second, front-line staff have been encouraged to empower themselves by the new public service paradigm, especially in Canada through the rhetoric of Public Service 2000. The exhortations of senior management may be greeted with scepticism by those on the front lines, but they reinforce citizen demands that those on the front lines be responsive to them.

Given the push to improve public services by decentralizing decision making down the line, the willingness of front-line staff to be more responsive and the restraints on resources, the challenge to senior management in departments and agencies is at least twofold. The first is to engage such staff in efforts to limit the rules and regulations governing service delivery to those with a clearly defined public interest and to fashion them in ways that can be understood by both staff and citizens. For the public service, this is critical to the idea of continuous learning. For citizens, this is critical to enhancing the credibility and integrity of the services they receive. Technical improvements that do not address these fundamental issues will merely invite staff distress and citizen dissatisfaction, given that clients cannot be treated in every respect as customers. Public servants simply do not have the authority to decide what services to deliver, the levels of services that can be afforded or whom their "customers" will be. They do not have the discretion of private sector managers to drop certain lines of products or services, or to tailor what they provide to particular markets of customers.[65] Nor, with precious few exceptions, can they create new market niches for public services, at least not for those funded by the public purse. For the vast majority of public servants, the call to be "entrepreneurial" and responsive to "customers" rings exceedingly hollow.

Conclusion

Enhancing performance by clarifying objectives is easier said than done. Muddling through not only appeals to ministers who wish to avoid being pinned down on specific intentions or priorities but also, to a point, represents a logical approach in the context of rapidly changing and turbulent environments. Flexibility, adaptiveness and corrective action can be more easily accommodated by those whose goals are not cast in stone. However, there is a price to be paid for this strategy. Governments characterized by major fluctuations in what is pursued are less able to have their policies translated into meaningful missions and operational tasks. Their policy objectives may reflect changing circumstances, yet their capacity to produce the desired outcomes is impeded by constant efforts to steer in different directions. What governments actually achieve is inevitably minimized by conflicting and inconsistent signals to those responsible for implementing policy, especially when policy objectives are multiple. Goal displacement by government departments and agencies is often the result.

The recent commitment of the Liberal government in Canada to a business plan model suggests that the advantages of being clear about policy objectives are once again to be pursued. The willingness of the government to use robust performance targets and measures, and to undertake program evaluations and make them part of the public record will constitute the test of its commitment to enhanced performance. Its resolve to adhere to a performance-based approach to maintain a strategic perspective in "getting government right" will also be tested by its ongoing program review exercise. Political considerations cannot be ruled out of strategic decision making, but if they begin to overwhelm attempts to enhance performance, as has too often been the Canadian experience over the last three decades, effective public policies and expenditure discipline will be the first casualties.

At the same time, the stated commitment to a client-focused approach to quality public services must move beyond the rhetoric that has too often resulted in scepticism among public servants and cynicism among citizens. In some large part, scepticism and cynicism have been fuelled by ministerial indifference to the plight of public servants who must seek simultaneously to maintain service levels and improve service quality with diminishing resources as well as by ministerial unwillingness to engage citizens directly on the issue of what can be afforded for particular services. Budgetary decisions that cut resources in the aggregate may reduce spending, but they do little to address either of these matters. Reshaping government priorities is as difficult a task as clarifying policy objectives; indeed it is part of the same exercise. It therefore also requires ministerial leadership if political consent is to be secured. If this leadership is not forthcoming, new forms of service delivery, as important as they may be to promoting quality service, will lack the necessary citizen and client support to achieve cost-effectiveness. In only a few cases can public servants respond to citizens and clients as customers; for the most part, there must be concerted political action to support efforts by public servants to involve citizens and clients in the design of services that meet their requirements, that are consistent with stated policy objectives and that are affordable. Unilateral or arbitrary decisions by public servants in redesigning public services and public service delivery are unlikely to satisfy these criteria. The crucial importance of developing and deploying service standards both as a process to involve citizens in the design of services and service delivery systems and as the means to enhance performance by specifying performance targets, measures and reporting requirements should not be underestimated. Without a commitment to performance management, even the best designs and delivery systems will succumb to bureaucratic pathologies as they are implemented.

Notes

1. Organisation for Economic Co-operation and Development, *Performance Management in Government: Performance Measurement and Results-Oriented Management* (Paris: OECD, 1994).

2. Canada, *New Management Initiatives: Initial Results from the Ministerial Task Force on Program Review* (Ottawa, May 1985), p. iii.

3. Public Policy Forum, "Toward a New Consultative Process: Lessons from the Nielsen Task Force," Ottawa, October 29, 1993.

4. Ian Clark, "Restraint, renewal, and the Treasury Board Secretariat," *Canadian Public Administration*, Vol. 37, no. 2 (Summer 1994), p. 215.

5. Quoted in Peter Aucoin and Herman Bakvis, *The Centralization-Decentralization Conundrum: Organization and Management in the Canadian Government* (Halifax: Institute for Research on Public Policy, 1988), p. 52.

6. Canada, Government of Canada, *The Expenditure Management System of the Government of Canada* (Ottawa: Minister of Supply and Services, 1995), pp. 5-6.

7. *The Expenditure Management System of the Government of Canada*, p. 6.

8. *The Expenditure Management System of the Government of Canada*, p. 6.

9. Canada, Steering Group on Special Operating Agencies, *Special Operating Agencies: Taking Stock. Final Report*, May 1994, p. 21.

10. *Special Operating Agencies*, p. 25.

11. *Special Operating Agencies*, p. 25.

12. *Special Operating Agencies*, p. 6.

13. *Special Operating Agencies*, p. 4.

14. Canada, Auditor General of Canada, *Report to the House of Commons for the Fiscal Year ended March 31, 1992* (Ottawa: Minister of Supply and Services, 1992), pp. 163-80; Canada, Auditor General of Canada, *Report of the Auditor General of Canada to the House of Commons, 1993* (Ottawa: Minister of Supply and Services, 1993), pp. 159-85.

15. A.W. Johnson, "Reflections on administrative reform in the government of Canada 1962-1991," Discussion Paper, Ottawa, Office of the Auditor General of Canada, 1992, p. 26.

16. Johnson, "Reflections on administrative reform," p. 27.

17. Arthur Kroeger, "The budget and the public service – good news with the bad," *Public Sector Management*, Vol. 6, no. 2 (1995), pp. 4-5.

18. Keith Mackay, "Evaluation – What's in it for You," paper prepared for Department of Finance SES Officers on "Trends in Public Sector Financial Management," Department of Finance, Commonwealth of Australia, July 14, 1994.

19. *Report of the Auditor General* (1993), chap. 6; Colin Campbell and John Halligan, *Political Leadership in an Age of Constraint: Bureaucratic Politics Under Hawke and Keating* (St. Leonards, Australia: Allen and Unwin, 1992), p. 192; R.J. Gregory, "The Attitudes of Senior Public Servants in Australia and New Zealand: Administrative Reform and Technocratic Consequence?", *Governance*, Vol. 4, no. 3 (July 1991), pp. 295-331; Spencer Zifcak, *New Managerialism: Administrative Reform in Whitehall and Canberra* (Buckingham: Open University Press, 1994), pp. 92-133.

20. United Kingdom, Prime Minister, Chancellor of the Exchequer and Chancellor of the Duchy of Lancaster, *The Civil Service: Continuity and Change* (London: HMSO, July 1994), pp. 24-25.

21. *The Civil Service*, pp. 23-24.

22. Christopher Pollitt, "Occasional Excursions: A Brief History of Policy Evaluation in the UK," *Parliamentary Affairs*, Vol. 46, no. 3 (July 1993), pp. 353-62; Neil Carter, "Learning to Measure Performance: The Use of Indicators in Organizations," *Public Administration*, Vol. 69 (Spring 1991), pp. 85-101.

23. *The Civil Service*, p. 14.

24. New Zealand, The Treasury, *Government Management* (Wellington: Government Printer, 1987), p. 76.

25. Jonathan Boston, "Purchasing Policy Advice: the Limits of Contracting Out," *Governance*, Vol. 7, no. 1 (January 1994), pp. 1-30.

26. Canada, Office of the Auditor General, *Toward Better Governance: Public Service Reform in New Zealand (1984-94) and its Relevance to Canada* (Ottawa: Minister of Supply and Services, 1995), p. 51.

27. *Toward Better Governance*, p. 48.

28. Quoted in *Toward Better Governance*, p. 48.

29. R.G. Laking, "Developing a culture of success: reflections on the New Zealand experiences," paper presented to the Commonwealth Association of Public Administration and Management, Charlottetown, Prince Edward Island, August 29-31, 1994.

30. Ian Ball, "Outcome Specification," paper presented at the Public Sector Convention of the New Zealand Society of Accountants, November 1992.

31. Donald J. Savoie, *Thatcher, Reagan, Mulroney: In Search of a New Bureaucracy* (Toronto: University of Toronto Press, 1994), pp. 270-74.

32. Canada, Government of Canada, *Public Service 2000: The Renewal of the Public Service of Canada* (Ottawa: Minister of Supply and Services, 1990), p. 90.

33. Clark, "Restraint, renewal, and the Treasury Board Secretariat," p. 235.

34. Canada, Clerk of the Privy Council and Secretary to the Cabinet, *Third Annual Report to the Prime Minister on the Public Service of Canada* (Ottawa: Minister of Supply and Services, 1995).

35. Sandford Borins, "Government in Transition: A New Paradigm in Public Administration," Report on the Inaugural Conference of the Commonwealth Association for Public Administration and Management, Charlottetown, Prince Edward Island, August 28-31, 1994.

36. Kenneth Kernaghan, "Partnership and public administration: conceptual and practical considerations," *Canadian Public Administration*, Vol. 36, no. 1 (Spring 1993), pp. 57-76; Canada, Clerk of the Privy Council and Secretary to the Cabinet, *Public Service 2000: A Report on Progress* (Ottawa: Minister of Supply and Services, 1992), p. 16.

37. Sandford Borins, "Public Sector Innovation: the Implications of New Forms of Organization and Work," in B. Guy Peters and Donald J. Savoie (eds.), *Governance in a Changing Environment* (Montreal: McGill-Queen's University Press, 1995), pp. 260-87; Kenneth Kernaghan, "Choose your partners – it's innovation time!", *Public Sector Management*, Vol. 3, no. 2 (Fall 1992), pp. 16-17; Donald J. Savoie, "Innovating to do better with less," *Public Sector Management*, Vol. 4, no. 1 (Spring 1993), pp. 15-17; F. Leslie Seidle, *Rethinking the Delivery of Public Services to Citizens* (Montreal: Institute for Research on Public Policy, 1995), chap. 1; G. Bruce Doern, *The Road to Better Public Services: Progress and Constraints in Five Canadian Federal Agencies* (Montreal: Institute for Research on Public Policy, 1994).

38. Canada, Task Force on Service to the Public, *Public Service 2000: Service to the Public. Report in Brief*, October 12, 1990.

39. *Public Service 2000: The Renewal of the Public Service of Canada*, p. 55.

40. Ian Clark, "On re-engineering the public service of Canada," *Public Sector Management*, Vol. 4, no. 4 (1994), p. 224; emphasis added.

41. Clark, "On re-engineering the public service of Canada," p. 224.

42. These points were made by departmental officials in studies of the restructuring, as experienced by the seven most affected departments, undertaken for the Canadian Centre for Management Development.

43. Canada, Treasury Board Secretariat, "Outlook on Program Priorities and Expenditures," June 5, 1995, p. 4.

44. Aucoin and Bakvis, *The Centralization-Decentralization Conundrum*, pp. 89-113.

45. Barbara Wake Carroll and David Siegel, "Two solitudes or one big happy family: head office-field office relations in government organizations," paper presented to the Annual meeting of the Canadian Political Science Association, Montreal, June 5, 1995.

46. James Q. Wilson, *Bureaucracy: What Government Agencies Do and Why They Do It* (New York: Basic Books, 1989), pp. 25-26.

47. Seidle, *Rethinking the Delivery of Public Services to Citizens*, chap. 1.

48. Norman Lewis, "The Citizen's Charter and Next Steps: A New Way of Governing?", *The*

Political Quarterly, Vol. 64, no. 3 (July-September 1993), pp. 316-26.

49. Bill Jenkins and Andrew Gray, "Reshaping the Management of Government: The Next Steps Initiative in the United Kingdom," in F. Leslie Seidle (ed.), *Rethinking Government: Reform or Reinvention?* (Montreal: Institute for Research on Public Policy, 1993), pp. 73-109; Christopher Pollitt, "Management Techniques for the Public Sector: Pulpit and Practice," in Peters and Savoie (eds.), *Governance in a Changing Environment*, pp. 203-38; Patricia Greer, *Transforming Central Government: The Next Steps Initiative* (Buckingham: Open University Press, 1994).

50. Les Metcalfe, "Conviction Politics and Dynamic Conservatism: Mrs. Thatcher's Managerial Revolution," *International Political Science Review*, Vol. 14, no. 4 (October 1993), pp. 351-71.

51. Seidle, *Rethinking the Delivery of Public Services to Citizens*, chap. 2.

52. Bryne Purchase and Ronald Hirshhorn, *Searching for Good Governance* (Kingston: School of Policy Studies, Queen's University, 1994), pp. 54-59.

53. Michael J. Trebilcock, *The Prospects for Reinventing Government* (Toronto: C.D. Howe Institute, 1994), pp. 52-61.

54. Jonathan Boston, John Martin and Pat Walsh, "Conclusion," in Jonathan Boston, John Martin, June Pallot and Pat Walsh (eds.), *Reshaping the State: New Zealand's Bureaucratic Revolution* (Auckland: Oxford University Press, 1991), p. 389.

55. Laking, "Developing a culture of success," p. 10.

56. Boston, Martin, Pallot and Walsh (eds.), *Reshaping the State.*

57. Michael Keating, "Managing for Results in the Public Interest," *Australian Journal of Public Administration*, Vol. 49, no. 4 (1990), p. 395.

58. Australia, Task Force on Management Improvement, *The Australian Public Service Reformed: An Evaluation of a Decade of Management Reform* (Canberra: Australian Government Publishing Service, December 1992), p. 400.

59. *The Australian Public Service Reformed*, p. 422.

60. Seidle, *Rethinking the Delivery of Public Services to Citizens*, chap. 3.

61. *The Australian Public Service Reformed*, p. 403.

62. Christopher Pollitt, Martin Cave and Richard Joss, "International benchmarking as a tool to improve public sector performance: a critical overview," in Organisation for Economic Co-operation and Development, *Performance Measurement in Government: Issues and Illustrations* (Paris: OECD, 1994), pp. 7-22.

63. Michael Keating and Malcolm Holmes, "Australia's Budgetary and Financial Management Reforms," *Governance*, Vol. 3, no. 2 (April 1990), pp. 180-81.

64. Jon Pierre, "The Marketization of the State: Citizens, Consumers, and the Emergence of the Public Market," in Peters and Savoie (eds.) *Governance in a Changing Environment*, pp. 55-81.

65. Peter Aucoin, "Administrative Reform in . Public Management: Paradigms, Principles, Paradoxes and Pendulums," *Governance*, Vol. 3, no. 2 (April 1990), pp. 128-29.

EIGHT

Securing Accountability

Perhaps the most elusive dimension of the new public management is its effect on accountability. Public management reformers in each of the four Westminster systems have spoken of the need to improve accountability of government and ministers to the legislature; of public servants to ministers; of public servants to their public service superiors; and, in certain respects, of public servants to legislators and even citizens directly. The several meanings attached to accountability derive from different understandings of the purposes of accountability and how they relate to one another.

Under the Westminster system, a government requires the confidence of the House of Commons to remain in office and carry out its program. Aside from determining who will occupy the executive offices of government and giving (or withholding) approval to government legislation, the principal obligation of the Commons is holding government to account for its management of public affairs, including the public purse.

Within this framework of parliamentary government, the exercise of executive powers by ministers, collectively and individually, is distinct from the exercise of legislative powers, which is shared between the government and the legislature that together constitute the Crown-in-Parliament. Ministers are the executive officers of government and public servants their subordinates. The tradition has been that public servants report and are accountable either directly to ministers, as with deputy ministers in Canada, or to their public service superiors through a hierarchical arrangement of offices. In a few cases, public servants report directly to Parliament, as in the case of "accounting officers" (see below). Otherwise, when public servants appear before parliamentary committees or speak publicly, they do so on behalf of their ministers. In this sense, they are deemed to be "servants of the Crown," whatever the statutory provisions of their employment.

Even before the advent of the new public management, the effectiveness of the Westminster system of ministerial responsibility and accountability was in question. As parliamentarians began to challenge the capacity of Parliament to control government, changes in institutional arrangements were made. But two aspects of the new public management have brought the issue of ministerial *and* public service responsibility and accountability to a head.

First, devolution initiatives raise the question of whether ministers can or should be held personally accountable for the actions of public servants to whom authority and responsibility have been delegated, particularly when formal agreements or contracts are the instruments of delegation. Second, the new public management demands that public servants be client-, even customer-focused. The responsiveness that this requires implies that public servants consider themselves to be the servants of citizens, and thus accountable to them.

The new public management also emphasizes the need for accountability in order to improve performance. The focus here goes beyond the matter of the control of government as such; the accountability regime, in other words, is meant to be a means not only to responsible government but also to good government. Some aspects of reporting, auditing and evaluating performance conform to traditional understandings of ministerial responsibility in securing accountability. But some, it is argued, do not. This is particularly true when public servants rather than ministers are deemed to be responsible for performance and therefore directly accountable to Parliament or to citizens.

In Search of the Missing Link

In its assessment of previous federal government efforts to improve public management, the 1990 White Paper, *Public Service 2000: The Renewal of the Public Service of Canada*, stated that: "The missing link all along has been effective accountability for the use of the authorities with which people have been entrusted."[1] The effective accountability sought by the Public Service 2000 initiative focused exclusively on enhancing accountability for "results" within government, that is, the accountability of deputy ministers and of officials down the line to each "level of management."[2] At no point in the elaboration of the principles on which Public Service 2000 was based was it thought necessary to depart from the traditional doctrine of public service accountability as accountability solely to ministers.

By 1990, the issue of accountability in the Canadian system had been transformed by several developments. On the control side, parliamentary committees were seeking to extract an accounting from public servants as well as ministers. Indeed, successive efforts at parliamentary reform, particularly after the Conservatives came to power in 1984, led to demands for direct public service accountability to newly empowered parliamentary committees. This idea had been recommended by the Royal Commission on Financial Management and Accountability in its 1979 report and had been reinforced by calls from Auditor General James Macdonell to bring public servants, as he put it to a parliamentary committee in 1982, "out of the closet."[3]

The accountability regime was transformed in several other respects. The Auditor General's mandate was enlarged in 1977 to encompass what was then called "comprehensive auditing" (now more modestly titled "value for money" auditing). Using these new powers, successive auditors general have sought to audit the quality of management and management systems in government departments and agencies by focusing on a broader scope of administrative behaviour. Although debate about public service accountability has largely centred on the roles of parliamentary committees and the Auditor General, there have been many other developments. These include the enactment of freedom of information legislation, an expansion in the number of parliamentary oversight agencies,[4] new administrative law regimes in which tribunals and the courts have greater control over executive and administrative powers, and the adoption of the constitutional Charter of Rights and Freedoms, with its implications for judicial review. All these have contributed to a public service that is much less anonymous and more tightly controlled than has been the Canadian norm.

Sharon Sutherland, writing in early 1991, argued convincingly that the traditional doctrine of ministerial responsibility was at odds with changing practice. As she noted: "On a haphazard basis officials are being held directly to account."[5] As a consequence, a number of "distortions" had been introduced into the traditional model of ministerial responsibility.[6]

Parliamentary committees deemed public servants, especially deputy ministers, to fall within their oversight mandates; the Auditor General argued for the right to subject policy advice to audit; and ministers were willing to name and blame officials in Parliament.

By the end of 1991, Sutherland had an even more damning critique to offer, given the behaviour of several ministers, a number of senior public servants, including the Clerk of the Privy Council, and a House of Commons committee in their handling of the celebrated Al-Mashat affair. In this instance, the government decided to hold a public servant and a political aide publicly accountable for a particular incident and to subject them to a parliamentary committee enquiry. Sutherland's incisive account of this affair demonstrated the inherent contradiction between ministerial responsibility and direct public service accountability to Parliament.[7] In this case, the political process denied these two officials recourse to the principles of natural justice because their obligations to respect ministerial confidences meant that they could not "speak fully in their own defence."[8] It also let ministers escape personal responsibility. As Sutherland put it: "The impression was created that accountability will rest with the most senior person unfortunate enough to miss the key meeting."[9]

In response, Paul Tellier, as the Head of the Public Service and the Clerk involved in this case, reasserted the traditional doctrine in his 1992 report to the Prime Minister and in a companion document to that report.[10] This reassertion did not suggest that any change was necessary with respect to how officials answer questions before parliamentary committees. Rather, the report stated that this process was best governed by "the practices that have grown up in Parliament's standing and legislative committees."[11] It "is not a matter of distinguishing clearly between policy and administration, as is sometimes suggested and which is generally difficult and often impossible to do. Rather, it is a question of distinguishing, case by case, between matters which are politically controversial, and those which are not." Politically controversial matters, the report went on to suggest, are those "that involve the House's confidence in Ministers."[12] How this distinction clarified the proper conduct of public servants in answering parliamentary questions, especially in light of Sutherland's account of "the essentially unpredictable style of discipline in the Al-Mashat affair,"[13] was not made clear.

This understanding of accountability, however, was not at odds with the views of ministers or senior officials. In his 1988 study of the accountability of deputy ministers, Gordon Osbaldeston reported that there was no support among the ministers and deputy ministers interviewed for his study for changes to traditional practice.[14] Ministers wished to have complete authority over the direction and management of their departments, and deputies confirmed that ministers did, in fact, concern themselves with virtually all aspects of departmental policy and operations, at least sporadically. They argued that it was not possible to separate ministerial and deputy ministerial authorities and responsibilities. Even when appearing before the Public Accounts Committee, with respect to their responsibilities for financial administration delegated to them by the Treasury Board, deputies considered themselves appearing "on behalf of their minister."[15] Both ministers and deputies, however, did admit that changes had led to some "confusion" among participants, "strains" between ministers and deputies, "conflicts" between ministers and parliamentarians and a general lack of "understanding" by parliamentarians of the respective roles of ministers, deputies and MPs on parliamentary committees.[16]

In his analysis, Osbaldeston acknowledged that "[c]onceptually, any accountability process should consist of three stages: the setting of expectations, the pursuit of expected goals, and the holding to account for performance." But he also stated that: "In the reality of government, the first stage can be incredibly difficult to achieve, casting doubt on how to carry out the second and third. In some cases, the setting of expectations by the minister never happens at all. What implications does this have for the accountability of the deputy minister?"[17] No answer to this question was given, either by Osbaldeston or those whom he interviewed. Although the latter admitted that confusion abounded in the system, this could be resolved, it was suggested, by establishing a basis of "trust" between ministers and deputies, in part by lengthening the time that deputies remained in their positions.[18]

The confusion is partly due to the many inexperienced ministers and parliamentarians in parliamentary-cabinet government in Canada as a result of the high turnover in parliamentary elections. In addition, the system itself is confusing because individual ministers do not, in fact, have complete authority over the direction and management of their departments. The Prime Minister, and not the minister, appoints deputy ministers (and associate deputies) and may give directions to them. The Public Service Commission appoints the senior executives below these two ranks as well as entry-level public servants; for the rest, it delegates staffing powers to deputies and not to ministers. The Treasury Board possesses a wide range of powers that limit the authority of individual ministers, as well as any authority delegated to deputies or other officials, over the direction and management of departments. And, without exhausting the list of limits, all major and many minor ministerial initiatives are subject to the approval of, and often amendment by, cabinet colleagues.

Accountabilities, accordingly, become "multiple," as Osbaldeston put it.[19] The failure to develop an accountability regime that sorts out these multiple accountabilities frustrates the efforts of parliamentary committees and others, including the Auditor General, to extract accountability from ministers, or anyone else, for departmental performance. Within government, deputies and departmental officials themselves feel frustrated by the absence of such a framework. Their accountabilities are multiple because there is a large and increasing number of functional control groups in the several branches of the Treasury Board Secretariat, the Public Service Commission and other oversight agencies that focus exclusively on particular dimensions of departmental management. In this design, no one is responsible for holding deputies to account for overall departmental management and performance as such.[20]

The extent to which authority has been delegated by central management authorities has merely compounded this deficiency in the accountability system, notwithstanding the rhetoric of such initiatives as the Increased Ministerial Authority and Accountability system or Public Service 2000. In each case, the multiplicity of accountabilities merely increased; questions of control and accountability became even further conflated and confused.

Efforts to improve accountability on several fronts continued to be made by the government, urged on by officials, parliamentary committees and agencies, especially the Auditor General. As noted in the previous chapter, the most recent manifestation is the 1995 announcement of the new Expenditure Management System (EMS), with the government's commitment to enhancing accountability by "focusing on performance."[21] The principal instruments for doing so include changes and improvements to reporting on performance against plans in the context of the Estimates process; published service standards and reporting on performance against these standards; and the publication of program evaluation plans and their findings.

The issues of public service accountability that Public Service 2000 sought to address are not unrelated to these commitments. The prospects for clearer accountability are greater now, at least to the extent that central agency controls over departments have been diminished. However, as the current Clerk acknowledged in her 1995 report, the "rigorous accountability regimes" adopted in other jurisdictions with the creation of "specialized organizations" for "program delivery" have not featured prominently in Canadian federal government reform efforts to date.[22]

Comparative Experiences

In the other three Westminster systems, the more aggressive adoption of the new public management has resulted in controversial efforts to secure accountability.

In Britain, accountability has been a focus of debate partly because of a series of celebrated cases in which ministers tried to evade responsibility even though the circumstances of the cases had little to do with changes in authority or responsibility structures. However, attempts to separate responsibility for policy and operations, as Colin Campbell and Graham Wilson note,[23] have had at least an indirect effect on the practice of ministerial responsibility. Many ministers now feel that they have a legitimate right to deny responsibility whenever they can pin it on public servants by claiming that the matter was an "operational" issue.

The British have long had a practice of designating permanent secretaries as "accounting officers" with the responsibility of providing an account, on their own behalf, on matters of financial management to the Public Accounts Committee. This practice has been extended to the chief executives of executive agencies, who also appear before parliamentary select committees. As recently as 1995, however, the government rejected the idea of an extension of direct public service accountability beyond the accounting officer regime.[24] Such an approach had been contemplated when the original idea of executive agencies was broached within government and, more recently, as proposed by the Treasury and Civil Service Committee in its 1994 report on the civil service.[25] The government had earlier accepted this same Committee's recommendation that chief executives respond directly to MPs' questions on the operational aspects of executive agencies, and these replies are now published in *Hansard*. However, it has continued to insist that public servants, including agency chief executives, are accountable to ministers and that only ministers are responsible to Parliament.

At the same time, the government has responded to its critics who charge that a "democratic deficit" has befallen the British practice of responsible government as a result of the adoption of the Next Steps executive agency regime.[26] In a 1993 speech, William Waldegrave, at the time minister responsible for the public service, argued that the several reporting requirements of the executive agencies (respecting framework documents, annual targets, reports and accounts, corporate and business plans, and citizen's charters) have "made transparent the links in the accountability chain which were pretty much obscure before." This means, he argued, that "management responsibility has actually never been clearer."[27]

The debate in Britain over the government's contention that management responsibility has become clearer and more transparent is complicated by the government's claim that the conventions of ministerial responsibility remain in place, especially when set against the practice of public service accountability to Parliament, its committees and agencies. Nonetheless, a comprehensive academic examination of relations between Parliament, including its parliamentary committees and parliamentary agencies, and executive agencies concludes that "the new arrangements do in fact bring the responsible officials (chief executives) much closer to Parliament." It goes on to state that "the greater openness about targets and objectives which has come with the agency program provides an opportunity for greater accountability to Parliament for both ministers and senior civil servants since what is publicly announced is more easily scrutinised and monitored."[28] It is also acknowledged that this has meant a decline in ministerial responsibility for government operations since ministers refuse to accept responsibility for matters that they state have been delegated. In the absence of a freedom of information regime, it is difficult for Parliament, or anyone else outside of government, to determine the exact nature of these ministerial-public service relationships beyond what the government decides to make public.[29]

While the government's critics insist that gaps remain in the accountability regime, most acknowledge that there has been considerable support across the partisan divide in Parliament for the new arrangements, at least insofar as they have enhanced *de facto* direct public service accountability to parliamentary committees.[30] Improved performance information and reporting have also strengthened ministerial responsibility despite efforts by ministers to escape accountability. Greater transparency has exacted a price because attempts to duck responsibility have become more difficult to hide. The Home Secretary recently discovered this when he sought to escape accountability for his responsibilities for the management of the Prison Service by sacking the service's chief executive.[31]

Within government, accountabilities have been clarified to a considerable extent, particularly with regard to the management of the executive agencies. As in Canada, however, the heavy hand of departments and central agencies has meant that various aspects of financial and personnel administration severely limit what chief executives and their subordinates can do to meet their responsibilities. More important, however, is the fact, as demonstrated in the 1995 firing of the head of the Prison Service, that chief executives and other senior officials not covered by civil service regulations are subject to arbitrary dismissal by ministers. When ministers and chief executives disagree on how to manage an agency (except in relation to specific financial transactions as covered by the accounting officer regime), there is no recourse for chief executives to provide an account to Parliament or any other governmental authority if their minister fires them. Pursuing legal action against a minister after the fact is hardly a satisfactory course from the perspective of good public management, let alone proper public accountability.

In Australia, the question of public accountability has been front and centre in the changes to public management for at least two reasons. First, because of the emphasis on results, considerable effort has been made to improve reporting on performance, both in the annual budgetary process and in departmental annual reports.[32] In each case, the aim was to enhance ministerial control over the public service by setting policy objectives, promoting a greater concern for the management of resources, focusing greater attention on outcomes and evaluating performance against desired results. The expectation was that the accountability of the government and individual ministers to Parliament would be strengthened.

The second reason was that, before these reforms, there were several initiatives aimed at enhancing accountability as control, including the creation of an administrative appeals tribunal, an ombudsman, a freedom of information act and measures to expand the scope of judicial review. The combined effect was the subjection of ministers and public servants to the most extensive array of external scrutiny and controls found in the four Westminster systems.

There has been a significant measure of debate over these approaches to accountability, in part because the government has continued to insist that public accountability within the Westminster system means ministerial responsibility as traditionally defined. The reality, however, is that public servants have become increasingly accountable to parliamentary committees, especially the Senate's estimates committees.[33] Because the government still claims that public servants do not speak on their own behalf, they are exposed to a kind of scrutiny in which they have few, if any, rights of self-defence. They are at the mercy of parliamentarians seeking to score political points or ministers who name and blame them and, in the case of those appointed by the prerogative power, who impose sanctions.[34]

The result is confusion, especially insofar as the Australian reforms have been predicated on the need to enhance public service responsiveness to ministers.[35] This has strengthened internal accountability in various ways but, when combined with reforms to enhance accountability for the performance of the government and departments, it has left public service accountability to Parliament and citizens even more muddled. Furthermore, the construction of an elaborate administrative law regime has added new forms of public service accountability that do not fit with the realities of public servants being left undefended in the arena of parliamentary committees or at the mercy of ministerial whims.

In New Zealand, the way ministers are required to direct departments was changed dramatically by statutory alterations in the relationships of ministers to their chief executives. Chief executives are responsible to ministers for the performance of their departments in providing the outputs that ministers purchase through an explicit contractual arrangement that binds ministers and chief executives and is transparent in the annual budgetary and parliamentary appropriations process. Ministers are thus accountable to Parliament not only for the outcomes they pursue but also for the specific outputs they purchase to realize these outcomes. In each of these respects, the traditional conventions of ministerial responsibility remain in force. Ministers are able to alter these contracts in response to unforeseen circumstances, but any such alterations must also be transparent. Ministers, in short, cannot change what has been agreed to without altering contracts for outputs.

Chief executives are thereby responsible and accountable to ministers, and not to Parliament directly. Their contracts for outputs are contracts with ministers. At the same time, their personal contracts are with the State Services Commissioner, and only this independent official can impose sanctions and rewards on chief executives. For instance, chief executives cannot be dismissed by their ministers individually or by Cabinet, although the State Services Commissioner will take ministerial or cabinet concerns into account in assessing the performance of chief executives. In turn, chief executives have full authority over their departmental subordinates. In these ways, the New Zealand approach combines the traditional conventions of ministerial responsibility with an independently staffed and managed public service, even though chief executives (and many of their subordinates) are no longer appointed for tenure but to fixed-term contracts. Indeed, tenure has disappeared from the personnel regime of the New Zealand public service.

The effectiveness of this regime in securing accountability depends on two major developments.[36] First, the process for determining ministerial and chief executive responsibilities is transparent. Parliament knows what has been agreed to with regard to both outcomes and outputs. This includes the specifications of output contracts as well as the accounting for the full costs of outputs, encompassing both direct costs and indirect costs of maintaining the capital and other assets of government. The use of accrual accounting in this context has increased the scope of information available to Parliament. Second, under the provisions of the statutory framework governing ministerial-chief executive relationships, and subject to their individual contracts, chief executives are assigned authority and responsibility for the management of the full range of financial, personnel and capital resources deployed in the provision of outputs. They are thus accountable for the use they make of these resources, including adherence to the corporate management policies of the government and its central authorities. In these ways, they are accountable to ministers for their performance in the provision of outputs as well as for the management of resources.

Although chief executives and their subordinates are not directly accountable to Parliament *via* its committees under this regime, the explicit and transparent character of their responsibilities has made it possible for parliamentary committees and parliamentary agencies to have a much clearer understanding of the respective responsibilities of ministers and departmental officials. The requirements of public reporting to Parliament and external auditing by parliamentary agencies make it easier for parliamentarians to assess the performance of chief executives and their departments in meeting their responsibilities. This has not led MPs to "terrorize" public servants, as Sutherland portrays the Canadian experience.[37] However, the exposure of public servants to parliamentary scrutiny has led, as elsewhere, to diminished anonymity. At the same time, the clarity and transparency of the accountability regime better enable MPs to focus their criticisms on ministers; they have less incentive to abuse public servants in an indirect attempt to get at their ministers. And public servants are better able than elsewhere to defend themselves against attacks by MPs because their responsibilities are more clearly specified.

The principal weakness in the New Zealand accountability regime has been the limited capacity of Parliament to make effective use of the significant improvements in performance reporting and transparency even though, as the Logan Report put it, "[a] principal objective of the Public Finance Act 1989 was to improve accountability to Parliament."[38] The size of Parliament, the absence of a second chamber, the relative paucity of support services for parliamentary committees and the disinclination of ministers to appear before committees have all weakened this crucial link in the accountability system. Furthermore, without the pressures emanating from Parliament, ministers are less inclined to hold their chief executives accountable for performance, particularly in meeting output requirements and in the stewardship of government resources. They are more inclined to hold them to account for the policy advice the executives give them, which invariably has a more immediate political consequence. Some of this is no doubt transitional. In any event, the adoption of a proportional representation electoral system, with its expected consequence of coalition government, may well alter relations between the government and Parliament in ways that advance parliamentary scrutiny and attention. What this might mean for public service accountability to Parliament cannot be predicted with any certainty, but any enhancement in the powers of Parliament is likely to bring a greater focus on performance management generally.

Comparative Perspectives

The incentive for improving accountability in each of the four systems has been the need both for enhanced ministerial control and enhanced control of ministers.[39] In this second regard, the capacities of Parliament in each system has hampered progress toward stronger accountability. In New Zealand, as noted, both the size and limited resources of the legislature have restricted significant improvements in reporting to Parliament. In Canada, the high turnover in the House of Commons means that relatively few MPs have the knowledge or experience to scrutinize government, notwithstanding the considerable resources provided to Parliament and its extensive array of audit and review agencies. But even in Australia and Britain, with their comparatively more independent legislatures, at least in terms of scrutiny, Parliament is seen to be ineffective in securing ministerial accountability.

However, despite Parliament's limited capacities, it is clear that governments are subject to greater exposure than they were even a decade or two ago, a development partially brought about by public management reforms including new reporting requirements. For the most part, these changes are due to larger political forces present in most western democracies. The media, interest groups and citizens generally have demanded a greater accounting from government, and governments, however reluctantly or haltingly, have been required to respond.

Within this new politics of public accountability, there have been questions about the fine line between the accounting extracted from ministers by Parliament, requiring them to justify and defend their management of public affairs, and the accounting extracted from public servants by parliamentary committees, requiring them to describe and explain the policies and programs of government. Because ministers possess executive authority and responsibilities, there are no executive designs for the delegation of ministerial authority and responsibilities that can justify ministers not assuming public accountability. Ministers have the constitutional power to delegate authority and responsibility to advance good government, but this does not relieve them of accountability for such delegations. For its part, Parliament has the constitutional obligation to extract an account from ministers. It also has the obligation, however, to extract an account from public servants, especially when authority and responsibility have been delegated. The precise ways by which committees exercise their powers vary across the four systems.

Ministers, of course, do at times act irresponsibly. They fail to give a full or accurate account of themselves; they obstruct the capacity of Parliament to obtain an account from their officials; or they deflect blame onto officials. Partisan dynamics may enable ministers to escape sanctions, but even though the interests of the government and opposition are not the same, this hardly serves the public interest in the proper functioning of responsible government.

Parliamentarians, at times, may also act irresponsibly, attempting to score political points against ministers by taking advantage of their interactions with public servants before parliamentary committees. For public servants, all of this can be unpleasant. They are caught in the crossfire between government and opposition in their efforts to meet two obligations: first, to answer questions about policy as well as administration; and second, to remain neutral to the ideological and political rationales for the decisions and actions of ministers. This situation has led to a confusion of public service *accountability* with *answerability* in parliamentary (and other public) forums.

Clearly, the conventions of ministerial responsibility have been increasingly corrupted by the view that ministers cannot personally "manage" their portfolios and, therefore, should not be held personally responsible for all that is done within their departments or agencies. While this view predates the new public management, it has gained greater currency as a result of the importance attached by the new public management to devolution and the separation of responsibilities for policy and operations. This concept of management is either excessively simplistic or excessively mechanistic or both. It presupposes that managers manage only when they can personally direct and supervise their subordinates, as a shopkeeper might, or otherwise set rules and regulations for subordinates that govern their behaviour in every respect, as in a highly routinized production factory.

While this view of management might be expected from parliamentarians who have had no direct experience in managing complex organizations, it is ironic that its propagation has largely come from the private sector, invariably from individuals whose experience is with major business corporations in which chief executive officers are held personally accountable for the performance of their organizations, no matter how complex, diversified and decentralized their management systems may be. This limited concept of management has corrupted the conventions of ministerial responsibility by denying the minister is the executive authority in charge of a portfolio and substituting the deputy minister (permanent head, departmental secretary or chief executive) as the "senior officer of the department," as a Canadian special committee on reform of the House of Commons expressed it.[40] Following the logic of this view, deputy ministers (and other officials) must be personally accountable to Parliament in ways that go beyond answering to parliamentary committees as witnesses in support of Parliament's obligation to scrutinize executive action.

If ministers are not personally responsible for the management of their portfolios because they must delegate authority, then, it is argued, those to whom authority is delegated must be. In addition to the obvious complications arising from the fact that deputy ministers or chief executives also delegate authority, the fundamental flaw in this idea of direct public service accountability is that there is no way for a Parliament to sort out who is responsible for specific policies, decisions and actions in the absence of well-defined contractual relationships between delegators and delegatees. Without such arrangements, the assumption is absurd that such assessments could be made in the ongoing management of complex organizations in politically controversial cases brought into the partisan arena of Parliament.

It is not merely self-interest, accordingly, that has led governments in the four Westminster systems to defend the traditional principle of ministerial responsibility. Public servants may benefit from this principle if they are not held publicly accountable for their use of delegated authority or their performance generally. But what is at issue is the public interest in responsible government. Direct public service accountability to Parliament, without clearly delineated contractual arrangements, such as exist in New Zealand for departmental chief executives and in Britain for the chief executives of agencies, diminishes the responsibility of ministers and therefore their control of their departments and agencies. Targeting ministers indirectly through direct public service accountability does not secure ministerial accountability; it merely invites partisan manipulation of the evidence before Parliament.

The reassertion of the traditional view of ministerial responsibility, however, has not prevented parliamentary committees from demanding that public servants appear before them to provide accounts of government and departmental performance or to respond to audits and reviews, especially those performed by parliamentary agents, most notably auditors general. Indeed, this exposure has increased, in part because audit agencies have extended their coverage of public management beyond the traditional verification of financial accounts to encompass value-for-money audits.

The objective of many parliamentarians is to direct or control the public service in line with their own policy agendas, despite their lack of any constitutional authority to do so. Although this has hardly resulted in the degree of micro-management practised by the American Congress, the intent is similar, namely to get the public service to do the bidding of Parliament. Indeed, many parliamentarians, especially in Australia and Canada, would welcome the powers possessed by congressional committees. The consequence of such a development, ironically, would be to heighten central agency micro-management within the executive structures of the state at the very time that there are calls in the United States to do the opposite.[41]

While most public servants do not welcome the increased exposure that results from more aggressive parliamentary committees and parliamentary auditing and review agencies, the conventions of ministerial responsibility do not provide a justification for restricting the capacities of Parliament and its agents to extract an account from public servants. Ministers have a constitutional right to insist on the confidentiality of advice rendered to them, by public servants or others, but this does not absolve public servants from the duty to report on executive policies, decisions and actions in the management of public affairs. In this sense, the traditional obligations of public servants to comply with the right of Parliament to secure and judge an audit of the "public accounts" are not affected by questions of centralized or decentralized management regimes within the executive structures of government. It simply does not matter whether ministers practise a "hands on" style of executive management (to "intervene in administration," as some might put it) or delegate authority. Even when they delegate, the public accounting is still an account of the government's, or a minister's, management of public affairs, including the management of the public purse.

Critics of the traditional system have failed to devise a new framework for public accountability that is itself not hopelessly muddled. This suggests not so much that the conventions of ministerial responsibility are outdated but that the assumptions about accountability within public management conflate the concepts of authority, responsibility and accountability. Accountability becomes synonymous with control over the exercise of authority rather than a method to extract an account from those who have been given authority (the means of government) to fulfil responsibilities (the ends of government).

In the context of parliamentary government, the conflation of these concepts is partly a function of partisan politics: the opposition will deploy any arguments that might enhance its control of the government, including control of the exercise of authority delegated by ministers to public servants. It is also partly a function of ministers seeking to escape accountability for their responsibilities whenever this is convenient: claims about delegated authority deflect attention to others. But it is also because the practice of responsible government assumes, as Sutherland puts it, that

> the government must be able to control and protect its own membership *to be able* meaningfully to accept responsibility for its direction and impact as a government. It would not be able to govern as one administration if the cabinet membership could be changed by the House of Commons exercising an authoritative veto on individual ministers.[42]

Sutherland's account underlines the fact that party government is what gives meaning to collective responsibility and that party government enables the electorate to pass judgement on the government *en bloc*.

However, the partisan structures of this same constitutional practice require the subordination of individual ministerial responsibility to collective responsibility, where responsibility in each instance means accountability. The result is twofold: ministers do not resign when instances of error or maladministration by officials in their department or agency are alleged to have occurred; and ministers have an incentive to blame officials in an attempt to escape any personal responsibility. The constitutional convention of ministerial responsibility as accountability, as a British scholar succinctly expressed it, "is what happens."[43]

If parliamentarians, especially but not only those in opposition, do not have the means to extract meaningful accounts from ministers, but do have the means to scrutinize the administration of public affairs, then it follows that they will try to hold officials to account directly in order to extract an account from someone. The role of individual ministers as heads of separate departments was a 19th-century innovation that brought about the very idea of individual ministerial responsibility *and* the end of the British Parliament's claim that public servants should report directly to Parliament. However, this no longer serves, in the minds of many parliamentarians, as a justification for restricting parliamentary committees from demanding an account directly from officials. Once the role of parliamentary committees was expanded, it was inevitable that the issue of direct public service accountability would come to the forefront. Ministers naming and blaming officials merely added another element to the equation. The expansion in the number and mandates of parliamentary audit and review agencies, freedom of information laws and judicial reviews completed that equation.

Reforms to public accountability in relation to organizations fully within ministerial portfolios must take into consideration the dynamics of responsible government and the requirements of good government. The former is driven by ideological or partisan forces; the latter requires objective or professional standards. Within the Westminster system, there has been a longstanding acceptance of the dual requirement that government provide Parliament with an annual statement of the public accounts, and that an independent parliamentary agency audit these public accounts. This constitutes a fundamental recognition that good government requires more than a government that merely maintains the confidence of the House and ministers being subjected to debate and questioning.

The dilemma in using the new public management to enhance good government is not just parliamentarians sometimes subjecting public servants to partisan-inspired enquiries and challenges. This is a fact of life from which public servants can no longer escape. Rather, the dilemma stems from the fact that neither government departments and agencies nor Parliament's audit and review agencies can produce performance reports, evaluate programs or conduct operational audits and reviews in ways that meet incontestable standards of objectivity. In certain technical respects they can, but beyond a very limited range of such activities, the bottom line is that these exercises constitute applied social and management sciences, with all their limitations. It follows that contestations over the economical, efficient and effective use of authority, as well as the appropriate discharge of responsibilities, are inevitably political and, in Westminster systems, invariably partisan.

For this reason a distinction between policy and administration cannot possibly capture the dynamics of delegated executive authority as applied to the management of the business of complex organizations. It is possible to devise a statutory regime to distribute authority in different ways, as is the case in Canada where Cabinet, individual ministers and boards of directors of Crown corporations have authorities and responsibilities for the direction and control of these quasi-autonomous government organizations. But, other than these kinds of arrangements, which raise their own accountability problems, accountability for delegated authority within the executive structures of government cannot be effectively built on the imprecise distinction between what is policy and what is administration. The distinction can be applied usefully *within* government, but this makes practical sense only because it is accepted that ultimate authority and accountability reside with the minister or Cabinet.

It should follow that even when ministers delegate their authority they remain accountable to Parliament for the management of public affairs within their portfolios. To the extent that Parliament does not challenge the basic management philosophy underpinning delegated executive authority as a means to good government, ministers should be held accountable for the design and management of delegated authority systems. This should include the responsibility for ensuring both that monitoring and control mechanisms are in place and that actions are taken whenever necessary to correct deficiencies resulting in either misuses of delegated authority or patterns of maladministration. There is nothing inherently new in any of this, of course, although the more extensive use of delegated authority that has accompanied the new public management, when combined with more assertive parliamentary committees, makes the challenge more difficult.

Improving Accountability

Efforts are continually being made to improve accountability in the service of good government. These include attempts to increase the specificity and transparency of ministerial policy objectives, expected services and outputs, and authority and responsibility relationships; to improve performance reporting; and to tailor public audits, reviews and evaluations to the limits of applied social and management sciences. Each of these measures has the capacity to provide officials, as Kenneth Stowe argues about the accounting officer regime in Britain, with a "weapon against political expediency."[44] Greater transparency, for instance, can be a defence against political expediency (that is, ministers doing what merely serves to advance their partisan interests) because it forces everything into the open where ministers must defend themselves. Performance reporting and public audits, reviews and evaluations can be a defence against the tendency of officials to seek protection in central controls and standardized procedures. Performance reporting requires departments and agencies to account for results as measured against specified targets. And public audits, reviews and evaluations serve to assess the effects of controls and procedures on performance.

Such efforts require a commitment on the part of government and Parliament to good government and a willingness to accept the limitations of these instruments of accountability; that is, there can be no absolute standards of clarity, performance or objectivity in any of these regards. The absence of such standards is not a justification for diminishing a commitment to pursuing good government. To deny the possibility of progress in these respects is to accept that responsible government can only be partisan; that half-truths, even falsehoods, must be accepted as the norm; and that parliamentarians and citizens must simply trust ministers and officials because public management is too complex and seamless to accommodate contractual distinctions in relation to authorities and responsibilities in the two areas of policy and operations.

At the same time, the health and vitality of the public service require that the rights of public servants be protected in the environment of increased scrutiny. It might be preferable to expect ministers to own up to their responsibilities, both for what they must be accountable and for their obligation to protect the institution and members of the public service. But since ministers cannot always be counted on to do so, and indeed in some instances are the perpetrators of violence against the rights and reputations of individual public servants, additional measures are required.

One such measure has been proposed by Chris Selby Smith and David Corbett in their analysis of the rights of public servants before parliamentary committees in Australia. They propose that when public servants are witnesses before parliamentary committees, especially when "direct accountability to parliamentary committees has been imposed on them" and/or they are "aggrieved by what takes place at a committee hearing or as a direct result of it," they should have "the right to be represented by counsel, call witnesses and have these witnesses examined under oath by counsel in order to test the truth of allegations damaging to character or reputation, or to determine whether [they have]...been subjected to damage, loss or disadvantage as a result of appearing as a witness."[45]

A second measure is to remove from ministers the right to dismiss public servants appointed by the prerogative power, as is the case in New Zealand, where only the State Services Commissioner can remove a chief executive and may do so only for reasons of poor performance. In Canada, this authority could be assigned to the Clerk of the Privy Council, the Public Service Commission or – a preferable route from the dual perspectives of informed knowledge and effective independence – a collective body of deputy ministers, including the Clerk and the Chair of the Commission.

Such measures in the Canadian context might create a certain tension between ministers and public servants as well as between members of Parliament and public servants. But this is an inevitable by-product of *de facto* direct public service accountability to parliamentary committees. In light of the discretionary powers of ministers in the way they respond to parliamentary questioning, and the parliamentary privileges of MPs, combined with the practical need to have public servants answer questions in parliamentary committee hearings, there must be a new regime to protect the rights of individual public servants. This is essential to the preservation and promotion of the public interest in a professional, nonpartisan public service.

Within government, the capacities of Canadian ministers to extract an account from officials who report directly to them requires, as in Britain and New Zealand, the increased use of performance contracts. This cannot rule out maintaining multiple sources of authority, because individual ministers do not have exclusive authority over their departmental or agency officials. But performance contracts can focus the accountability of these officials much more effectively than can all the exhortations about building better relations between ministers and deputy ministers based on trust. Effective performance contracts must be explicit about the requirements of securing accountability for the corporate management responsibilities of government that extend across the public service as well as for the management of those operations that cannot serve larger public purposes if managed in complete isolation from other operations of government.

The challenges here are not new. What is new is the extent to which the centre of government, in the form of central management and policy agencies, must be able to secure corporate objectives and policy interdependencies in ways that allow for extensive devolution without diminishing accountability. This requires attention to at least two critical dimensions of central agency-line department/agency relationships.

First, those at the centre of government must lead the public service. Central agency officials should not be mere adjuncts to the political leadership. They must ensure that the political leadership is provided with the kind of strategic advice that speaks to their policy agenda. More is required, however. Central agency officials must also provide the strategic leadership of the public service that helps strengthen the present and future management of the public service. To ensure accountability in the context of devolved authority, the framework of public administration must extend responsibility for securing corporate objectives and attending to policy interdependencies to those in line departments or agencies. And it must hold these managers to account for their performance in these respects. If front-end controls (rules and regulations) and centralized decision making (pre-transaction central agency approvals) are not to characterize central agency-line department/agency relations, greater emphasis must be given to ensuring that line managers execute their corporate management and policy responsibilities. Those who do should be rewarded; those who do not should face sanctions.

Second, central agencies must ensure that the accountability of line managers is not polluted by a politicization of the public service. The responsibilities of line managers now make them more vulnerable to inescapable political challenges. In ensuring that line managers are accountable, central agencies must have standards of best practice if managers are to be assessed according to professional norms and not by the vagaries of the broader political process. These norms will be considered legitimate only to the degree that line managers themselves are involved in their development. The leadership role of the central agencies thus implies a greater collaboration with line managers in setting public management standards for corporate and horizontal responsibilities.

Because of the greater exposure of public servants to direct public accountability, guidelines are needed for risk management where central controls are diminished, especially with respect to the expanded use of contracts, not only for the procurement of goods and services, but also for the delivery of services. A code of ethics is needed to govern the behaviour of public servants in the context of delegated authority, especially on the front lines of service delivery. And mechanisms are needed to enhance the rights of citizens to appeal administrative decisions and to seek redress, if necessary by legal action.[46] Each of these requirements constitutes, in part, a concern for the effects of the new public management insofar as it expands public service authority. The need for public service leadership, especially in providing the necessary support and protection for individual public servants, is obviously a prerequisite if middle managers and front-line staff are to resist the temptation to hunker down in the face of these new accountability requirements.

Finally, there is the challenge that arises from the new public management's encouragement for public servants to consider themselves "accountable" to their clients or customers. A critical dimension here is that front-line managers and staff must be supported in their efforts, not only to provide services in ways that adhere to public policy, but also to provide accounts to citizens that address the public policy objectives in those services. This is especially necessary where these public services impose restrictions or requirements that citizens object to or challenge. Effective delivery entails more than having public complaint and redress mechanisms. It also demands meaningful consultations that go beyond mere expressions of citizen wants and demands.

Front-line public servants must be able to conduct dialogues with citizens to understand and meet their needs better in the design of delivery systems. This requires that they have a better appreciation of the public interests to be advanced and protected in the design of public services, as well as a greater capacity to articulate these interests than has been the norm, given that public services have traditionally been designed at headquarters. Where the delivery of public services is managed by way of multidepartmental mechanisms, contracted out or conducted through partnership arrangements, this element of direct accountability to citizens is even more important.

In all of this, citizens cannot be treated as customers. They have rights and entitlements but, as individuals or as groups, they are not sovereign. Public service accountability at this level, accordingly, is similar to public service accountability to Parliament: it requires information and explanation of government policies and regulations but not a partisan defence or justification of government policy, decisions or actions. Public accountability remains with ministers. Citizen complaint and redress mechanisms may allow issues of responsibility for public service actions or inactions to be addressed; yet this does not make the public service accountable directly to the public.

Service standards or citizen's charters can be key instruments of public service accountability. But they must be the standards of the government or individual ministers, even if developed in the first instance by public servants in consultation with citizens. They cannot be the sole responsibility of deputies and their departments or chief executives of agencies; they must be part and parcel of an organization's performance contract with its minister.

Conclusion

Without effective accountability regimes, ministers and public servants are insufficiently subject to the discipline of democratic controls over the use of state power and public resources, including the public purse. In public management, furthermore, the various pathologies of bureaucracy are most evident where accountability regimes are weak or weakly enforced. Reforms to strengthen democratic control over the exercise of state power and public resources have been predicated on the need to increase the transparency of government and to subject executive and administrative decisions to parliamentary and judicial, including quasi-judicial, review and oversight. Reforms to accountability regimes designed to enhance performance are equally critical, particularly to efforts to improve good government.

Improving government by strengthening ministerial accountability in Parliament and public service accountability, both to ministers and public service superiors, is not easily accomplished. Performance management, measurement and reporting require ministers and public servants to do what does not come naturally to those interested in the exercise of power. They do not always take kindly to having their discretion restricted by the need to clarify objectives, to specify expected results and to subject themselves to an account of their decisions and actions. If parliamentarians are unwilling or unable to enforce a robust accountability regime on ministers and officials, there will be little incentive for a rigorous accountability regime within government. Poor governance, in short, produces poor public management.

Notes

1. Canada, Government of Canada, *Public Service 2000: The Renewal of the Public Service of Canada* (Ottawa: Minister of Supply and Services, 1990), p. 89.

2. *Public Service 2000: The Renewal*, p. 89.

3. Quoted in S.L. Sutherland, "Responsible Government and Ministerial Responsibility: Every Reform has its Own Problem," *Canadian Journal of Political Science*, Vol. 24, no. 1 (March 1991), p. 111.

4. S.L. Sutherland and G.B. Doern, *Bureaucracy in Canada: Control and Reform*, Vol. 43 of the Research Studies of the Royal Commission on the Economic Union and Development Prospects for Canada (Toronto: University of Toronto Press, 1985), pp. 43-55.

5. Sutherland, "Responsible Government and Ministerial Responsibility," p. 92.

6. Sutherland, "Responsible Government and Ministerial Responsibility," p. 120.

7. S.L. Sutherland, "The Al-Mashat affair: administrative responsibility in parliamentary institutions," *Canadian Public Administration*, Vol. 34, no. 4 (Winter 1991), pp. 573-603.

8. Sutherland, "The Al-Mashat affair," p. 596.

9. Sutherland, "The Al-Mashat affair," p. 602.

10. Canada, Government of Canada, *Public Service 2000: First Annual Report to the Prime Minister on the Public Service of Canada* (Ottawa: Minister of Supply and Services, 1992), p. 7; and Canada, Clerk of the Privy Council and Secretary to the Cabinet, *Public Service 2000: A Report on Progress* (Ottawa: Minister of Supply and Services, 1992), pp. 94-99.

11. *Public Service 2000: A Report on Progress*, p. 98.

12. *Public Service 2000: A Report on Progress*, pp. 98-99.

13. Sutherland, "The Al-Mashat affair," p. 603.

14. Gordon F. Osbaldeston, *Keeping Deputy Ministers Accountable* (London, Ontario: National Centre for Management Research and Development, 1988), pp. 14-23.

15. Osbaldeston, *Keeping Deputy Ministers Accountable*, p. 47.

16. Osbaldeston, *Keeping Deputy Ministers Accountable*, pp. 47-48.

17. Osbaldeston, *Keeping Deputy Ministers Accountable*, p. 11.

18. Osbaldeston, *Keeping Deputy Ministers Accountable*, pp. 154-56.

19. Osbaldeston, *Keeping Deputy Ministers Accountable*, p. 9.

20. Osbaldeston, *Keeping Deputy Ministers Accountable*, pp. 72-74.

21. Canada, Government of Canada, *The Expenditure Management System of the Government of Canada* (Ottawa: Minister of Supply and Services, 1995), p. 4.

22. Canada, Clerk of the Privy Council and Secretary to the Cabinet, *Third Annual Report to the Prime Minister on the Public Service of Canada* (Ottawa: Minister of Supply and Services, 1995), p. 41.

23. Colin Campbell and Graham K. Wilson, *The End of Whitehall: Death of a Paradigm?* (Oxford: Blackwell, 1995), pp. 249-88.

24. United Kingdom, Prime Minister, Chancellor of the Exchequer and Chancellor of the Duchy of Lancaster, *The Civil Service: Taking Forward Continuity and Change* (London: HMSO, January 1995), pp. 27-29.

25. United Kingdom, House of Commons, Treasury and Civil Service Committee, *Fifth Report: The Role of the Civil Service*, Vol. 1 (London: HMSO, 1994), pp. lv-lvii.

26. Andrew Dunshire, "Administrative Theory in the 1980s: A Viewpoint," *Public Administration*, Vol. 73, no. 1 (1995), pp. 25-34; and Chancellor of the Duchy of Lancaster (William Waldegrave), "The Reality of Reform and Accountability in Today's Public Service," speech to the Public Finance Foundation, July 5, 1993.

27. "The Reality of Reform and Accountability," pp. 11, 13.

28. Philip Giddings, "Next Steps to Where?", in Philip Giddings (ed.), *Parliamentary Accountability: A Study of Parliament and Executive Agencies* (London: Macmillan, 1995), pp. 230, 235. In addition to Giddings' introductory and

concluding chapters, 10 chapters examine various aspects of executive agencies and parliamentary accountability.

29. Diana Woodhouse, *Ministers and Parliament: Accountability in Theory and Practice* (Oxford: Clarendon Press, 1994), pp. 275-76.

30. Campbell and Wilson, *The End of Whitehall*, pp. 279-80.

31. *The Economist*, October 21, 1995, pp. 61-62.

32. Don Fuller and Bet Roffey, "Improving Public Sector Accountability and Strategic Decision-Making," *Australian Journal of Public Administration*, Vol. 52, no. 2 (June 1993), pp. 149-63.

33. Colin Campbell and John Halligan, *Political Leadership in an Age of Constraint: Bureaucratic Politics Under Hawke and Keating* (St. Leonards, Australia: Allen and Unwin, 1992), pp. 215-17.

34. Chris Selby Smith and David Corbett, "Parliamentary Committees, Public Servants and Due Process," *Australian Journal of Public Administration*, Vol. 54, no. 1 (March 1995), pp. 19-34.

35. Elizabeth Harmon, "Accountability and Challenges for Australian Governments," *Australian Journal of Political Science*, Vol. 29 (1994), pp. 1-17.

36. Jonathan Boston, "Assessing the performance of departmental chief executives: perspectives from New Zealand," *Public Administration*, Vol. 70, no. 3 (Autumn 1992), pp. 405-28.

37. Sharon L. Sutherland, "The Public Service and Policy Development," in Michael M. Atkinson (ed.), *Governing Canada: Institutions and Public Policy* (Toronto: Harcourt Brace Jovanovich Canada, 1993), p. 103.

38. New Zealand, State Services Commission Steering Group, *Review of State Sector Reforms* (Wellington: State Services Commission, November 29, 1991), p. 39.

39. Bruce Stone, "Administrative Accountability in the Westminster Democracies: Towards a New Conceptual Framework," *Governance*, Vol. 8, no. 4 (October 1995), pp. 505-26.

40. Canada, House of Commons, Special Committee on the Reform of the House of Commons, *Third Report* (Ottawa: Queen's Printer, June 1985), p. 20.

41. Donald F. Kettl, "Building Lasting Reform: Enduring Questions, Missing Answers," and Christopher H. Foreman, Jr., "Reinventing Politics? The NPR Meets Congress," in Donald F. Kettl and John J. Dilulio, Jr. (eds.), *Inside the Reinvention Machine: Appraising Governmental Reform* (Washington: Brookings Institution, 1995), pp. 9-83, 152-68.

42. Sutherland, "Responsible Government and Ministerial Responsibility," p. 96; emphasis in the original.

43. J. Griffiths, quoted in Selby Smith and Corbett, "Parliamentary Committees, Public Servants and Due Process," p. 32, note 9.

44. Kenneth Stowe, "Good Piano Won't Play Bad Music: Administrative Reform and Good Governance," *Public Administration*, Vol. 70, no. 3 (Autumn 1992), p. 393.

45. Selby Smith and Corbett, "Parliamentary Committees, Public Servants and Due Process," p. 29.

46. Phillip J. Cooper, "Accountability and Administrative Reform: Toward Convergence and Beyond," in B. Guy Peters and Donald J. Savoie (eds.), *Governance in a Changing Environment* (Montreal: McGill-Queen's University Press, 1995), pp. 173-99; B. Guy Peters and Donald J. Savoie, "Civil Service Reform: Misdiagnosing the Patient," *Public Administration Review*, Vol. 54, no. 5 (September-October 1994), pp. 418-25.

NINE

Conclusion:
An Agenda for Public Management

The fiscal crisis of the Canadian federal government will continue to influence its approach to public management for the foreseeable future. Like many other governments, it will continue to roll back the state and to rely more and more on markets to allocate resources. The government will also need to cope with the exigencies of an increasingly globalized economy[1] and a more demanding body politic.[2]

As the Canadian government seeks to manage the public household in a global economy, it must formulate policies that address the interdependencies between and among its various initiatives. Only to the extent that it deals effectively with these horizontal policy issues will it be able to "steer the state" in ways that secure desired policy results, however incomplete or temporary these must be.

As the government responds to domestic pressures for quality public services, it will need to improve the integration of its service delivery systems. Individual citizens, client groups and businesses increasingly are demanding services that do not subject them to the inconveniences and costs of fragmented government. While those on the front lines of service delivery are sometimes accused of being unresponsive in their relations with citizens and clients, the reverse is more often the case.[3] The fundamental challenge at this level is not the logistics of designing integrated service delivery systems. In fact, the examples presented in Leslie Seidle's *Rethinking the Delivery of Public Services to Citizens* illustrate that many such systems have already been initiated in Canada and elsewhere.[4] Rather, the challenge is to ensure the survival of the corporate values and practices of the public service – respecting the equality of citizens, the equitable treatment of individuals and groups, adherence to public service ethics and the accountable management of resources – in the context of new organizational forms and methods of managing client entitlements and expectations.

Steering the state and providing quality service at a time of ongoing program review will require that the Canadian government pursue a vigourous public management reform program. Following the 1993 overhaul of the machinery of government initiated by Prime Minister Kim Campbell and continued by Jean Chrétien, the present government has introduced a new Expenditure Management System and committed itself to enhanced performance management and reporting. These important steps should bring Canada into line with the other three Westminster systems. Yet all this comes at a time when the operations of government are being subjected to major surgery, including a downsizing of the public service. To improve public management under such circumstances, it is urgent that the government address a number of crucial matters in a coherent and consistent manner.

Designs for Public Management

In its assessment of public management reform in the four Westminster systems, the 1993 study by the Canadian Office of the Auditor General underlined how critical political and public service leadership is to the success of reform initiatives.[5] It also called for greater coherence in design, and consistency in practice. The comparative experience suggests that several conditions must be met to improve public management within our contemporary system of responsible government.

The Separation of Responsibilities for Policy and Operations

It is unrealistic to expect ministers to manage their portfolios effectively in the minister-as-manager mode or to make a meaningful distinction between policy and administration (or as it is sometimes expressed, politics and administration). It follows that, to discharge their executive responsibilities, ministers must delegate authority.

New Zealand and Great Britain have accepted this precept. They recognize that the hierarchical and integrated structure of the traditional ministerial department imposes severe restraints on the capacity of departments both to serve ministers well *and* to manage operations cost-effectively. Their decision to adopt organizational designs to separate responsibilities for policy and operations has led to many accomplishments. With respect to the dynamics of ministerial government, the logic is straightforward, yet subtle.

First, the separation of policy and operational responsibilities encourages ministers, individually and collectively, to be more strategic in their decision making, to address horizontal issues up front with their colleagues and to be more demanding of the advice they receive from officials or others. Ministers can steer the state better if they spend more time determining their objectives and the means to achieve them, the activities they will support, the targets they will set, the measures they will use to assess performance, and the criteria and methods they will apply when evaluating the effectiveness of government operations.

Second, the separation of policy and operational responsibilities encourages those responsible for operations to serve ministers well by doing what ministers want done. Ministers' expectations are clearer and more likely to be met by their officials, although this does not make their tasks simple. It can, however, clarify what ministers want undertaken and what ministerial priorities are attached to each of these tasks. The British and New Zealand experiences demonstrate that this approach can work in Westminster systems, as it has long worked in several continental European countries. Although it does not eliminate the basic conundrums of governance, it has the potential to improve governance if other conditions, as outlined below, are accepted as integral to good public management.

The reforms of these two systems represent an explicit acknowledgement that the traditional ministerial department no longer achieves meaningful ministerial direction, control and accountability for public policy and administration. They have destroyed the myth that responsibilities for policy and operations cannot be separated without a loss of political control over administration. This myth had served largely to legitimize the discretion of ministers to use the powers of the state for partisan purposes. For senior public servants, it had served to maintain their power, given that ministers had to delegate extensive powers to them.

The experiences of Britain and New Zealand before they adopted the new model, as well as the continuing experiences of Australia (where greater interest in this model is now emerging) and of Canada, make it clear that ministers cannot have it both ways. If they wish to maintain their authority to intervene in the implementation and management of programs whenever they see fit, they must accept that their subordinates will behave in certain ways. For example, ministers could have their objectives displaced by those of their departmental operating units. Theoretically, this could be prevented by ensuring that ministerial policy objectives are sufficiently clear and precise to direct the management and delivery of operations. But this is rarely the case. Ministers wish to keep objectives as general as possible to retain maximum flexibility to change direction in the course of policy implementation.

Because the models adopted in Britain and New Zealand restrict the exercise of ministerial discretion, strong ministerial commitment to good government is required. Ministers interested in pursuing partisan interests in the management of their portfolios are unlikely to make that commitment. Nor will deputies and other senior officials who relish the power they wield in traditional ministerial departments favour changes that curtail their discretion. It is thus not surprising that in both Britain and New Zealand concerted prime ministerial and central administrative leadership was necessary to restructure government along these lines.

Contractual Relations Between Ministers and the Heads of Operational Agencies

To have an effective separation of responsibilities for policy and operations, relations between ministers and their officials must be structured on a contractual-type basis, at least with those officials responsible for the management and delivery of public services. This can be extended to encompass relations between ministers and the heads of their policy departments, as in New Zealand where policy advice is considered an output purchased by ministers. At a minimum, however, contractual arrangements must be applied to heads of operational agencies because greater authority must be delegated to them for the management and delivery of services.

Under this model, ministers remain responsible for both policy and operations. There is no separation of responsibilities between ministers and officials (as is implied by notions of a policy-administration or politics-administration dichotomy), but there is between the responsibilities of policy advisers to ministers and operational managers. This is most evident in Britain where a minister's department and a minister's executive agency (or agencies) constitute different organizations. This model is fundamentally different from the special operating agency (SOA) model used in Canada. Because the heads of SOAs report to deputy ministers and not to ministers, the Canadian model does not meet the most important condition in the separation of responsibilities for policy and operations, namely to have different officials responsible for assisting ministers with respect to policy and operations.

The key issue here is the need for ministers, assisted by their policy advisers, to clarify the objectives of operational units, to set performance targets and service standards, to establish corporate policy and management requirements and to institute performance measures and reporting mechanisms to hold to account those who manage operations. These conditions constitute the basic contracts between ministers and those responsible for operations. The heads of operational agencies must accept the conditions stipulated in their contracts with ministers. They give advice through this process and thus bring operational considerations to bear on the negotiation of their contracts, if only to ensure that they do not agree to do what cannot be achieved. Although operational heads are involved in setting their own contracts, they do not have the discretion to write them. Since the contracts are ministerial instruments, ministers may change the terms of the contract, for instance in response to changing circumstances.

The recent Canadian adoption of business plans for departmental operations is a move in this direction. But unless ministers are willing to make these plans explicit and transparent, the new initiatives are unlikely to improve public management. It is ironic that traditionalists suggest that such transparency in responsibilities is not only unrealistic in the Westminster model, but would undermine the principles of ministerial responsibility. How a lack of specificity and transparency of ministerial objectives supports the principles of ministerial responsibility is not at all clear. A similar argument was made centuries ago in England against the publication of the proceedings and debates of Parliament!

If the Canadian federal government is to accept the separation of policy and operational responsibilities in its organizational design, it must avoid the shortcomings of the special operating agency model, with agency heads subordinate to deputy ministers. The heads of operational departments or agencies must be chief executives in their own right and have their own contracts with ministers. Separate organizations are thus required to distinguish between policy ministries and operational agencies.

Devolution of Authority for the Management of Operations

If ministers accept the first two conditions of good public management, then they must allow managers of operations sufficient authority over the operational dimensions of policy implementation, including the financial and personnel resources, to meet the terms of their contracts. In Britain and New Zealand, ministers have accepted this condition, and significant degrees of authority have been devolved from ministers. In this regard, New Zealand has gone furthest and has also established a statutory framework for this devolution.

The most critical development in each of these cases has been the acceptance of the idea of devolution of authority from central agencies. This includes the transfer of responsibility for ensuring adequate management controls, effective administrative processes, adherence to best practices and the promotion of public service values from central agencies (and in Britain, from "parent" departments) to those who head operational units.

Australia has not adopted the contractual approach in precisely this way but has pursued significant devolution from central agencies to line departments and agencies. This has occurred primarily because much of the management reform in that country has been led by the Department of Finance, its central management agency.

In Canada, the Treasury Board has adopted several devolutionary measures but with a less coherent approach and less consistency in its aims. Unfortunately, there is still reliance on the ill-conceived notion that management reform means increased managerial discretion and the empowerment of public servants. The assumption has been that, to achieve better results, public servants (both senior management and those on the front lines) must be freed from controls, rules and compliance with procedures. To the extent that Canadian reformers have framed the agenda in terms of discretion and empowerment (even at times implying that "entrepreneurial" public servants should ignore controls and procedures to overcome bureaucracy), it is not surprising that ministers and Members of Parliament have been less than enthusiastic supporters of the new public management. And with good reason: such ideas are contrary to good government.

This notion is due largely to the reliance of Canadian advocates of reform on North American private-sector management gurus for their inspiration. In contrast, reformers in the other three Westminster systems have done their own thinking. It should be noted here that the National Performance Review of the Clinton administration in the United States (which in several respects is a rerun of the Canadian initiative, Public Service 2000) has faltered badly[6] because of its reliance on these same notions of managerial discretion and empowerment, as promoted in the popular, but flawed, manifesto of David Osborne and Ted Gaebler, *Reinventing Government*.[7]

The purpose of devolution is not to eliminate controls, procedures and rules, but to reduce them where they hinder good management and do not promote or accommodate best practices in particular settings. Rules and controls are essential to good management. By devolving authority to operational agencies, these essentials do not disappear. They are established, however, by those to whom authority is devolved for the management and delivery of public services and who are thus responsible and accountable to their ministers for meeting the requirements of good public management.

Contrary to what is often assumed in Canadian thinking, devolution does not mean that the responsibilities for good corporate management policies are discarded and that organizations autonomous from ministerial or parliamentary control take over. It does mean, however, that these responsibilities do not necessarily belong to central agencies.[8] Such devolution of responsibilities implies changes to the basic statutory frameworks that now govern the corporate management of the public service and regulate the management of government operations.

Rigorous Performance Management Systems

If ministers devolve authority and responsibility, they need to be assured that rigorous performance management regimes are in place. Otherwise they have merely increased public service discretion. In each of the other three Westminster systems, the adoption of performance management measures has been accorded high priority. Although not perfect, these measures have certainly enhanced good government.

In Britain, a major effort has been made to measure performance, including adherence to the service standards central to the Citizen's Charter initiative. In New Zealand, performance measurement is at the heart of the new system of expenditure budgeting, contracting for outputs and reporting requirements, including the use of a highly transparent accrual accounting system. In Australia, a wide range of measures has increased the priority given to performance management with positive results. In particular, program evaluation as a means to measure the effectiveness of policy initiatives has had a positive influence on decision making, especially on resource allocation.

Although academic criticism is widespread, there is a grudging recognition that progress has been made in this most difficult area.[9] In fact, much of the practical criticism is possible only because of the introduction of performance targets, their indicators or measures, and reporting regimes.

Methodologies and reporting instruments can be questioned, gaps in coverage and application can be challenged, and partisan political manipulation of data can be exposed. Equally important, as Donald Kettl notes: "Performance-based management is most fundamentally about communication, not measurement. Moreover, this communication occurs within a broader political process, in which the players have a wide array of different incentives. Performance-based management will have meaning only to the degree to which it shapes and improves these incentives."[10]

Hardly a newcomer to this important area, the Canadian government has been attempting to improve performance management since the late 1960s. As the litany of Canadian efforts attests, however, performance management – as performance measurement – will not take hold unless embedded in a comprehensive approach that alters the incentives on which good public management must be based.

Lack of commitment to performance management in recent years has been largely due to the assumption, explicitly displayed in the Public Service 2000 exercise, that performance is best improved by changing the culture of the public service. In particular, it has been assumed that if managers improve their skills in managing people, morale will improve, and then staff will work better. Unfortunately, there is little evidence that cultural change happens independent of changes to structure, management systems or leadership. In the other three Westminster systems, the assumption was just the opposite, namely that structural changes are required to effect changes in culture, including improved morale.

The failures of successive governments and parliaments to acknowledge the importance of performance management are obviously due to a complex set of factors, some of which do not reflect well on either the competence of Canada's political class or its commitment to good government. Canadian public service leaders have also contributed to this state of affairs.

While political and administrative leadership means more than assigning quantitative targets and playing with crude numbers, good government demands attention to the difficult requirements of improved performance. The support for the principal reform measures in the other Westminster systems – which extends beyond the political parties that launched them – underlines not only ministers' interest in good public management but also the extent to which these measures represent citizen expectations. The Canadian myth that there are no votes in good public management is simply bad political analysis, unsupported by the experiences of several provincial political systems.

A Robust Accountability Regime

While criticisms abound regarding the supposed shortcomings of the new public management with respect to accountability, the fact is that accountability – of ministers to Parliament, public servants to ministers, and through them to Parliament – has been enhanced in the other three Westminster systems. Structural changes have clarified responsibilities, and improved performance management has resulted in better performance reporting inside government and to Parliament and citizens alike. Governmental activities have become more transparent in each respect.

In Britain, more so than in New Zealand or Australia, ministers have had difficulty in reconciling their commitment to greater transparency in the work of the public service with their own accountability to Parliament. Despite the best efforts of some ministers, including at times the prime minister, to evade responsibility, the greater transparency and division of responsibilities have made it more difficult for ministers to escape exposure. Even though a good deal of farce has characterized ministerial responsibility in Britain during the last decade,[11] the accountability regime has actually improved.

Acceptance of the first four conditions of good public management described above has resulted in enhanced accountability. By conscious design or not, reform measures in these systems grew from the roots of responsible government because public management reform was closely linked to governance, especially when ministers supported reforms to enhance their strategic control over the bureaucracy. The purpose here was not simply to ensure that state activities were responsive to political direction, but that improved policies, improved services and thus improved governance would result. It was recognized that this demanded more transparency across a range of activities. Improved accountability, including public accountability, was the consequence.

In Canada, there has also been progress. But because reforms have not been a priority of ministers, coherence in design and consistency in practice have suffered. Moreover, because reforms have been largely driven by the senior public service and based on the assumptions of increased discretion and empowerment, the connection to both internal and external accountability has been weak. In this conception of public management, accountability is regarded as a constraint to productive management: the less of it the better. It is not viewed as an instrument to enhance productive management, as is the case in the other three systems.

In the Canadian view, the ultimate constraint, naturally, is public accountability to Parliament, parliamentary committees and parliamentary agencies. While lip-service is given to the primacy of ministerial responsibility, this myth is largely a cover for doing as little as possible to enhance public accountability. Such an approach has done little to promote public confidence in and respect for our parliamentary system of government. The ultimate irony is that ministers, individually and collectively, are themselves among the principal victims of this failure to secure better accountability.

An Independent Institution of Public Service
While bureaucracy bashing was initially a prominent feature of public management reform, especially in Britain and Canada, much rhetoric has been expended more recently on the importance to good government of a professional, nonpartisan public service.

Even the sweeping public management reforms in New Zealand retained a significant measure of independence for the public service as an institution of government separate from partisan politics. In this respect, the New Zealand reforms differed from those in the other three systems, which in themselves have important variations, such as in the impact of the personalization of senior public service appointments where they are subject to the prime minister's prerogative. In Britain and Canada, the impact helped set the tone both for what was expected of those at the top and those wishing to make it to the top, and for what was acceptable behaviour on the part of senior managers.

The individual personalities and correspondingly different management styles of prime ministers, senior ministers and the most senior public servants loom large in this equation, and there have been important variations among the four political systems. More so than in the other three countries, the Canadian public service has suffered from what is widely perceived as an excess of ruthlessness, powermongering and cronyism in the upper echelons of government, extending to the senior public service. The pervasiveness and entrenchment of this culture in the public service itself may be disputed, in part because management in government inherently has a corrupting influence. Both the high politics of governance and the low politics of organizational life exact their price as power is wielded in public institutions.

This would all be only of interest to academic study were it not that such culture corrodes public service creativity, competence and commitment. Ministers are not well served when alternatives to the status quo are discouraged by the conformist mentality of superiors, when substantive policy knowledge takes second place to Machiavellian skills at manipulating the process, or when fear of retaliation causes public servants to hunker down in anticipation of aggressive reaction against any signs of non-conformity. Great damage is caused to the long-term health and vitality of the public service by this culture because even its victims are prone to adopt the same bullying tactics in relation to their own subordinates.

There is no easy way to eliminate the basis for this culture. Yet the system can afford only so many cases of blatant brutality, such as exhibited in the Al-Mashat affair or the 1993 restructuring, before it degenerates into a Hobbesian state of uncivil society. Curbing the power of prime ministers and ministers to dismiss those senior public service executives appointed by prerogative is one important step. Ensuring that recommendations for appointments to these same positions, as well as decisions on dismissals from them, are made by a formally constituted collective body of the senior public service is a second. Requiring the prime minister to disclose publicly appointments not recommended by such a body is a third. Strengthening the role of the Public Service Commission in this process and in relation to positions in the executive ranks below these positions is a fourth. Instituting an effective public service code under the jurisdiction of the Public Service Commission to expose ministerial or senior public service misconduct is a fifth. A complementary measure is ensuring that public servants are accorded the rights of natural justice in appearing before parliamentary committees, or when identified by ministers in the proceedings of Parliament, its committees or other public forums.

The Canadian system is not alone in its failings in these respects, although the other three systems have adopted or are seriously considering some of the above measures. Equally important, Canada's shortcomings with regard to the conditions described above have exacerbated the problem. The prevailing orthodoxy that all is well in Canada because we have maintained the formalities of a professional, nonpartisan public service, despite the threat to this formal system posed by the Mulroney government, assumes too much. Institutional changes alone will not transform behaviour. But without institutional changes, the *de facto* norms, expectations and assumptions about what is acceptable behaviour are unlikely to change significantly. Those who have succeeded in this culture have little incentive to alter their behaviour, even though they may exhort those below them to behave differently.

Admittedly, this generalization does not apply to all senior public servants; many at the top are genuinely committed to change and have taken steps to improve matters. At the same time, the disinclination to discuss shortcomings in the system in a frank, forthright and public manner, and to urge political leaders in Cabinet and Parliament to institute reforms, constitutes a disservice to political leaders, the public service itself and the Canadian public.

Looking Ahead

The new public management has not generated sustained or informed public discussion in Canada, at least at the federal level. What little debate that has resulted has either been confined within the public service itself, and therefore not public, or limited to a few skirmishes between former public servants[12] and academics.[13]

The relative dearth of debate over the last two decades has been due in large part to the fact that the governments in power – first Trudeau's and then Mulroney's – let government get out of hand, leading to a serious fiscal crisis, a bloated Cabinet, an excessively centralized command and control style of public management and a demoralized public service.

A significant consequence of this legacy has been the need for a massive assault on the structures, programs and personnel of the Canadian federal government. Given the continuing fiscal situation, the government cannot afford to rest. More must be done. The central question in reforming public management is whether an effective accommodation can be reached in reforming both the partisan dynamics of responsible government and the nonpartisan requirements of good government. The agenda presented here is offered as food for thought, in the hope that it will assist the process of reforming Canadian public management.

Notes

1. Donald J. Savoie, "Globalization, Nation States and the Civil Service," in B. Guy Peters and Donald J. Savoie (eds.), *Governance in a Changing Environment* (Montreal: McGill-Queen's University Press, 1995), pp. 82-110.

2. F. Leslie Seidle, "The Angry Citizenry: Examining Representation and Responsiveness in Government," *Policy Options*, Vol. 15, no. 6 (July-August 1994), pp. 75-80.

3. Barbara Wake Carroll and David Siegel, "Two solitudes or one big happy family: head office-field office relations in government organizations," paper presented to the Annual Meeting of the Canadian Political Science Association, Montreal, June 5, 1995.

4. F. Leslie Seidle, *Rethinking the Delivery of Public Services to Citizens* (Montreal: Institute for Research on Public Policy, 1995), especially chap. 6.

5. Canada, Auditor General of Canada, *Report of the Auditor General of Canada to the House of Commons, 1993* (Ottawa: Minister of Supply and Services, 1993), pp. 159-85.

6. Donald F. Kettl, *Reinventing Government? Appraising the National Performance Review* (Washington: Brookings Institution, 1994), especially pp. 47-53.

7. David Osborne and Ted Gaebler, *Reinventing Government: How the Entrepreneurial Spirit is Transforming the Public Sector* (New York: Plume, 1993).

8. John L. Manion, "The organization and management of government," notes for an address to the Advanced Management Program of the Canadian Centre for Management Development (Ottawa: Canadian Centre for Management Development, 1993); and Peter Aucoin, "Re-engineering the Centre," *Public Sector Management*, Vol. 6, no. 1 (1995), pp. 15-16.

9. Christopher Pollitt, "Management Techniques for the Public Sector: Pulpit and Practice," in Peters and Savoie (eds.), *Governance in a Changing Environment*, pp. 214-18.

10. Donald F. Kettl, "Building Lasting Reform: Enduring Questions, Missing Answers," in Donald F. Kettl and John J. DiIulio, Jr. (eds.), *Inside the Reinvention Machine: Appraising Governmental Reform* (Washington: Brookings Institution, 1995), p. 65.

11. Colin Campbell and Graham K. Wilson, *The End of Whitehall: Death of a Paradigm?* (Oxford: Blackwell, 1995), pp. 264-88.

12. For example, Paul M. Tellier, "No time for half-measures: the urgency of re-engineering the public service of Canada," remarks to the Canadian Institute, Ottawa, February 21, 1994 (an abridged version of Tellier's remarks is printed in *Canadian Speeches: Issues of the day*, Vol. 8, issue 1 (April 1994), pp. 45-48; Ian Clark, "On Re-engineering the Public Service of Canada: A Comment on Paul Tellier's Call for Bold Action," *Public Sector Management*, Vol. 4, no. 4 (1994), pp. 20-22.

13. For example, Donald J. Savoie, "What is wrong with the new public management?", *Canadian Public Administration*, Vol. 38, no. 1 (Spring 1995), pp. 112-21; Sandford Borins, "The new public management is here to stay," *Canadian Public Administration*, Vol. 38, no. 1 (Spring 1995), pp. 122-32.

Selected Bibliography

Aberbach, Joel, and Bert Rockman. "Civil Servants and Policymakers: Neutral or Responsive Competence?", *Governance*, Vol. 7, no. 4 (October 1994), pp. 461-69.

Albo, Gregory, David Langille and Leo Panitch (eds.), *A Different Kind of State? Popular Power and Democratic Administration* (Toronto: Oxford University Press, 1993).

Atkinson, Michael M., and William D. Coleman. "Bureaucrats and politicians in Canada: an examination of the political administration model," *Comparative Political Studies*, Vol. 18, no. 1 (April 1985), pp. 58-80.

Aucoin, Peter. "The Politics and Management of Restraint in Government: An Overview," in Peter Aucoin (ed.), *The Politics and Management of Restraint in Government* (Montreal: Institute for Research on Public Policy, 1981), pp. 1-23.

Aucoin, Peter. "Organizational Change in the Canadian Machinery of Government: From Rational Management to Brokerage Politics," *Canadian Journal of Political Science*, Vol. 19, no. 1 (March 1986), pp. 3-27.

Aucoin, Peter. "Contraction, Managerialism and Decentralization in Canadian Government," *Governance*, Vol. 1, no. 2 (April 1988), pp. 144-61.

Aucoin, Peter. "The Mulroney Government, 1984-1988: Priorities, Positional Policy and Power," in Andrew Gollner and Daniel Salée (eds.), *Canada Under Mulroney: An End-of-Term Report* (Montreal: Vehicle Press, 1988), pp. 335-56.

Aucoin, Peter. "Administrative Reform in Public Management: Paradigms, Principles, Paradoxes and Pendulums," *Governance*, Vol. 3, no. 2 (April 1990), pp. 115-37.

Aucoin, Peter. "Cabinet government in Canada: corporate management of a confederal executive," in Colin Campbell and Margaret Jane Wyszomirski (eds.), *Executive Leadership in Anglo-American Systems* (Pittsburgh: University of Pittsburgh Press, 1991), pp. 139-59.

Aucoin, Peter. "Re-engineering the Centre," *Public Sector Management*, Vol. 6, no. 1 (1995), pp. 15-16.

Aucoin, Peter, and Herman Bakvis. "Regional responsiveness and government organization: the case of regional economic development policy in Canada," in Peter Aucoin (ed.), *Regional Responsiveness in the National Administrative State* (Toronto: University of Toronto Press, 1985), pp. 51-118.

Aucoin, Peter, and Herman Bakvis. *The Centralization-Decentralization Conundrum: Organization and Management in the Canadian Government* (Halifax: Institute for Research on Public Policy, 1988).

Australia, Management Advisory Board. *Building a Better Public Service* (Canberra: Australian Government Publishing Service, 1993).

Australia, Task Force on Management Improvement. *The Australian Public Service Reformed: An Evaluation of a Decade of Management Reform* (Canberra: Australian Government Publishing Service, December 1992).

Axworthy, Thomas. "Of secretaries to princes," *Canadian Public Administration*, Vol. 31, no. 2 (Summer 1988), pp. 247-64.

Bakvis, Herman. *Regional Ministers: Power and Influence in the Canadian Cabinet* (Toronto: University of Toronto Press, 1991).

Bakvis, Herman, and David Mac Donald. "The Canadian Cabinet: organization, decision-rules, and policy impact," in Michael M. Atkinson (ed.), *Governing Canada: Institutions and Public Policy* (Toronto: Harcourt Brace Jovanovich Canada Inc., 1993), pp. 57-59.

Ball, Ian. "Outcome Specification," paper presented at the Public Sector Convention of the New Zealand Society of Accountants, November 1992.

Banting, Keith. "The Way Beavers Build Dams: Social Policy Change in Canada," in Keith Banting and Ken Battle (eds.), *A New Social Vision for Canada?* (Kingston: Queen's University School of Policy Studies, 1994), pp. 131-37.

Barzelay, Michael. *Breaking Through Bureaucracy: A New Vision for Managing in Government* (Berkeley: University of California Press, 1992).

Blais, André, and Stéphane Dion. "Conclusion: Are Bureaucrats Budget Maximizers?", in André Blais and Stéphane Dion (eds.), *The Budget-Maximizing Bureaucrat: Appraisals and Evidence* (Pittsburgh: University of Pittsburgh Press, 1991), pp. 355-61.

Blais, André, and Stéphane Dion. "Introduction," in André Blais and Stéphane Dion (eds.), *The Budget-Maximizing Bureaucrat: Appraisals and Evidence* (Pittsburgh: University of Pittsburgh Press, 1991), pp. 3-12.

Borins, Sandford. "Public Choice: 'Yes Minister' Made it Popular, But Does Winning the Nobel Prize Make it True?", *Canadian Public Administration*, Vol. 31 (1988), pp. 12-26.

Borins, Sandford. "Government in Transition: A New Paradigm in Public Administration," Report on the Inaugural Conference of the Commonwealth Association for Public Administration and Management, Charlottetown, Prince Edward Island, August 28-31, 1994.

Borins, Sandford. "Public Sector Innovation: The Implications of New Forms of Organization and Work," in B. Guy Peters and Donald J. Savoie (eds.), *Governance in a Changing Environment* (Montreal: McGill-Queen's University Press, 1995), pp. 260-87.

Borins, Sandford. "The new public management is here to stay," *Canadian Public Administration*, Vol. 38, no. 1 (Spring 1995), pp. 122-32.

Boston, Jonathan. "The Theoretical Underpinnings of Public Sector Restructuring in New Zealand," in Jonathan Boston, John Martin, June Pallot and Pat Walsh (eds.), *Reshaping the State: New Zealand's Bureaucratic Revolution* (Auckland: Oxford University Press, 1991), pp. 1-26.

Boston, Jonathan. "Assessing the performance of departmental chief executives: perspectives from New Zealand," *Public Administration*, Vol. 70, no. 3 (Autumn 1992), pp. 405-28.

Boston, Jonathan. "Purchasing Policy Advice: the Limits of Contracting Out," *Governance*, Vol. 7, no. 1 (January 1994), pp. 1-30.

Boston, Jonathan, John Martin and Pat Walsh. "Conclusion," in Jonathan Boston, John Martin, June Pallot and Pat Walsh (eds.), *Reshaping the State: New Zealand's Bureaucratic Revolution* (Auckland: Oxford University Press, 1991), pp. 388-400.

Bourgault, Jacques, and Stéphane Dion. "Brian Mulroney a-t-il politisé les sous-ministres?", *Canadian Public Administration*, Vol. 32, no. 1 (1989), pp. 63-83.

Bourgault, Jacques, and Stéphane Dion. "Governments Come and Go, But What of Senior Civil Servants? Canadian Deputy Ministers and Transitions in Power (1867-1987)," *Governance*, Vol. 2, no. 2 (1989), pp. 124-51.

Bourgault, Jacques, and Stéphane Dion. "Canadian senior civil servants and transitions of government: the Whitehall model seen from Ottawa," *International Journal of Administrative Science*, Vol. 56, no. 1 (1990), pp. 149-69.

Bourgault, Jacques, and Stéphane Dion. *The Changing Profiles of Federal Deputy Ministers: 1968 to 1988* (Ottawa: Minister of Supply and Services and Canadian Centre for Management Development, 1991).

Braybrooke, David, and Charles Lindblom. *A Strategy of Decision* (London: Free Press, 1963).

Brodie, Janine, and Jane Jenson. "Piercing the Smokescreen: Brokerage Parties and Class Politics," in Alain G. Gagnon and A. Brian Tanguay (eds.), *Canadian Parties in Transition* (Scarborough, Ontario: Nelson Canada, 1989), pp. 24-44.

Brodtrick, Otto. "A Second Look at the Well-Performing Organization," in James C. McDavid and Brian Marson (eds.), *The Well-Performing Government Organization* (Toronto: Institute of Public Administration of Canada, 1991), pp. 16-22.

Brooks, Stephen. *Public Policy in Canada: An Introduction* (Toronto: McClelland and Stewart, 1993).

Burnham, J., and G.W. Jones. "Advising Margaret Thatcher: the Prime Minister's Office and the Cabinet Office Compared," *Political Studies*, Vol. 41, no. 2 (1993), pp. 299-314.

Caiden, Gerald. *Administrative Reform Comes of Age* (Berlin: Walter de Gruyter, 1991).

Campbell, Colin. *Governments Under Stress* (Toronto: University of Toronto Press, 1983).

Campbell, Colin. "Cabinet committees in Canada: pressures and dysfunctions stemming from the representational imperative," in Thomas T. Mackie and Brian W. Hogwood (eds.), *Unlocking the Cabinet: Cabinet Structures in Comparative Perspective* (London: Sage, 1985), pp. 61-85.

Campbell, Colin. "Mulroney's Broker Politics: The Ultimate in Politicized Incompetence," in Andrew Gollner and Daniel Salée (eds.), *Canada Under Mulroney: An End-of-Term Report* (Montreal: Vehicule Press, 1988), pp. 309-34.

Campbell, Colin. "The Political Roles of Senior Government Officials in Advanced Democracies," *British Journal of Political Science*, Vol. 18 (April 1988), pp. 243-72.

Campbell, Colin. "I've Never Met a Transition I Didn't Like: Some Reflections on Sixteen Years of Comparative Research," in Donald J. Savoie (ed.), *Taking Power* (Toronto: Institute of Public Administration of Canada, 1993), pp. 73-98.

Campbell, Colin. "The search for coordination and control revisited: for machinery of government, ten lost years?", paper prepared for the Ten-Year Reunion, Structure and Organization of Government Research Committee, International Political Science Association, Manchester, England, September 22-24, 1994.

Campbell, Colin, and John Halligan. *Political Leadership in an Age of Constraint: Bureaucratic Politics Under Hawke and Keating* (St. Leonards, Australia: Allen and Unwin, 1992).

Campbell, Colin, and George J. Szablowski. *The Super-Bureaucrats: Structure and Behaviour in Central Agencies* (Toronto: The Macmillan Company of Canada Ltd., 1979).

Campbell, Colin, and Graham K. Wilson. *The End of Whitehall: Death of a Paradigm?* (Oxford: Blackwell, 1995).

Canada. *New Management Initiatives: Initial Results from the Ministerial Task Force on Program Review* (Ottawa, May 1985).

Canada, Auditor General of Canada. *Report to the House of Commons for the Fiscal Year ended March 31, 1983* (Ottawa: Minister of Supply and Services, 1983).

Canada, Auditor General of Canada. *Report to the House of Commons for the Fiscal Year ended March 31, 1988* (Ottawa: Minister of Supply and Services, 1988).

Canada, Auditor General of Canada. *Report to the House of Commons for the Fiscal Year ended March 31, 1992* (Ottawa: Minister of Supply and Services, 1992).

Canada, Auditor General of Canada. *Report of the Auditor General of Canada to the House of Commons, 1993* (Ottawa: Minister of Supply and Services, 1993).

Canada, Clerk of the Privy Council and Secretary to the Cabinet. *Public Service 2000: A Report on Progress* (Ottawa: Minister of Supply and Services, 1992).

Canada, Clerk of the Privy Council and Secretary to the Cabinet. *Third Annual Report to the Prime Minister on the Public Service of Canada* (Ottawa: Minister of Supply and Services, 1995).

Canada, Government of Canada. *Public Service 2000: The Renewal of the Public Service of Canada* (Ottawa: Minister of Supply and Services, 1990).

Canada, Government of Canada. *Public Service 2000: First Annual Report to the Prime Minister on the Public Service of Canada* (Ottawa: Minister of Supply and Services, 1992).

Canada, Government of Canada. *The Expenditure Management System of the Government of Canada* (Ottawa: Minister of Supply and Services, 1995).

Canada, House of Commons, Special Committee on the Reform of the House of Commons. *Third Report* (Ottawa: Queen's Printer, June 1985).

Canada, Office of the Auditor General. *Toward Better Governance: Public Service Reform in New Zealand (1984-94) and its Relevance to Canada* (Ottawa: Minister of Supply and Services, 1995).

Canada, Royal Commission on Financial Management and Accountability. *Final Report* (Ottawa: Minister of Supply and Services, 1979).

Canada, Royal Commission on Government Organization. *Report*, Vol. 1 (*Management of the Public Service*), abr. ed. (Ottawa: The Queen's Printer, 1963).

Canada, Steering Group on Special Operating Agencies. *Special Operating Agencies: Taking Stock, Final Report*, May 1994.

Canada, Task Force on Service to the Public. *Public Service 2000: Service to the Public. Report in Brief*, October 12, 1990.

Canada, Treasury Board Secretariat. "Outlook on Program Priorities and Expenditures," June 5, 1995.

Canadian Centre for Management Development. *Continuous Learning* (Ottawa: Minister of Supply and Services and Canadian Centre for Management Development, 1994).

Carroll, Barbara Wake. "Politics and Administration: A Trichotomy?", *Governance,* Vol. 3, no. 4 (October 1990), pp. 345-66.

Carroll, Barbara Wake. "The structure of the Canadian bureaucratic elite: some evidence of change," *Canadian Public Administration,* Vol. 34, no. 2 (Summer 1991), pp. 359-72.

Carroll, Barbara Wake, and David Siegel. "Two solitudes or one big happy family: head office-field office relations in government organizations," paper presented to the Annual Meeting of the Canadian Political Science Association, Montreal, June 5, 1995.

Carter, Neil. "Learning to Measure Performance: The Use of Indicators in Organizations," *Public Administration,* Vol. 69, (Spring 1991), pp. 85-101.

Clark, Ian. "Recent changes in the cabinet decision-making system in Ottawa," *Canadian Public Administration,* Vol. 28, no. 2 (Summer 1985), pp. 185-201.

Clark, Ian. "On Re-engineering the Public Service of Canada: A Comment on Paul Tellier's Call for Bold Action," *Public Sector Management,* Vol. 4, no. 4 (1994), pp. 20-22.

Clark, Ian. "Restraint, renewal, and the Treasury Board Secretariat," *Canadian Public Administration,* Vol. 37, no. 2 (Summer 1994), pp. 209-48.

Cooper, Phillip J. "Accountability and Administrative Reform: Toward Convergence and Beyond," in B. Guy Peters and Donald J. Savoie (eds.), *Governance in a Changing Environment* (Montreal: McGill-Queen's University Press, 1995), pp. 173-99.

Craswell, Emma, and Glyn Davis. "Does the Amalgamation of Government Agencies Produce Better Policy Co-ordination?", in Patrick Weller, John Forster and Glyn Davis (eds.), *Reforming the Public Service: Lessons From Recent Experience* (South Melbourne: Macmillan Education Australia Ltd., 1993), pp. 180-207.

Crozier, Michel. *The Bureaucratic Phenomenon* (Chicago: University of Chicago Press, 1964).

Crozier, Michel. *The Crisis of Democracy* (New York: New York University Press, 1975).

Derlien, Hans-Ulrich. "Historical legacy and recent developments in the German higher civil service," *International Review of Administrative Sciences,* Vol. 57, no. 3 (September 1991), pp. 385-401.

Desveaux, James A. "Anticipating Uncertainty: The Structure-Strategy Problem in Public Bureaucracy," *Governance,* Vol. 7, no. 1 (1994), pp. 31-58.

DiIulio, John J., Jr., Gerald Garvey and Donald F. Kettl. *Improving Government Performance: An Owner's Manual* (Washington: Brookings Institution, 1993).

Doern, G. Bruce. "The development of policy organizations," in G. Bruce Doern and Peter Aucoin (eds.), *The Structures of Policy Making in Canada* (Toronto: Macmillan Company, 1971), pp. 39-78.

Doern, G. Bruce. *The Road to Better Public Services: Progress and Constraints in Five Canadian Federal Agencies* (Montreal: Institute for Research on Public Policy, 1994).

Drewry, Gavin, and Tony Butcher. *The Civil Service Today* (Oxford: Basil Blackwell, 1988).

Dunshire, Andrew. "Administrative Theory in the 1980s: A Viewpoint," *Public Administration*, Vol. 73, no. 1 (1995), pp. 25-34.

Dupré, Stefan. "The Workability of Executive Federalism in Canada," in Herman Bakvis and William Chandler (eds.), *Federalism and the Role of the State* (Toronto: University of Toronto Press, 1987), pp. 236-58.

Foreman, Christopher H., Jr. "Reinventing Politics? The NPR Meets Congress," in Donald F. Kettl and John J. Dilulio, Jr. (eds.), *Inside the Reinvention Machine: Appraising Governmental Reform* (Washington: Brookings Institution, 1995), pp. 9-83.

French, Richard D. *How Ottawa Decides* (Toronto: Canadian Institute for Economic Policy, 1980).

Fuller, Don, and Bet Roffey. "Improving Public Sector Accountability and Strategic Decision-Making," *Australian Journal of Public Administration*, Vol. 52, no. 2 (June 1993), pp. 149-63.

Galvin, Bernard. *Policy Co-ordination, Public Sector and Government* (Wellington: Victoria University Press, 1991).

Giddings, Philip. "Next Steps to Where?", in Philip Giddings (ed.), *Parliamentary Accountability: A Study of Parliament and Executive Agencies* (London: Macmillan, 1995), pp. 221-41.

Gray, Andrew, and Bill Jenkins with Andrew Flynn and Brian Rutherford. "The management of change in Whitehall: the experience of the FMI," *Public Administration*, Vol. 69 (Spring 1991), pp. 41-61.

Greer, Patricia. *Transforming Central Government: The Next Steps Initiative* (Buckingham: Open University Press, 1994).

Gregory, R.J. "The Attitudes of Senior Public Servants in Australia and New Zealand: Administrative Reform and Technocratic Consequence?", *Governance*, Vol. 4, no. 3 (July 1991), pp. 295-331.

Halligan, John. "The career public service and administrative reform in Australia," *International Review of Administrative Studies*, Vol. 57, no. 3 (1991), pp. 345-60.

Halligan, John. "The Art of Reinvention: the United States National Performance Review," *Australian Journal of Public Administration*, Vol. 53, no. 2 (June 1994), pp. 135-43.

Harmon, Elizabeth. "Accountability and Challenges for Australian Governments," *Australian Journal of Political Science*, Vol. 29 (1994), pp. 1-17.

Hennessey, Peter. *Cabinet* (Oxford: Basil Blackwell, 1986).

Hodgetts, J.E. *The Canadian Public Service* (Toronto: University of Toronto Press, 1973).

Hodgetts, J.E., William McCloskey, Reginald Whitaker and V. Seymour Wilson. *The Biography of an Institution* (Montreal: McGill-Queen's University Press, 1972).

Hogwood, Brian W. "Whitehall families: core departments and agency forms in Britain," *International Review of Administrative Sciences,* Vol. 61, no. 4 (December 1995), pp. 511-30.

Hogwood, Brian W., and Thomas T. Mackie. "The United Kingdom: decision sifting in a secret garden," in Thomas T. Mackie and Brian W. Hogwood (eds.), *Unlocking the Cabinet: Cabinet Structures in Comparative Perspective* (London: Sage, 1985), pp. 36-60.

Holmes, Malcolm. "Corporate Management – A View from the Centre," in G. Davis, P. Weller and C. Lewis (eds.), *Corporate Management in Australian Government* (South Melbourne: Macmillan, 1989), pp. 29-47.

Hood, Christopher. "A Public Management for All Seasons?", *Public Administration,* Vol. 69, no. 1 (Spring 1991), pp. 3-19.

Hood, Christopher, and Michael Jackson. *Administrative Argument* (Aldershot, England: Dartmouth Publishing Company, 1991).

Ives, Denis. "Next Steps in Public Management," *Australian Journal of Public Administration,* Vol. 53, no. 3 (1994), pp. 335-40.

Jenkins, Bill, and Andrew Gray. "Reshaping the Management of Government: The Next Steps Initiative in the United Kingdom," in F. Leslie Seidle (ed.), *Rethinking Government: Reform or Reinvention?* (Montreal: Institute for Research on Public Policy, 1993), pp. 73-109.

Johnson, A.W. "Reflections on administrative reform in the government of Canada 1962-1991," Discussion Paper, Ottawa, Office of the Auditor General of Canada, 1992.

Jones, G.W. "Presidentialization in a parliamentary system," in Colin Campbell and Margaret Jane Wyszomirski (eds.), *Executive Leadership in Anglo-American Systems* (Pittsburgh: University of Pittsburgh Press, 1991), pp. 111-37.

Keating, Michael. "Managing for Results in the Public Interest," *Australian Journal of Public Administration,* Vol. 49, no. 4 (1990), pp. 387-98.

Keating, Michael. "Mega-departments: The Theory and Objectives," in Patrick Weller, John Forster and Glyn Davis (eds.), *Reforming the Public Service: Lessons From Recent Experience* (South Melbourne: Macmillan Education Australia Ltd., 1993), pp. 1-15.

Keating Michael, and Malcolm Holmes. "Australia's Budgetary and Financial Management Reforms," *Governance,* Vol. 3, no. 2 (April 1990), pp. 168-85.

Kernaghan, Kenneth. "Career Public Service 2000: road to renewal or impractical vision?", *Canadian Public Administration,* Vol. 34, no. 4 (1991), pp. 551-72.

Kernaghan, Kenneth. "Choose your partners – it's innovation time!", *Public Sector Management*, Vol. 3, no. 2 (Fall 1992), pp. 16-17.

Kernaghan, Kenneth. "Partnership and public administration: conceptual and practical considerations," *Canadian Public Administration*, Vol. 36, no. 1 (Spring 1993), pp. 57-76.

Kernaghan, Kenneth. "The emerging public service culture: values, ethics, and reforms," *Canadian Public Administration*, Vol. 37, no. 4 (Winter 1994), pp. 614-30.

Kettl, Donald F. *Reinventing Government? Appraising the National Performance Review* (Washington: Brookings Institution, 1994).

Kettl, Donald F. "Building Lasting Reform: Enduring Questions, Missing Answers," in Donald F. Kettl and John J. Dilulio, Jr. (eds.), *Inside the Reinvention Machine: Appraising Governmental Reform* (Washington: Brookings Institution, 1995), pp. 152-68.

Kroeger, Arthur. "The budget and the public service – good news with the bad," *Public Sector Management*, Vol. 6, no. 2 (1995), pp. 4-5.

Laframboise, H.L. "Administrative reform in the federal public service: signs of a saturation psychosis," *Canadian Public Administration*, Vol. 14, no. 3 (Fall 1971), pp. 303-25.

Laframboise, H.L. "Here come the program-benders!", *Optimum*, Vol. 7, no. 1 (1976), pp. 40-48.

Laking, R.G. "Developing a culture of success: reflections on the New Zealand experiences," paper presented to the Commonwealth Association of Public Administration and Management, Charlottetown, Prince Edward Island, August 29-31, 1994.

Laking, R.G. "The New Zealand Management Reforms," *Australian Journal of Public Administration*, Vol. 53, no. 3 (September 1994), pp. 313-24.

Landry, Réjean. "Administrative reform and political control in Canada," *International Political Science Review*, Vol. 14, no. 4 (1993), pp. 335-50.

Lewis, Norman. "The Citizen's Charter and Next Steps: A New Way of Governing?", *The Political Quarterly*, Vol. 64, no. 3 (July-September 1993), pp. 316-26.

Lindquist, Evert. "Think tanks or clubs? Assessing the influence and roles of Canadian policy institutes," *Canadian Public Administration*, Vol. 36, no. 4 (Winter 1993), pp. 547-79.

Lindquist, Evert. "Citizens, Experts and Budgets: Evaluating Ottawa's Budget Process," in Susan D. Phillips (ed.), *How Ottawa Spends 1994-95: Making Change* (Ottawa: Carleton University Press, 1994), pp. 91-128.

MacDonald, Flora. "The Minister and the Mandarins," *Policy Options*, Vol. 1, no. 3 (September-October 1980), pp. 29-31.

Mackay, Keith. "Evaluation – What's in it for You," paper prepared for Department of Finance SES Officers on "Trends in Public Sector Financial Management," Department of Finance, Commonwealth of Australia, July 14, 1994.

Mackie, Thomas T., and Brian W. Hogwood. "Cabinet committees in context," in Thomas T. Mackie and Brian W. Hogwood (eds.), *Unlocking the Cabinet: Cabinet Structures in Comparative Perspective* (London: Sage, 1985), pp. 32-33.

Manion, J.L. "Career public service in Canada: reflections and predictions," *International Review of Administrative Sciences*, Vol. 57, no. 3 (September 1991), pp. 361-72.

Manion, John L. "The organization and management of government," notes for an address to the Advanced Management Program of the Canadian Centre for Management Development (Ottawa: Canadian Centre for Management Development, 1993).

Manion, John L., and Cynthia Williams. "Transition Planning at the Federal Level in Canada," in Donald J. Savoie (ed.), *Taking Power: Managing Government Transitions* (Toronto: Institute of Public Administration of Canada, 1993), pp. 99-114.

Martin, John. *A Profession of Statecraft?* (Wellington, New Zealand: Victoria University Press, 1988).

Massé, Marcel. "Getting Government Right," address to the Public Service Alliance of Canada, Longueuil, Quebec, September 12, 1993.

Meisel, John. *The Canadian General Election of 1957* (Toronto: University of Toronto Press, 1962).

Merton, Robert K. "Bureaucratic structure of personality," *Social Forces*, Vol. 18 (May 1940), pp. 560-68.

Metcalfe, Les. "Conviction Politics and Dynamic Conservatism: Mrs. Thatcher's Managerial Revolution," *International Political Science Review*, Vol. 14, no. 4 (October 1993), pp. 351-71.

Metcalfe, Les, and Sue Richards. *Improving Public Management* (London: Sage, 1987).

Mintzberg, Henry. *The Structuring of Organizations: A Synthesis of the Research* (Englewood Cliffs: Prentice-Hall, 1979).

Mintzberg, Henry, and Jan Jorgensen. "Emergent strategy for public policy," *Canadian Public Administration*, Vol. 30, no. 2 (Summer 1987), pp. 214-29.

Moon, Jeremy. "Innovative Leadership and Policy Change: Lessons from Thatcher," *Governance*, Vol. 8, no. 1 (January 1995), pp. 1-25.

New Zealand, State Services Commission. *New Zealand – Public Sector Reform* (Wellington: State Services Commission, 1993).

New Zealand, State Services Commission Steering Group. *Review of State Sector Reforms* (Wellington: State Services Commission, November 29, 1991).

New Zealand, The Treasury. *Government Management* (Wellington: Government Printer, 1987).

Niskanen, William. "A reflection on *Bureaucracy and Representative Government*," in André Blais and Stéphane Dion (eds.), *The Budget-Maximizing Bureaucrat: Appraisals and Evidence* (Pittsburgh: University of Pittsburgh Press, 1991), pp. 13-31.

Noble, John. "Reflections on the Not-so-Well-Performing Organizations," in James C. McDavid and Brian Marson (eds.), *The Well-Performing Government Organization* (Toronto: Institute of Public Administration of Canada, 1991), pp. 37-41.

O'Connor, Loretta J. "Chief of Staff," *Policy Options*, Vol. 12, no. 3 (April 1991), pp. 23-26.

Organisation for Economic Co-operation and Development. "Serving the Economy Better," Public Management Occasional Papers, Paris (1991).

Organisation for Economic Co-operation and Development. *Public Management Developments: Survey 1993* (Paris: OECD, 1993).

Organisation for Economic Co-operation and Development. *Performance Management in Government: Performance Measurement and Results-Oriented Management* (Paris: OECD, 1994).

Osbaldeston, Gordon F. "How Deputies are Accountable," *Policy Options*, Vol. 8, no. 7 (September 1987), pp. 10-13.

Osbaldeston, Gordon F. *Keeping Deputy Ministers Accountable* (London, Ontario: National Centre for Management Research and Development, 1988).

Osbaldeston, Gordon F. *Organizing to Govern*, Vols. 1 and 2 (Toronto: McGraw-Hill Ryerson, 1992).

Osborne, David, and Ted Gaebler. *Reinventing Government: How the Entrepreneurial Spirit is Transforming the Public Sector* (New York: Plume, 1993).

Painter, Martin. *Steering the Modern State: Changes in Central Coordination in Three Australian State Governments* (Sydney: Sydney University Press, 1987).

Pallot, June. "Financial Management Reforms," in Jonathan Boston, John Martin, June Pallot and Pat Walsh (eds.), *Reshaping the State: New Zealand's Bureaucratic Revolution* (Auckland: Oxford University Press, 1991), pp. 166-97.

Palmer, Matthew S.R. "Cabinet Ministers and Single Party Majority Government in New Zealand: the Collective Decision-Making Approach," paper presented to the Joint Sessions of Workshops on "The Political Role of Cabinet Ministers in the Process of Parliamentary Government," European Consortium for Political Research, University of Limerick, March 30-April 4, 1992.

Parris, Henry. *Constitutional Bureaucracy* (London: George Allen and Unwin, 1969).

Peters, B. Guy, and Donald J. Savoie. "Civil Service Reform: Misdiagnosing the Patient," *Public Administration Review*, Vol. 54, no. 5 (September-October 1994), pp. 418-25.

Peters, Thomas, and Robert Waterman. *In Search of Excellence* (New York: Harper and Row, 1982).

Pfeffer, Jeffrey. *Managing With Power: Politics and Influence in Organizations* (Boston: Harvard Business School Press, 1992).

Pierre, Jon. "The Marketization of the State: Citizens, Consumers, and the Emergence of the Public Market," in B. Guy Peters and Donald J. Savoie (eds.), *Governance in a Changing Environment* (Montreal: McGill-Queen's University Press, 1995), pp. 55-81.

Plasse, Micheline. "Ministerial Chiefs of Staff in the Federal Government in 1990: Profiles, Recruitment, Duties and Relations with Senior Public Servants," paper prepared for the Canadian Centre for Management Development, Ottawa, April 1994.

Plumptre, Tim. "Reform at the crossroads: efforts to implement an integrated strategy for renewal in the Canadian federal government," mimeo, June 1994.

Pollitt, Christopher. *Managerialism and the Public Services: The Anglo-American Experience* (Oxford: Basil Blackwell, 1990).

Pollitt, Christopher. "Occasional Excursions: A Brief History of Policy Evaluation in the UK," *Parliamentary Affairs*, Vol. 46, no. 3 (July 1993), pp. 353-62.

Pollitt, Christopher. "Management Techniques for the Public Sector: Pulpit and Practice," in B. Guy Peters and Donald J. Savoie (eds.), *Governance in a Changing Environment* (Montreal: McGill-Queen's University Press, 1995), pp. 203-38.

Pollitt, Christopher, Martin Cave and Richard Joss. "International benchmarking as a tool to improve public sector performance: a critical overview," in Organisation for Economic Co-operation and Development, *Performance Measurement in Government: Issues and Illustrations* (Paris: OECD, 1994), pp. 7-22.

Pross, A. Paul. "The pressure group conundrum," in James P. Bickerton and Alain-G. Gagnon (eds.), *Canadian Politics*, 2nd ed. (Peterborough: Broadview Press, 1994), pp. 173-87.

Public Policy Forum. "Toward a New Consultative Process: Lessons from the Nielsen Task Force," Ottawa, October 29, 1993.

Purchase, Bryne, and Ronald Hirshhorn. *Searching for Good Governance* (Kingston: Queen's University School of Policy Studies, 1994).

Ridley, F.F. "Career service: a comparative perspective on civil service promotion," *Public Administration*, Vol. 61 (Summer 1983), pp. 179-96.

Roberts, Alasdair. "Building a Common Services Department: The Establishment of Public Works and Government Services Canada" (Ottawa: Canadian Centre for Management Development, forthcoming).

Roberts, J. *Politicians, Public Servants and Public Enterprise* (Wellington: Victoria University Press, 1987).

Roberts, John. "Ministers, the Cabinet and Public Servants," in Jonathan Boston and Martin Holland (eds.), *The Fourth Labour Government: Radical Politics in New Zealand* (Auckland: Oxford University Press, 1987), pp. 89-110.

Royal Institute of Public Administration. *Top Jobs in Whitehall: Report of a Working Group* (London, 1987).

Savoie, Donald J. "Innovating to do better with less," *Public Sector Management*, Vol. 4, no. 1 (Spring 1993), pp. 15-17.

Savoie, Donald J. *Thatcher, Reagan, Mulroney: In Search of a New Bureaucracy* (Toronto: University of Toronto Press, 1994).

Savoie, Donald J. "Globalization, Nation States and the Civil Service," in B. Guy Peters and Donald J. Savoie (eds.), *Governance in a Changing Environment* (Montreal: McGill-Queen's University Press, 1995), pp. 82-110.

Savoie, Donald J. "What is wrong with the new public management?", *Canadian Public Administration*, Vol. 38, no. 1 (Spring 1995), pp. 112-21.

Savoie, Donald J. "Restructuring the government of Canada: leading from the centre" (Ottawa: Canadian Centre for Management Development, forthcoming).

Séguin, Francine. "Service to the public: a major strategic change," *Canadian Public Administration*, Vol. 34, no. 3 (Autumn 1991), pp. 465-73.

Seidle, F. Leslie. "Interest Advocacy through Parliamentary Channels: Representation and Accommodation," in F. Leslie Seidle (ed.), *Equity and Community: the Charter, Interest Advocacy and Representation* (Montreal: Institute for Research on Public Policy, 1993), pp. 189-225.

Seidle, F. Leslie. "The Angry Citizenry: Examining Representation and Responsiveness in Government," *Policy Options*, Vol. 15, no. 6 (July-August 1994), pp. 75-80.

Seidle, F. Leslie. *Rethinking the Delivery of Public Services to Citizens* (Montreal: Institute for Research on Public Policy, 1995).

Selby Smith, Chris, and David Corbett. "Parliamentary Committees, Public Servants and Due Process," *Australian Journal of Public Administration*, Vol. 54, no. 1 (March 1995), pp. 19-34.

Self, Peter. *Government by the Market? The Politics of Public Choice* (Boulder: Westview Press, 1993).

Smith, Martin. "The core executive and the resignation of Mrs. Thatcher," *Public Administration*, Vol. 72 (Autumn 1994), pp. 341-63.

Sproule-Jones, Mark. "Science as art and art as science: a response to Professor Borins' paper," *Canadian Public Administration*, Vol. 31, no. 1 (1988), pp. 34-41.

Stone, Bruce. "Administrative Accountability in the Westminster Democracies: Towards a New Conceptual Framework," *Governance*, Vol. 8, no. 4 (October 1995), pp. 505-26.

Stowe, Kenneth. "Good Piano Won't Play Bad Music: Administrative Reform and Good Governance," *Public Administration*, Vol. 70, no. 3 (Autumn 1992), pp. 387-94.

Sutherland, S.L. "The Consequences of Electoral Volatility: Inexperienced Ministers 1949-90," in Herman Bakvis (ed.), *Representation, Integration and Political Parties in Canada* (Toronto: Dundurn Press, 1991), pp. 303-54.

Sutherland, S.L. "Responsible Government and Ministerial Responsibility: Every Reform has its Own Problem," *Canadian Journal of Political Science*, Vol. 24, no. 1 (March 1991), pp. 91-120.

Sutherland, S.L. "The Al-Mashat affair: administrative responsibility in parliamentary institutions," *Canadian Public Administration*, Vol. 34, no. 4 (Winter 1991), pp. 573-603.

Sutherland, Sharon L. "The Public Service and Policy Development," in Michael M. Atkinson (ed.), *Governing Canada: Institutions and Public Policy* (Toronto: Harcourt Brace Jovanovich Canada Inc., 1993), pp. 81-113.

Sutherland, S.L., and G.B. Doern. *Bureaucracy in Canada: Control and Reform*, Vol. 43 of the Research Studies of the Royal Commission on the Economic Union and Development Prospects for Canada (Toronto: University of Toronto Press, 1985).

Swift, Frank. *Strategic Management in the Public Service: The Changing Role of the Deputy Minister* (Ottawa: Minister of Supply and Services and Canadian Centre for Management Development, 1993).

Tellier, Paul M. "No time for half-measures: the urgency of re-engineering the public service of Canada," remarks to the Canadian Institute, Ottawa, February 21, 1994 (an abridged version of Tellier's remarks is printed in *Canadian Speeches: Issues of the day*, Vol. 8, issue 1 (April 1994), pp. 45-48).

Thain, Colin, and Maurice Wright. "Planning and Controlling Public Expenditure in the UK, Part 1: The Treasury's Public Expenditure Survey," *Public Administration*, Vol. 70 (Spring 1992), pp. 3-24.

Thain, Colin, and Maurice Wright. "Planning and Controlling Public Expenditure in the UK, Part 2: The Effects and Effectiveness of the Survey," *Public Administration*, Vol. 70 (Summer 1992), pp. 193-224.

Theakston, Kevin, and Geoffrey K. Fry. "Britain's administrative elite: permanent secretaries 1900-1986," *Public Administration*, Vol. 67 (Summer 1989), pp. 129-47.

Trebilcock, Michael J. *The Prospects for Reinventing Government* (Toronto: C.D. Howe Institute, 1994).

Trosa, Sylvie. *Next Steps: Moving On*, prepared for the Office of Public Service and Science (United Kingdom), February 1994.

United Kingdom, Cabinet Office, Next Steps Team. *Briefing Note*, September 1, 1995.

United Kingdom, Chancellor of the Duchy of Lancaster. "The Reality of Reform and Accountability in Today's Public Service," speech to the Public Finance Foundation, July 5, 1993.

United Kingdom, Committee on the Civil Service. *Report* (London: HMSO, 1968).

United Kingdom, Efficiency Unit. *Improving Management in Government: The Next Steps* (London: HMSO, 1988).

United Kingdom, House of Commons, Treasury and Civil Service Committee. *Fifth Report: The Role of the Civil Service*, Vol. 1 (London: HMSO, 1994).

United Kingdom, Prime Minister, Chancellor of the Exchequer and Chancellor of the Duchy of Lancaster. *The Civil Service: Continuity and Change* (London: HMSO, July 1994).

United Kingdom, Prime Minister, Chancellor of the Exchequer and Chancellor of the Duchy of Lancaster. *The Civil Service: Taking Forward Continuity and Change* (London: HMSO, January 1995).

United States, Vice President Al Gore. *Creating a Government that Works Better and Costs Less: Report of the National Performance Review* (Washington: US Government Printing Office, 1993).

Wainwright, Hilary. "A New Kind of Knowledge for a New Kind of State," in Gregory Albo, David Langille and Leo Panitch (eds.), *A Different Kind of State? Popular Power and Democratic Administration* (Toronto: Oxford University Press, 1993), pp. 112-21.

Walter, James. *The Ministers' Minders* (Melbourne: Oxford University Press, 1986).

Weber, Max. "Bureaucracy," in H.H. Gerth and C. Wright Mills (eds.), *From Max Weber: Essays in Sociology*, translated (New York: Oxford University Press, 1946), pp. 196-244.

Weller, Patrick. "Cabinet committees in Australia and New Zealand," in Thomas T. Mackie and Brian W. Hogwood (eds.), *Unlocking the Cabinet: Cabinet Structures in Comparative Perspective* (London: Sage, 1985), pp. 86-113.

Weller, Patrick. "Politicization and the Australian Public Service," *Australian Journal of Public Administration*, Vol. 48, no. 4 (December 1989), pp. 369-78.

Weller, Patrick. "Party rules and the dismissal of prime ministers: comparative perspectives from Britain, Canada and Australia," *Parliamentary Affairs*, Vol. 47, no. 1 (January 1994), pp. 133-43.

Wildavsky, Aaron. *Speaking Truth to Power: The Art and Craft of Policy Analysis* (Boston: Little, Brown and Company, 1979).

Wilson, James Q. *Bureaucracy: What Government Agencies Do and Why They Do It* (New York: Basic Books, 1989).

Wilson, Graham K. "Prospects for the public service in Britain. Major to the rescue?", *International Review of Administrative Sciences*, Vol. 57, no. 3 (September 1991), pp. 327-44.

Woodhouse, Diana. *Ministers and Parliament: Accountability in Theory and Practice* (Oxford: Clarendon Press, 1994).

Wright, J. David, and Graeme Waymark. *Special Operating Agencies: Overview of the Special Operating Agency Initiative* (Ottawa: Canada Centre for Management Development/Minister of Supply and Services, 1995).

Yeatman, Anna. "The Reform of Public Management: An Overview," *Australian Journal of Public Administration*, Vol. 53, no. 3 (September 1994), pp. 287-95.

Zifcak, Spencer. *New Managerialism: Administrative Reform in Whitehall and Canberra* (Buckingham: Open University Press, 1994).

Zussman, David. "Walking the Tightrope: the Mulroney Government and the Public Service," in Michael Prince (ed.), *How Ottawa Spends 1986-87: Tracking the Tories* (Toronto: Methuen, 1986), pp. 250-82.

Zussman, David, and Jak Jabes. *The Vertical Solitude: Managing in the Public Sector* (Halifax: Institute for Research on Public Policy, 1989).

Note on the Author

Peter Aucoin is McCulloch Professor in Political Science and Professor of Public Administration at Dalhousie University. He is President of the Canadian Political Science Association, a Fellow of the Institute for Research on Public Policy, a Senior Fellow of the Canadian Centre for Management Development and a Director of the Institute on Governance. He is a former Vice-President of the Institute of Public Administration of Canada. He has served as a Research Coordinator for the Royal Commission on the Economic Union and Development Prospects for Canada, Research Director for the Royal Commission on Electoral Reform and Party Financing, and Research Director for the Halifax Commission on City Government. He has been Director of the School of Public Administration and Chair of the Department of Political Science at Dalhousie. He has authored or edited 10 books and published more than 40 journal articles and book chapters on Canadian and comparative government and public administration.

Recent IRPP Publications

Governance

F. Leslie Seidle, *Rethinking the Delivery of Public Services to Citizens*

Kirk Cameron, Graham White, *Northern Governments in Transition: Political and Constitutional Development in the Yukon, Nunavut and the Western Northwest Territories*

G. Bruce Doern, *The Road to Better Public Services: Progress and Constraints in Five Canadian Federal Agencies*

Donald G. Lenihan, Gordon Robertson, Roger Tassé, *Canada: Reclaiming the Middle Ground*

F. Leslie Seidle (ed.), *Seeking a New Canadian Partnership: Asymmetrical and Confederal Options*

F. Leslie Seidle (ed.), *Equity and Community: The Charter, Interest Advocacy and Representation*

F. Leslie Seidle (ed.), *Rethinking Government: Reform or Reinvention?*

Telecommunications

W.T. Stanbury (ed.), *Perspectives on the New Economics and Regulation of Telecommunications*

Yves Rabeau, *Les télécommunications: problématique d'une industrie en évolution rapide*

Charles Sirois, Claude E. Forget, *The Medium and the Muse: Culture, Telecommunications and the Information Highway*

Charles Sirois, Claude E. Forget, *Le Médium et les Muses: la culture, les télécommunications et l'autoroute de l'information*

Education

Thomas T. Schweitzer, *The State of Education in Canada*

Stephen B. Lawton, *Busting Bureaucracy to Reclaim our Schools*

Bruce Wilkinson, *Educational Choice: Necessary But Not Sufficient*

Peter Coleman, *Learning About Schools: What Parents Need to Know and How They Can Find Out*

Edwin G. West, *Ending the Squeeze on Universities*

Social Policy

Adil Sayeed (ed.), *Workfare: Does it Work? Is it Fair?*

Monique Jérôme-Forget, Joseph White, Joshua M. Weiner (eds.), *Health Care Reform Through Internal Markets: Experience and Proposals*

Ross Finnie, *Child Support: The Guideline Options*